CHILDREN OF THE THIRD REICH

Catrine Clay is an acclaimed historian and documentary filmmaker. Her books include *The Good Germans* (2020), *Labyrinths* (2016) and *Trautmann's Journey* (2010).

CHILDREN OF THE THIRD REICH

Three Pasts, Three Futures

Catrine Clay

W&N
WEIDENFELD & NICOLSON

First published in Great Britain in 2026 by Weidenfeld & Nicolson,
an imprint of The Orion Publishing Group Ltd
Carmelite House, 50 Victoria Embankment
London EC4Y 0DZ

An Hachette UK Company

The authorised representative in the EEA is Hachette Ireland,
8 Castlecourt Centre, Dublin 15, D15 XTP3, Ireland
(email: info@hbgi.ie)

1 3 5 7 9 10 8 6 4 2

A CIP catalogue record for this book is
available from the British Library.

ISBN (Hardback) 978 1 4746 2258 5
ISBN (Export Trade Paperback) 978 1 4746 2259 2
ISBN (Ebook) 978 1 4746 2261 5
ISBN (Audio) 978 1 4746 2262 2

Typeset at The Spartan Press Ltd,
Lymington, Hants

Printed and bound in Great Britain by Clays Ltd,
Elcograf S.p.A.

FSC www.fsc.org MIX Paper | Supporting responsible forestry FSC® C104740

www.weidenfeldandnicolson.co.uk
www.orionbooks.co.uk

In Memory of Dan Bar-On
1938–2008

CONTENTS

INTRODUCTION

The underlying theme of this book is power in the wrong hands. What happens to ordinary people leading ordinary lives, caring for their children, going to work, tending their gardens, once power gets into the wrong hands. People like you and me. Looking back, I see that most of my books and many of my BBC documentaries which preceded them are about that. My mother was Swiss, so I grew up speaking German and French as well as English, and that almost inevitably led me to twentieth-century European history. And that century was crammed with power in the wrong hands. Two world wars, civil wars, terror regimes, the Holocaust, you name it.

The fact is, there's little the small individual can do about it. It's too late. The angel has flown. This book is about three such small, anonymous individuals, each profoundly affected by the fallout from the Third Reich: Renate, Joe and Dan. And one further individual – not small, not anonymous – who was the living example of what can happen: *Reichsführer-SS* Heinrich Himmler.

Ideology is often at the heart of it. In this case it was the ideology of racial purity in Nazi Germany – the Aryan, the Master Race, the Thousand-Year German Reich and all that baloney, as one of the American GIs invading Germany at the end of the Second World War put it. And baloney it was, as I hope to show in this book, but that didn't stop over 45 million people, those small individuals, being killed, including the extermination of 6 million Jews in the Holocaust. It was there from the start, that baloney, when Hitler wrote his 700-page manifesto *Mein Kampf* way back in 1924. It was still there in Hitler's will. Heinrich Himmler and his SS put it into terrifying practice.

Renate was born in Nazi Germany in 1941, at Steinhöring in Bavaria, in a *Lebensborn* home. Heinrich Himmler founded the *Lebensborn* 'charity' to breed the pure Aryan. The fathers were unknown SS officers, the mothers, some married, some not, were racially tested before they could produce 'a child for Hitler'. Once the babies were born, most mothers left them in the homes. But not Renate's mother.

Joe was born in a Displaced Persons camp in Germany in 1946. His parents, Lonia and Mendel, were survivors of the Holocaust. First it was the Warsaw ghetto, then Poniatowa concentration camp, then the miraculous survival. Finally they made it to a new life in America. But the dark past wouldn't go away.

Dan was born in Haifa, Israel, in 1938, though it wasn't Israel then, it was Palestine. His parents fled Hamburg early on, in 1933. Dan's father was a doctor. From April 1933, hardly two months after the Nazis came to power, Jewish doctors were no longer allowed to practise. That's how fast power acts once it's in the wrong hands. Dan's parents decided on Palestine, still under British rule at the time. So Dan grew up a patriotic Israeli, until he wasn't so sure any more.

Many years later, Renate, Joe and Dan met. It was in Israel, in 1993, at Neve Shalom, a peace centre halfway between Jerusalem and Tel Aviv. And they discovered that in spite of their very different lives, the one in Germany, the other in America, the last in Israel, they, quite unexpectedly, shared one thing: growing up in silence about the past. Their parents, wishing to protect their children, and perhaps themselves too, never spoke about that dark past. In Renate's case it was just her mother, since she didn't know who her father was. Her mother was called Else. And Else had her own secrets. In Joe's case, his parents, Lonia and Mendel, couldn't tell their stories even if they'd wanted to. For their own sanity. Because the stories were too horrific. In Dan's case it was easier, because his parents had escaped the Nazi terror, just in time.

As they told each other their stories, they realised that trauma is passed from generation to generation, from parent to child, without mention, silently, invisibly. Although Renate, Joe and Dan didn't live through the Nazi period themselves, they discovered they were all still Children of the Third Reich.

Catrine Clay
London, October 2025

PART ONE

DARK PASTS

CHAPTER ONE

RENATE: A CHILD FOR HITLER

Three drumrolls. Then the announcement on German radio: 'Our Führer Adolf Hitler, fighting to the last breath against Bolshevism, fell for Germany this afternoon at his operational headquarters in the Reich Chancellery.' It was 1 May 1945.

So it ended as it had begun, in lies. The Führer hadn't 'fallen', which is what soldiers do fighting a war. And he hadn't heroically shot himself either, as was announced. He'd taken poison. Now it was all over. The Nazi's Thousand-Year German Reich had lasted just twelve years, leaving over 45 million dead. Their dream of the Master Race was buried in the rubble of Berlin and London, Warsaw and Smolensk, Monte Cassino and Stalingrad and far-flung outposts of Empire. And now the Allies – British, American, Russian and French – were making their way across Germany, invading, occupying, pacifying, quelling. Millions of refugees were on the move, fleeing the Russians from the east or the Allies from the west, one path crossing the other in the chaos of defeat.

And among that chaos, in a chaos all her own, we find Renate. Renate turned four in 1945, living with foster parents in Kohren, a small town east of Leipzig. But she was born at the Hochland children's home at Steinhöring in Bavaria on 21 November 1941 – the father an unknown SS officer, the mother Else Röder, aged thirty-five, unmarried. Hochland was not a normal children's home. It was a *Lebensborn* home – part of a 'charity' set up in 1936 by Heinrich Himmler, the *Reichsführer* leader of the SS, to breed the racially pure Aryan. Eventually there were nineteen *Lebensborn* homes scattered across the German Reich and the German-occupied countries beyond, including Norway – a special favourite of Himmler's because the women were so blond and blue-eyed.

'Every mother of good blood will be sacred to us,' wrote Himmler, choosing those words as the motto for his charity *Lebensborn e.V*; *Lebensborn* meant 'fount of life'. 'We shall survive or we shall perish with this best blood of Germany. If the good blood is not perpetuated we will be unable to rule over the world.'

Racial purity was at the very heart of Nazi ideology – a religion almost. In fact, the Naming Ceremony to mark the birth of a child in one of the *Lebensborn* homes looked very much like a religious service: the baby placed on a white embroidered cushion before an altar draped with the swastika flag and adorned with flowers and plants, a framed photograph of Hitler in place of the image of Christ. There were flaming torches on either side of the altar and the black standard of the SS hung above, together with a wreath festooned with twelve candles signifying the solstice, surrounded by foliage. Two SS officers officiated in full dress uniform – black, with black jackboots and black caps adorned with the white *Totenkopf* (Death's Head) badge. Plus a ceremonial sword. No prayers, but an SS officer who intoned:

> Wc bclicvc in thc God of all things
> And in the mission of our German blood
> Which grows ever young from German soil
> We believe in the race, carrier of blood
> And in the Führer, chosen for us by God

It sounded like a prayer but it was composed by Heinrich Himmler, not the Church. There were instructions too, also written by Himmler. After the 'prayer' the senior officiating SS officer was to turn and address the baby thus: 'We take you into our Community as a limb of our body, you shall grow up in our protection and bring honour to your name, pride to your brotherhood and inextinguishable glory to your race.' To which the 'congregation', that is, the nurses of the *Lebensborn* home and the mother, responded: 'We bow in reverence before the ancestors, whose blood, as mission and obligation, circulates in our veins. We ourselves will become ancestors. Our children are the witnesses of our breeding and of our being. And our children will proclaim our greatness.' Only the Amen was missing.

'Yes, I think I had a Naming Ceremony,' said Renate some fifty years later, still trying to make sense of what happened to her during those first five years of her life. 'My mother said they used a sword and placed it across the baby. She said the sword was bigger than me! In the ceremony they gave you the name. It's written on my

Lebensborn certificate: the name of my mother, and the name of the *Lebensborn* home, Hochland, and then underneath there is my name: Renate.' She smiled and shook her head. 'Only when I was grown up I realised I was born into a special ideology. The Nazis said, never mind you are not married. Make a child for Hitler. It is completely alien to me. I know the ideology, but I can't connect to it.'

When she finally visited Steinhöring in 1982 – a first step into her dark past – the villagers told her there were many bonfires in the gardens of the Hochland *Lebensborn* home during the last days of the war. Apart from that they were reluctant to talk about the home, insisting there'd been no contact between them. 'It was the SS, not us,' they kept repeating. Still, it turned out that the birth register had been saved from the bonfires and was now kept in the local mayor's office. Apparently there was a steady stream of people coming to check the register, trying, like Renate, to find out who they were and who their parents had been. But it was an impossible task. Few of the mothers' names were listed, and certainly not the names of the SS officers who were the fathers, which were always intended to remain secret. Addresses, if given at all, used the same few Munich addresses, belonging to the SS. Most of the children ended up in children's homes, because once the war was lost and the Nazis' dream of their Thousand-Year German Reich lay dead in the bombed-out ruins, no one wanted anything to do with these so-called racially pure 'children for Hitler'. Even with the help of the Red Cross and the Catholic charity Caritas, the fathers and most of the mothers remained an unsolvable mystery.

When Renate checked the Birth Register she found one birth listed on 1 May 1945 and five more on 5 May, presumably catching up with those babies born during the last days of the war when everything was in chaos. And she found her own entry: 21 November 1941, with her mother's name and, although no name of the father, an acknowledgement of paternity, which was unusual. Puzzling.

So Renate's story was different from those of most other *Lebensborn* children. Worse, as it turned out. But that is to get ahead of ourselves.

Back in 1945, on the afternoon of 3 May, just two days after Hitler's death was announced and four days before the official end of the Second World War, ten men of C Company of the US Army's 86th Division arrived in Steinhöring. The place was little more than a large village, a single main street with rich farming land on either side. There was no one about, everyone hiding in their houses, curtains drawn. The US soldiers made their way cautiously through the village, rifles cocked, covering both sides of the road. You never knew. Even though the war was over, there were last-ditch snipers everywhere – one-time Hitler Youths most of them, still ready to die for the Führer though the Führer himself was already dead in his bunker in Berlin. In fact, there were no snipers, but still the men of C Company were in for a big surprise.

At the end of the village they came across a large building. It had a pitched roof and a round white tower in the old Bavarian style, high wrought-iron gates decorated with mysterious Germanic runes, and a wide gravel forecourt featuring a monumental statue of a mother and child carved in stone. It was the Hochland home. The gates were padlocked but the Americans kicked them in, likewise the massive oak front door, and made their way through the ground floor – a spacious entrance hall with polished wooden floors and chandeliers, an airy white-tiled kitchen, store rooms, pantry, and a large sunny room like a nursery, scattered with toys, all silent and empty, deserted. They made their way up a wide wooden staircase to the landing above, rifles still cocked. And there, in another large room, they found forty toddlers and children, some dressed, some naked. In other rooms on the same floor and the attic floor they found many more, crammed in, crying – almost 200 in all, some just babies in their cots. There were a few nurses too, in their NS uniforms, hiding in a back room. The men of C Company had experienced many surprises during this war, but few more surprising than this. What the hell was going on?

While half the men checked the grounds – high wall, playground with abandoned toys, small lake, neat kitchen gardens, woodland – the rest went in search of someone who could explain. There was a church in the village, surrounded by a well-tended cemetery. Where there is a church there is a priest. They found him hiding in his house, like everyone else. The priest told them the building was a mother and baby home called Hochland, and had opened in 1936. Beyond that he was vague, saying the villagers had no contact with the home and knew little about it. The nursing staff had kept pretty much to themselves. '*Es tut mir Leid*, I'm sorry, I can't enlighten you any further,' he said. Mighty strange, thought the men of C Company. Something didn't smell right.

In fact there was some truth to what he said. Many of the Catholic priests in Bavaria had early on in the Nazi regime taken to greeting their parishioners with the traditional '*Grüss Gott!*', God be with you, not the required '*Heil Hitler!*' – a small thing, one might think, but punishable by a stint in a concentration camp. Some had also started hoisting the regional blue and white flag rather than the swastika on their church towers on feast days. Meanwhile, the Communists and Socialists had gone underground to continue their opposition to the Nazi regime. Each had active party headquarters outside the Reich – the Communists in Moscow, the Social Democrats first in Prague, then Paris – and active cells within the Reich, organising underground resistance and sabotage, reporting back to their headquarters with the help of couriers, often women. They all knew the risks: a concentration camp at best, death at worst.

'The way in which Youth is being prepared today for the coming war can be seen clearly once again in the end of year celebrations in X,' reported SOPAD, the Social Democratic Party Intelligence network, from an unknown town in Bavaria in 1936. 'In the largest room in the town, which was decorated for the celebration, around 130 boys and as many girls who had just finished their eighth year at school were assembled. Over the stage, in big lettering, stood: WE ARE BORN TO DIE FOR GERMANY. In his talk, as reported by one of the boys who was not named, the school principal emphasised that "we must give our faithful heart to the Führer, and, since he is Germany's liberator and greatest hero, our whole life belongs to him. In the fight for the national freedom of all Germans, even Youth may not shy away from offering itself up selflessly." At the end there was the oath: "And if it must be, we know why: We are born to die for Germany."'

'As part of our mission to preserve the German *Volk* we shall have to develop a technique of depopulation. By which I mean the removal of entire racial units,' as Hitler put it in one of his 'Table Talks'. 'If I can send the flower of the German *Volk* into the hell of war without the smallest pity for the spilling of precious German blood, then surely I have the right to remove millions of an inferior race that breeds like vermin!' And this was in 1932, seven years before war was declared. But then war was already part of the plan, as stated in *Mein Kampf*, which refers not only to Hitler's personal struggle for existence but the struggle of the entire German Aryan race.

The priest at Steinhöring didn't expect the American soldiers to understand about the home. It was beyond comprehension really. He put them in touch with a local landowner, Freiherr Otto von Feury, who agreed to act as liaison with the locals, but wasn't especially forthcoming about the mother and baby home. 'It was run by the SS,' he repeated, 'not us.' Apparently the nurses would go to the butcher to buy meat, to the baker for bread and the dairy for milk, then go straight back inside the home again. They hardly spoke to the villagers, who hardly spoke to them. Von Feury put C Company in touch with Johann Grander, who ran the local dairy and was a

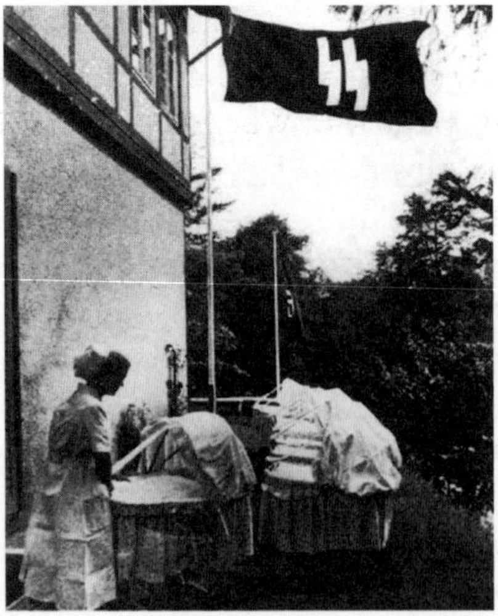

known anti-Nazi. Johann Grander was much more forthcoming. It was a home run by *Reichsführer* Heinrich Himmler's SS, he told them, for making the *Arische* babies. A *Lebensborn* home.

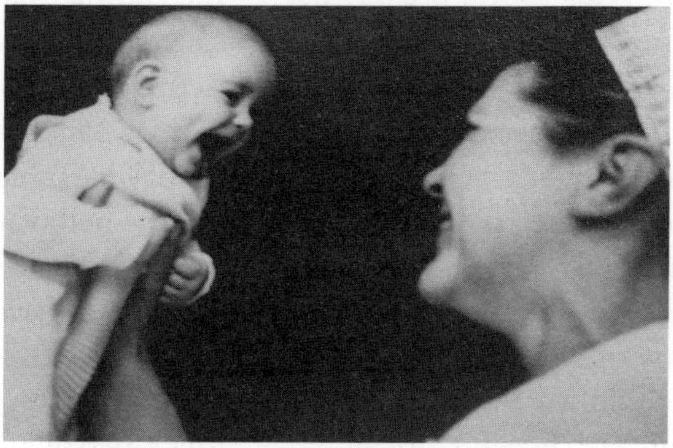

Say again? The American GI recalling that moment fifty years later was still astonished by it, shocked.

Herr Grander's English wasn't great, but he tried again: 'to make the *Arische Rasse*, *wissen Sie*, you know? *Reichsführer-SS* Heinrich Himmler's *Lebensborn* homes for the *Arische*.'

'*Arische*?'

One of the other Americans spoke some German. 'Aryans,' he said. 'Master Race and all that baloney.'

The men of C Company couldn't believe what they were hearing. 'Where are the mothers?'

'Oh, they don't stay. They just come to have the child. A child for Hitler, *wissen Sie*.'

Well, C Company happened to know there were a few mothers left, some evidently pregnant. 'Where are the staff?'

'They ran. In the Alps now.'

'Who are the fathers?'

'SS officers. *Arisch*, *natürlich*, of course.' Johann Grander laughed. Good joke, wasn't it?

This was more than the men of C Company could take in. It was plain crazy.

They made Johann Grander the new mayor of Steinhöring and put Freiherr Otto von Feury in charge of the Hochland home. It was US Army regulations: in each town or village they occupied they had to find a responsible local man, preferably anti-Nazi though it was hard to tell, to act as liaison with the occupying forces. Also to get rid of the previous mayor and replace him with someone who had not been involved with the local Nazi Party. Then move on. C Company moved on, leaving Freiherr von Feury to sort out what should happen to the 200 babies and children abandoned in the Hochland home.

Freiherr von Feury turned out to be a man of some initiative. Before C Company left he did a deal with the American officers. He needed petrol and a pass to get about. He had a small car, but it was standing immobile and useless in the garage of his country house on the outskirts of Steinhöring. All the shops were shut, so he needed to get from farm to farm to buy the milk and bread, and with luck some sausages, to feed the children. And he needed to contact a doctor: Dr Kleinle in Wasserburg, twenty kilometres away – some of the women were about to give birth. One midwife had stayed, but they needed a doctor. The trouble was, the Americans had interned Dr Kleinle for suspected Nazi sympathies. Before C Company left they procured some petrol and a pass for von Feury, and informed him that the next wave of Americans would be occupying the area for the duration, so Steinhöring would come under their administration. He should refer the case of Dr Kleinle to them.

'It is impossible now to understand how Himmler could do such things – could even think of them,' Renate said years later. 'And what about my father? What was he?'

Renate was a teacher, so she knew how to do her research. She started to read everything she could about *Lebensborn e.V*, hunting for clues. Apparently Himmler had founded the Ancestral Heritage Society in 1935, a year before he founded *Lebensborn*. Its purpose: to trace the origins of Nordic families and races, an 'ancient, holy legacy', older even than Greece or Rome. Special significance was given to 'ancient' runes, including the geometric S for his SS, which was a symbol for victory in ancient times, or so Himmler and his SS Race and Settlement experts believed. The pierced V, similarly 'ancient', representing life, became the symbol for *Lebensborn*. If Renate had looked closely at the gates of the Hochland home at Steinhöring she'd have seen both symbols worked into the wrought-iron pattern, like a secret code. Himmler was keen to change the names of the months back to ancient times – May to *Wonnemond*, the month of ecstasy, August to *Heurent*, the month of haymaking, and the like. But someone somewhere vetoed that. Enough was enough.

'A marriage with few children is little more than an affair,' stated Himmler at the start of *Lebensborn*. 'I hope members of the SS, and especially its officers, will set a good example. Four children is the minimum necessary for a good and healthy marriage. In the event of childlessness it is the duty of every SS leader to adopt racially valuable children, free of hereditary illness. The *Lebensborn* organisation will aid SS men in the selection and adoption of racially valuable children.' Girls were valuable as future racially pure mothers, but especially prized were the sons, who were destined to fight in the future war and die for the Führer if necessary. Thus four sons: two to die, two to live and procreate. Apparently the *Reichsführer-SS* quite forgot that he and his wife Marga only had one child, a girl named Gudrun.

But you didn't have to be married to bear a child. It was how the Nazi system worked: disguise a racial law by making it sound like social progress. *Lebensborn* was described as being modern by rejecting the bourgeois stigma of the unmarried woman bearing an illegitimate child. But the real point was that woman and child had to be racially pure. There could be no interbreeding. Only 'racially healthy' children were produced. Aryan children. The Slav and the 'Negro' were racial sub-specimens. After them came the Jew, who was not only racially impure but 'evil'.

Once in power, the Nazis' racial laws came thick and fast. It started in June 1933 with the Committee of Experts for Population and Racial Policy, which included Himmler. By 1935 came the laws: the Law for the Protection of the Hereditary Health of the German *Volk*, requiring the 'racially less valuable' to be registered. And the Law for the Prevention of Offspring with Hereditary Diseases. And the Marriage Health Law requiring a Certificate of Fitness (Racial) to marry. And the Law for the Protection of German Blood and German Honour of 14 November 1935, which made it illegal for anyone who threatened the 'purity of German blood' to engage in a sexual act with a German.

This was first and foremost the Jews. But not only. It soon extended to those with physical deformities and the 'generally feeble-minded', including homosexuals, schizophrenics, manic depressives, epileptics, chronic alcoholics. Hereditary Health Courts were set up, using primitive intelligence tests to measure mental deficiencies, with a lawyer and two doctors making the decision in secret: whether to sterilise or not. Already in 1934, hardly a year after the *Machtergreifung* (seizure of power), there were 181 Hereditary Health Courts. The National Socialist League of German Physicians, set up in 1929 for the purpose of purifying the *Vaterland*, had 2,786 members in January 1933. By the end of the year the number had risen to 11,000. By 1943 it was 46,000. Naturally, none were Jews.

The problem was a pressing one, as stated in the preamble to the Hereditary Law: 'Whereas hereditary healthy families have for the most part adopted a policy of having only one or two children, countless numbers of racial inferiors and those suffering from hereditary conditions are reproducing without restraint, allowing their sick and disadvantaged offspring to be a burden on the community.' Later came castration for sex offenders and abortion for 'unfit' pregnant women. Later still, euthanasia. A great raft of 'experts' was needed to implement this branch of medicine and fill the new institutions conducting the research: biologists, racial hygienists, anthropologists, sociologists, historians of Germanic studies. If you didn't want to lose your job, best keep your head down and do as you were told. Nazi Germany was soon filled with 'beefsteaks': people who were brown (Nazi) on the outside, pink inside.

Renate discovered that when she was three she'd been transferred to a *Lebensborn* home at Kohren, near Leipzig; who knows why? That's where *Tante* (aunt) Hilde, as she learned to call her foster mother, arrived to choose a child to adopt sometime in 1944.

The site of the home had again been personally chosen by Himmler, who liked to reuse buildings which had previously been clinics or sanatoria owned by Jews. Busy as he was with the great matters of state and war, he nevertheless found time to concern himself with every last detail of his *Lebensborn* homes. The names should suggest beauty and calm and be built in the old Germanic farm style with pitched roofs and pretty window boxes, surrounded by gardens with vegetables and flowers and orchards. *Blut und Boden*. Blood and Soil. There should be large, sunny rooms on the ground floor with French windows leading into the garden where the children could play in sandpits or on the swings. If the weather was clement the children should run about naked, because sun and fresh air were essential for health. The babies should sleep in their cots under the apple and cherry trees. The furnishings came from looted Jewish properties and were thus of the very best quality. There was a special treat for babies born on 7 October, Himmler's birthday: a candlestick made at Dachau concentration camp, plus a candle and one Reichsmark for every birthday till they were twenty-one, though that never materialised as the Nazi regime didn't last that long. The hard labour building the homes was done by inmates from the local concentration camp, the heavy domestic work by women prisoners shipped in from Ravensbrück camp. Everything went pleasingly hand in hand. Give and take.

The health of the children was of the greatest concern to the *Reichsführer-SS* because they would one day inherit the Thousand-Year German Reich. As the original statutes of *Lebensborn* stated, the whole purpose was to support racial and genetically valuable families and to give pregnant women, whether married or not, a healthy place to bear their racially pure children. Along with all the other instructions to his *Lebensborn* SS administration, Himmler made precise lists of the children's daily diet. Vegetables should always be steamed and potatoes served in their jackets. There should be plenty of fresh salads and fresh fruit and sunflower seeds and regular doses of castor oil. Wholemeal bread was advised, as was porridge for the children's breakfast because he'd heard that the British aristocracy were keen on it, especially Lord Halifax. The British were Aryans, of course, just like the Germans, which was a serious factor, Himmler knew, when Hitler decided not to invade the British Isles in May 1940 after the victory at Dunkirk, turning away from the English Channel at the last moment to face east and conquer the racially subhuman Russians instead. His *Wehrmacht* – army – generals were appalled. They didn't yet understand that this war was first and foremost a racial war. If they'd read *Mein Kampf* they might have understood: it was already there in 1924, in black and white. But who on earth could plough through all that?

Still. Had they read *Mein Kampf* the generals would have known that the Nazis' racial theories were the key to everything else. Equally, they could have paid more attention to the racial laws, which came fast after the *Nationalsozialistische Deutsche Arbeiterpartei*'s – NSDAP, Nazi Party – *Machtergreifung* in January 1933. Already in April, hardly two months later, came the Law for the Restoration of the Professional Civil Service, dismissing anyone politically or racially undesirable and barring Jews from being doctors, dentists, teachers and students. Dachau was opened the same month. Then came *Gleichschaltung*, whereby anyone not 'politically aligned' lost their job. From July doctors had to register each case of hereditary illness, except in women over forty-five who were past the age of childbearing. Doctors who didn't do their duty would be fined. If Germany got a million racially healthy children a year, and removed 700,000 or 800,000 of the weakest people, the strength of the *Vaterland* would be accordingly increased, as Hitler announced at the 1929 Nuremberg Party Rally.

Racial theories were all the rage in the Western world in the nineteenth century and early years of the twentieth. Many books were written on anthropology and eugenics, with some arguing the case for sterilisation of the unfit. Anti-Semitism was widespread. The British Empire was a typical colonial society where the 'pure' Anglo-Saxon did not mix with the 'native' or the 'half-breed', and certainly never intermarried. But nowhere were these theories taken to their logical conclusion as in Nazi Germany: the extermination of the racially inferior. And nowhere did extermination go hand in hand with a programme to breed a racially superior Master Race. In other countries, those theories were a small part of a varied whole. In Nazi Germany, they were the whole. The basis of everything else.

The Nazis had not won the election in November 1932 – the last democratic election in Germany for twelve years. They'd only got their *Machtergreifung* in January 1933 because of a fateful coalition with the centre parties, who were more afraid of the Communists than they were of the Nazis. But once in power, there was no stopping them, especially in matters concerning race. The First Nuremberg Law of 1935 'to protect German Blood and Honour' barred marriage and any sexual relations between Jews and non-Jews, punishable by time in a concentration camp, later by death. Jews were not allowed to employ German servants, and were not allowed to fly the German national flag. The same applied to Gypsies and 'Negroes'. The Marriage Health Law stipulated that all couples had to undergo a medical examination to avoid 'racial damage'. Either that or be sterilised. A German citizen was defined as being of German or related blood, who was willing and able faithfully to serve the German people and the Reich. The rest of the population was classified as residents, not citizens, so had no privileges. 'When determining racial characteristics it is not enough to look at the external shape of the body,' stated the *Nation and Race Journal*. 'We must go beyond, to explore differences in the inner organs of the body, differences that may reflect deeper psychological differences between races. Best known of this area is "racial smell".'

Presumably *Tante* Hilde and her husband, as members of the Nazi Party, knew some if not all of this as they joined other prospective parents going up and down a line-up of children at the *Lebensborn* home, inspecting and choosing a racially pure child. Did they want a boy? Did they want a girl? Did they prefer a baby or an older child? Was the child blond enough – a key question, because there were cases of parents giving back the children once they grew older and less blond. Perhaps *Tante* Hilde, filling in the forms, said she preferred a child, not a baby. And a girl. Her reasons, like so many details of Renate's early life, are lost in the fog of time. She made her choice easily. Renate was a sturdy, striking child – fair hair done in stumpy pigtails, her eyes bright blue – the very image of the Nazis' pure Aryan.

How could Renate know that this was a turning point in her life, mirroring in its own small way the turning point in Germany's war? By mid-1944, shortly after the D-Day landings in Normandy, there was no doubt the Allies would win. They were only waiting for Hitler's unconditional surrender, which he refused to concede, preferring to sacrifice another million lives till the inevitable end in May 1945. For now, there was chaos. When Renate was born in 1941 at the Steinhöring home it housed no more than 100 children and babies and was well staffed with nurses and doctors and an efficient administration, which occupied a large office on the first floor – all members of Himmler's SS. But in this last year of the war, with an influx of children from other *Lebensborn* homes across the Reich fleeing the advancing Western Allies from one direction or the Russians from the other, it was mayhem in the remaining homes.

One day about a year later, after the *Götterdämmerung* of defeat, a woman arrived at the small house at Kohren where Renate was living with *Tante* Hilde. The woman was in her late thirties, and she came with her mother. It turned out they were Renate's mother and grandmother. Most of the other mothers had abandoned their children in the *Lebensborn* homes, now ordinary children's homes, preferring to forget they'd ever been prepared to bear a child for Hitler now that the dream of the Thousand-Year German Reich lay dead and buried. But Frau Röder, as Renate's mother had been encouraged to call herself by Nazi law though she was not married, wanted her child back. In fact she'd managed, in spite of the war and the great distance from her home in Cologne, with all the train disruptions and the dangers of the bombing raids, to visit her child once or twice in the *Lebensborn* homes over the past four years, though Renate had virtually no recollection of it. So now here was Else Röder, come to collect her child and take her home. Perhaps *Tante* Hilde was only ever a foster mother, taking care of Renate till her real mother was able to look after her. Who knows? Renate often asked her mother about it in later years, but she never got a straight answer.

How was the child Renate to understand what was happening to her? How could any of the 11,000 children born in Heinrich Himmler's *Lebensborn* homes know? Not even Renate's mother Frau Röder really understood, though she'd been a willing, not to say keen, volunteer to produce a child for Hitler back in 1941. In fact, she'd been in love with Friedrich, the SS officer who was Renate's father. The only trouble was that Friedrich was already married. With five children. And then he had one or two more, outside marriage, doing his bit to breed racially pure children for *Lebensborn*, as instructed by his chief, *Reichsführer-SS* Heinrich Himmler.

But Else Röder didn't know that when the couple met, back in the summer of 1937. Renate thought it was at a hotel in the Black Forest and that Else had gone there for a holiday, on her own or possibly with a group from the *Kraft durch Freude* (Strength through Joy) organisation introduced by the Nazis. Else worked at a local savings bank in Cologne which gave their employees one week's holiday a year. Perhaps she was sitting on the hotel terrace reading one of her books when an SS officer came to sit at the table next to her. However hard Renate tried to get the facts of that fateful meeting from her mother in later years, Else never did divulge them. Perhaps she didn't want to share them with anyone, not even her daughter, Friedrich's child. All she would say, repeating it again and again, eyes shining, was that he was tall and handsome, and that he smiled at her. And that she was quite taken aback, astonished that such a grand officer might want to talk to her. Else didn't think of herself as very attractive: she was small and shy, with blue button eyes and wispy blond hair, and although she'd had some suitors over the years she was still unmarried, aged thirty-one.

After that they met from time to time, and each time Else couldn't believe her luck. It was love at first sight for her. Who knows what it was for him?

Once or twice Friedrich, as he was called, even came to visit her at home in Cologne, bringing her *Mutti* flowers. When the rest of the family heard about those visits they were quite overcome. They didn't know exactly what Friedrich did in the SS, but he was clearly high up, and they were willing accomplices in the relationship. Eventually Friedrich told Else what she'd already guessed: that he was married, with children. He didn't mention that he'd been married before, to a half-Jewess he'd divorced early after the Nazi *Machtergreifung*, and that one of their children, the disabled one, had 'disappeared'. But he went on to explain something important to Else: there was no reason why she shouldn't have a child herself, if she wanted. All this bourgeois rubbish about illegitimate children – there was no need for it. *Reichsführer-SS* Heinrich Himmler said the most important people in the Reich today were the mothers, the ones who bore the children for the future Thousand-Year German Reich. It really didn't matter whether they were married or not. In fact the *Reichsführer-SS*, whom he knew personally, was so keen on this that he'd founded a charity called *Lebensborn* consisting of mother and baby homes where the mothers could have their babies in the most healthy and beautiful places, with the very best care, whether married or not. Had she heard of *Lebensborn*? Else hadn't. But she longed to have a child. His child.

He explained that she'd have to undergo the usual racial tests at RuSHA, the SS Race and Settlement Main Office, before she was accepted as a *Lebensborn* mother, to attest to her sound health, mental as well as physical, and her racial purity going back to her great-grandparents. Only half the women who applied were accepted, he explained, so stringent were the requirements of race. None of this presented a problem for Else, who really couldn't wait to get pregnant. Of course Friedrich had already undergone all the racial tests or he couldn't have been an SS officer in the first place. He was an early member of the Nazi Party and an early member of the SS. He had few educational qualifications, having only attended the local polytechnic, but the SS recruitment office wasn't bothered about that. The key thing, as the *Reichsführer-SS* insisted, was that the recruits be Aryan, with a soldierly bearing. Friedrich certainly was both.

From Friedrich's point of view, Else must have seemed the perfect choice: not only racially pure, but pure in other ways too – ways *Lebensborn* knew how to appreciate. As Dr Gregor Ebner, the Chief Medical Officer, wrote to Max Sollmann, running the *Lebensborn* head office in Munich: 'As you know, the *Reichsführer-SS* is a strong opponent of excessive beauty care in our women. He considers it unworthy of the German woman to paint her lips, pluck her eyebrows and paint her nails. We hold to this very strongly in *Lebensborn* homes, and ensure the mothers do not start these unfortunate habits. Unfortunately I have noticed that women working at head office do indulge in these deplorable practices. Some of the mothers have noticed it and are somewhat confused about what the real attitude of the SS is in this respect. It would therefore be better if the women who work for *Lebensborn* set a proper example.'

Else was modest and attractive in a quiet, natural sort of way. Born in 1906, she had grown up during the hard years of the First World War, swiftly followed by the chaos of the Weimar Republic with its economic crises and virtual civil war between Fascists and Communists, fought out daily in violent street battles. They were harsh times, especially for ordinary people like her family. Her father worked in a market garden cultivating fruit and vegetables. Her mother ran the household. Then her father died, leaving the two women living alone, managing as best they could. Else was working at her local savings bank as a stenotypist in 1933 when Hitler and the Nazis came to power, promising to restore order and pride to the German nation and give the Jews what they had coming to them. Mother and daughter were not ardent Nazi supporters, but supporters nevertheless. After all, hadn't the Führer saved the German Reich from ruin?

You only had to read the newspapers and listen to the wireless. Everything was on the up: unemployment solved, law and order restored, clean, safe streets, better conditions for the working man and, best of all, the *Kraft durch Freude* movement. Imagine: there were paid holidays now, and marvellous leisure opportunities for the workers – sports clubs, entertainments, many new feast days like the Führer's birthday, and subsidised trips to beautiful parts of the Reich. 'The popularity of these trips is having a great effect,' went a secret SOPAD report in the summer of 1934:

> Their cheapness is astonishing. Examples: visits to mountain villages. I met a couple from Cologne. For an eight-day stay in Frasdorf, including the journey there and back, plus costs and board, they paid 60 marks. Otherwise the journey alone with a holiday card would have cost 100 marks. In any case a worker earning 53 pfennigs an hour cannot manage it on his own. Again: 1,200 workers from Bavaria went to Spitsbergen. The trip lasted 10 days. Inclusive of board, the whole trip cost 76 marks per person. And another: 900 men from Munich, workers from BMW and other local firms, went on an eight-day trip to the Mosel. The trip cost 35 marks per person. The participants got a glass of wine with each midday meal. At one place on the Mosel there was a wine-tasting at a public spa, and the participants of the trip were allowed to drink to their hearts' content. You can imagine how enthusiastic they were!

Not to mention the triumph of the 1936 Olympic Games, caught on film by the brilliant Leni Riefenstahl on the orders of her boss Joseph Goebbels at the Ministry of Propaganda and Enlightenment, when the whole world was in awe of Germany and the achievements of the Nazi Party. And not an unhappy Jew in sight.

'*Liebes Elsele!* Dear little Else,' went the first letter from Friedrich, dated 20 July 37, hardly two weeks after that first meeting on the hotel terrace in the Black Forest. Astonishingly it was headed *Der Führer des SS-Oberabschnittes Mitte* on the left, and *Braunschweig, den Landtagsgebäude*, the regional parliament, on the right. So he lived in Braunschweig and he was the *Führer* of the entire region.

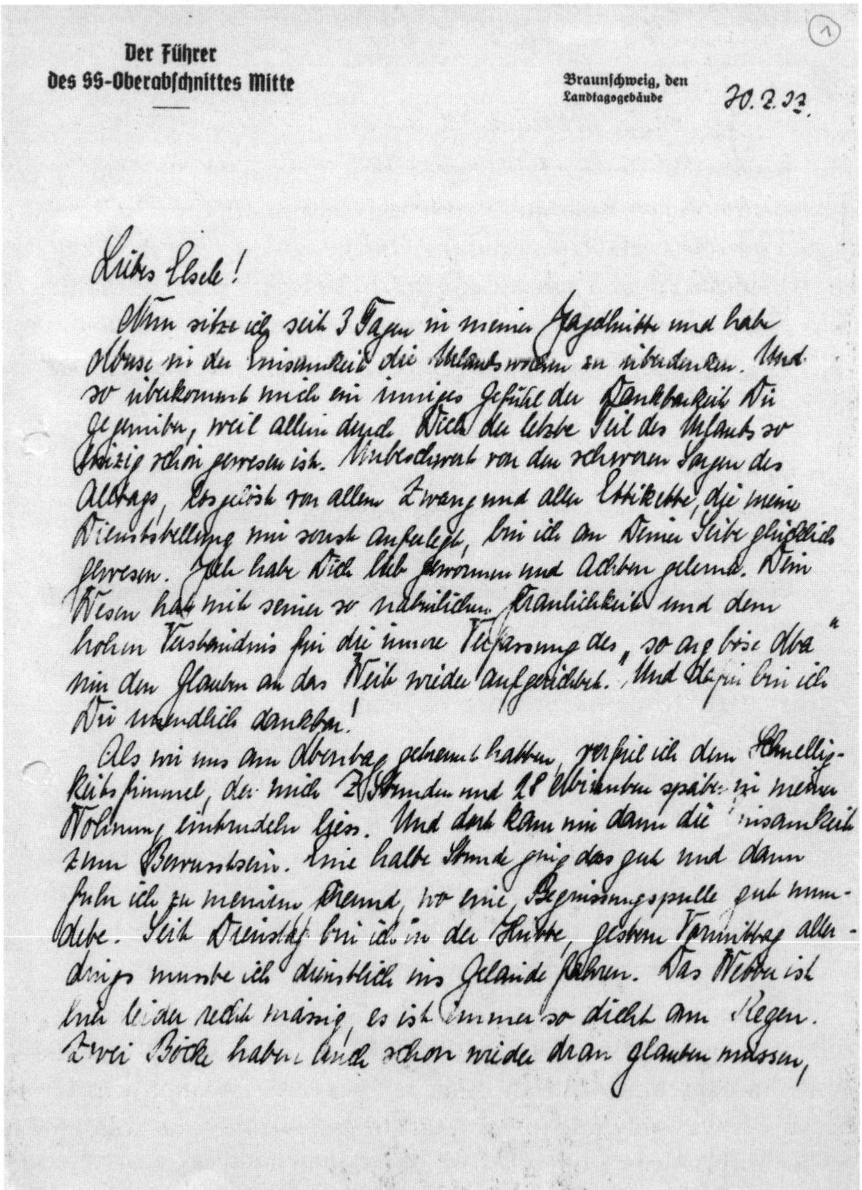

(1)

Der Führer
des SS-Oberabschnittes Mitte

Braunschweig, den
Landtagsgebäude 20.7.37.

Liebes Elsele!

Nun sitze ich seit 3 Tagen in meiner Jagdhütte und habe Muße in der Einsamkeit die Urlaubswochen zu überdenken. Und so überkommt mich ein inniges Gefühl der Dankbarkeit Dir gegenüber, weil allein durch Dich der letzte Teil des Urlaubs so einzig schön gewesen ist. Unbeschwert von den schweren Sorgen des Alltags, losgelöst von allem Zwang und aller Etikette, die meine Dienststellung mir sonst auferlegt, bin ich an Deiner Seite glücklich gewesen. Ich habe Dich lieb gewonnen und achten gelernt. Dein Wesen hat mit seiner so natürlichen Fraulichkeit und dem hohen Verständnis für die innere Verfassung des „so arg bösen Alten" mir den Glauben an das Weib wieder aufgerichtet. Und dafür bin ich Dir unendlich dankbar!

Als wir uns am Abend getrennt hatten, verfiel ich dem Schnelligkeitstaumel, der mich 2 Stunden und 28 Minuten später in meiner Wohnung einlaufen ließ. Und dort kam mir dann die Einsamkeit zum Bewusstsein. Eine halbe Stunde ging das gut und dann fuhr ich zu meinem Freund, wo eine Begrüßungsquelle gut mundete. Seit Dienstag bin ich in der Hütte, gestern Vormittag allerdings musste ich dienstlich ins Gelände fahren. Das Wetter ist hier leider recht mäßig, es ist immer so dicht am Regen. Zwei Böcke haben auch schon wieder dran glauben müssen,

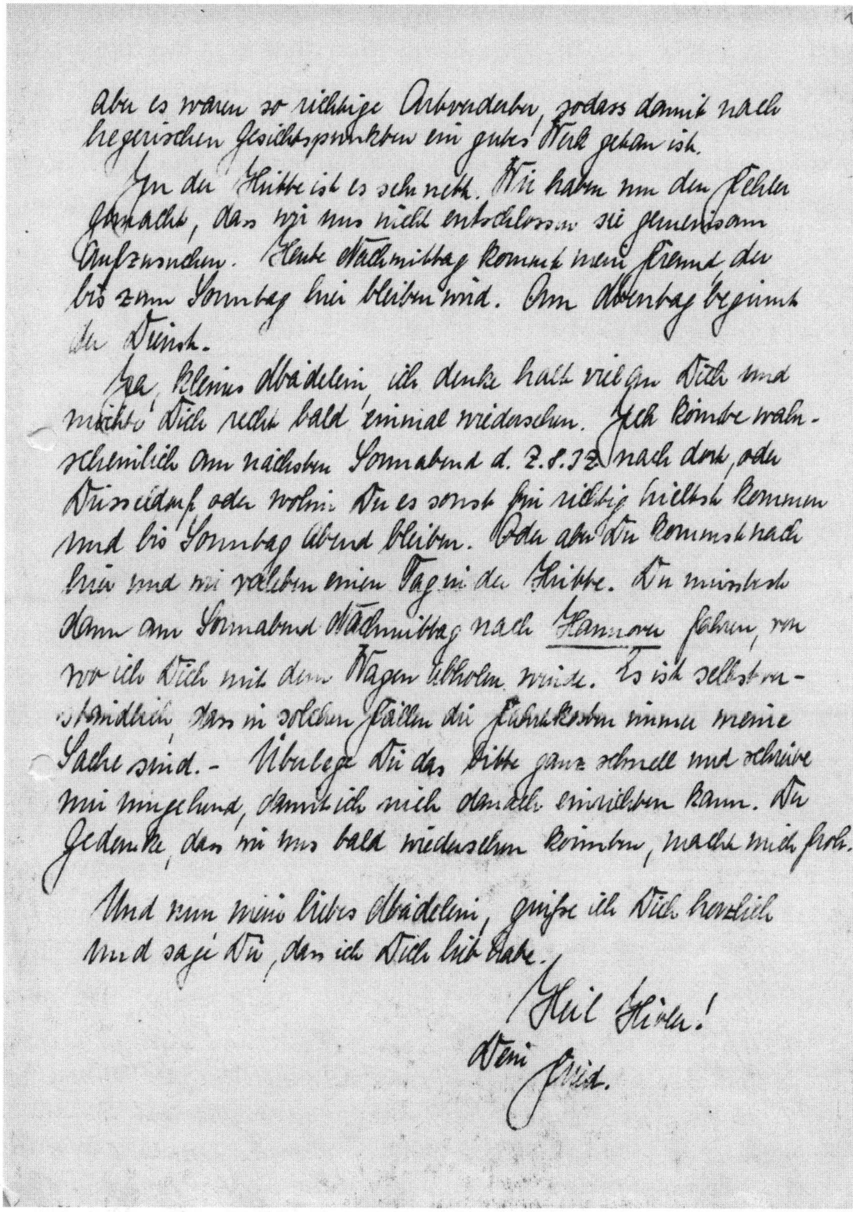

1

Aber es waren so richtige Arbeitertaten, sodass damit nach hegerischen Gesichtspunkten ein gutes Werk getan ist.

In der Hütte ist es sehr nett. Wir haben nur den Fehler gemacht, dass wir uns nicht entschlossen sie gemeinsam aufzusuchen. Heute Nachmittag kommt mein Freund der bis zum Sonntag hier bleiben wird. Am Montag beginnt der Dienst.

Ja, kleines [illegible], ich denke halt viel an Dich und möchte Dich recht bald einmal wiedersehen. Ich komme wahrscheinlich am nächsten Sonnabend d. 2.8.[illegible] nach dort, oder Düsseldorf oder wohin Du es sonst für richtig hieltest kommen und bis Sonntag abend bleiben. Oder aber Du kommst nach hier und wir erleben einen Tag in der Hütte. Du müsstest dann am Sonnabend Nachmittag nach Hannover fahren, von wo ich Dich mit dem Wagen abholen würde. Es ist selbstverständlich, dass in solchen Fällen die Fahrkosten immer meine Sache sind. – Überlege Du das bitte ganz schnell und schreibe mir umgehend, damit ich mich danach einrichten kann. Der Gedanke, dass wir uns bald wiedersehen können, macht mich froh. –

Und nun mein liebes [illegible], grüße ich Dich herzlich und sage Dir, dass ich Dich lieb habe.

Heil Hitler!

Dein [illegible].

'I've been in my hunting hut for the last three days, so I've had the time, sitting here on my own, to think about the weeks of holiday. And I'm overcome with an inner feeling of gratitude towards you because it was only due to you that the last week of the holiday was so beautiful. Away from all the heavy concerns of my everyday life, free of any pressures and matters of etiquette, I was happy in the knowledge of your love. I have learnt to love and respect you. Your natural and direct character, and your deep understanding of people's inner feelings, have restored my faith in womankind. And for that I am deeply grateful!'

When they met he'd felt a quickening of his heart, he wrote, and once he was back home he became aware of a loneliness. The weather was unfortunately not so good, always raining. But it was nice in the hut. His friend Struppi was arriving that afternoon and staying till Sunday. Monday it was back to work. 'Well, *kleines Mädelein*, little girl, I think of you often and would like to see you again very soon. I could probably come and see you next Sunday afternoon, and stay till evening. Or we could meet wherever you prefer. Or we could spend the Saturday night and Sunday in my hut. You'd have to take the train to Hanover on the Saturday, and I'd pick you up in my car there. It goes without saying that I would pay your travel expenses. Please think this over quickly, so I can arrange matters accordingly. You can imagine how happy it makes me to think we'll be seeing each other again soon. And now, little one, I embrace you tightly, and tell you how much I care for you. *Heil Hitler!* Your Fried.'

So Fried it was, from then on.

On 21 August 1937 he wrote again: '*Mein liebes Mädelein!* My dear little girl!' He thanked her heartily for her letter. The work he was doing had to be seen through, and that increased his longing for Cologne. 'I think of you often too, and have a great longing for you.' Unfortunately he couldn't see her again till 3 October, work was too pressing – other than 5 September, when he had to be on SS troop manoeuvres for several days in the Heide, but could take some time off during the first two days when his presence was not absolutely necessary. Or he could come to Cologne. But how to manage this? He asked her to suggest something quickly, so he could arrange matters. 'Anyway, we must see one another, or it's not much of a life.' Otherwise things were going well. There had been a happy meeting with the *Kamaraden*. Struppi sent best wishes. Tomorrow was Sunday, but not for him, because he had a long meeting in Magdeburg. He had to give a speech at the *Volksgemeinschaft-Wehrgemeinschaft* exhibition, on *Volk* and defence, and he had no idea what he was going to say! 'You are my dear, sweet little one. So we'll meet, and I'm already looking forward to it very much. Stay healthy, and enjoy your day off. I embrace you heartily, your Fried.'

On 17 September 1937 he wrote again, to thank her for the 'sweet photograph'. He thought of her often, and wished she was with him. He was very tired after a heavy day's work. But work was going well. Nuremberg had been a success. On Friday he was having to go to Munich to greet Mussolini. So it was difficult to meet. Unless she took Saturday off work (he knew her chief was absent) and kept it free, in case he could get away. In which case she could take an omnibus to B, and they could spend the night together in the hotel. He would organise it. 'I'm longing to see you because you're a darling girl! I embrace you heartily, your Fried.'

On 28 September he wrote from Berlin, headed Reichstag, *Abgeordneter*, delegate. Evidently Friedrich liked to use official notepaper. He was already in his office at 6 a.m., he wrote, he had so much work. He never said what kind of work he did, there in Braunschweig. 'I hope you enjoyed our time together. I am already looking forward to the next.' He was too busy for a few days, but on Friday he was off to B with the *Reichsführer-SS*. They could try another Hanover plan – she should wait for him in the railway station waiting room, second-class, which was less obvious. He hoped to be there on time. 'I'll be in full uniform, so I'll wait for you in the car at the *back* of the station. All the rest, overnight, travel to B, leave to me. I am thinking of you. I embrace you, your Fried.'

If ever Fried had a moment of guilt about Else it was quickly assuaged by his chief, Heinrich Himmler. As the *Reichsführer-SS* jokily put it in one of his interminable talks to his *Gruppenführer*s earlier that year: 'We are all men here, consequently it is safe to say – the moment you have to select a stenotypist and you have two candidates before you, one fearfully hideous fifty-year-old who does 300 words a minute, a sheer genius in this sphere, and another a racially good, pretty twenty-year-old who does a bare 150 words, you will, unless I completely misjusdge you – probably with the most serious air and with a thousand moral reasons – because the other is old and therefore could become ill more easily – I know, take the lovely young twenty-year-old, who does fewer words.' What a wag, his SS officers said to one another, laughing heartily.

Another Fried letter came from the Reichstag on 18 October 1937 thanking Else for both her letters, which always gave balsam for his nerves. He was sorry he hadn't written for so long. 'But you'll forgive me, I know. And that I feel warmly for you and often think of you, you already know! There is so much happening, I'll tell you about it another time. The last ten days I have had to work late into the night. That's why I've had to postpone our meeting. As soon as I've finished my SS work, I'll probably be able to go to the hut for a few days. And then I want to see you as soon as possible. I embrace you heartily dear girl, your Fried.'

Why was Fried so busy that summer of 1937? To put it simply, he was carrying out Joseph Goebbels's expressed intention, written in his private diary on 7 August 1936, anticipating the triumph of the Berlin Olympics: 'After the Olympics we'll get ruthless. Then there will be some shooting.'

Braunschweig had, from the earliest days of the Nazi Party, been a hotbed of Fascist violence, with Friedrich active there from the first, renowned for his brutality, hounding Communists and other opponents of the Nazi regime. Wolfenbüttel prison, a vast nineteenth-century building, was only seven kilometers south of Braunschweig. In 1937 the Reich Ministry of Justice decided to make it the main execution centre for northern Germany, in addition to its day-to-day work of imprisoning and torturing resisters of the Nazi regime. Now that the world was no longer watching, the Party *Führer*s could get back to work, with thousands of arrests of Communists and Socialists, thousands of Jewish assets and properties 'appropriated' – the 'Actions' often going happily hand in hand: Communists and Jews, Jews and Communists – two birds with one stone.

In fact there was endless trouble to deal with throughout the Reich. You only had to read the police reports being sent to local Gestapo offices to see how powerful the opposition to the Nazi regime still was, in spite of the 'Actions'.

'Funeral of a Communist' in Darmstadt was dated 21 April 1937: 'Concerning a Communist demonstration on the occasion of the burial of Adam Schaefer who was a prisoner in protective custody in Dachau. The investigations into the above affair have so far discovered: On 24 March 1937 Adam Schaefer (born 25 August 1907 in Mainz-Kostheim and who was in the camp due to expressing anti-state opinions) was shot by an SS guard whom he attacked.

About 800 people were present at the burial itself. Those present were almost exclusively opponents of the state. About 40 per cent were known former associates and members of the SPD Social Democrat Party and the centre parties; perhaps 60 per cent were former KPD Communists. Participants appeared from distant suburbs and even Mainz itself. The Communists stood together during the ceremony at the graveside...'

Sabotage was a perennial problem in the armaments factories: 'There have been complaints for several months about inadequate work production at the armaments firm of Middle German Steelworks in Groeditz, district Grossenhain, which has a workforce of about 6,000 people,' went another police report, this time in Dresden. 'Absence from work and sickness is very high, up to 1,200 workers temporarily missing. In several cases damage to machinery caused suspicion of sabotage. Since October the Gestapo has become involved in about 50 cases.'

The Churches were another problem, especially the Catholic Church, roughly half their priests being arrested at one time or another. They were using feast days and pilgrimages as a cover for political action. Thus a police report about the night of 17 March 1937 from Cologne: 'Pilgrims flocked to the meeting point for the procession's 22.50 departure from the Hay Market and went on till shortly after midnight. It is estimated that 25,000 attended. Each parish group carried a large cross in front of it to the cathedral. The devotion was made by Archbishop Schulte. Politically it was noteworthy that the Catholic population of Cologne, in recent times, have banded together strongly. They are taking part in church celebrations and events in numbers of such size that have hardly been seen in previous years.' This one was not unique: in Bamberg 60,000 people participated in its 700-year-old Dornweihe festival, and 800,000 travelled to Aachen for the Heiligtum Fest.

Yes, there was endless work for Friedrich – day work, night work, you-name-it work. His next letter to Else came from Braunschweig again, *SS-Oberschnitte Mitte*, on 25 October 1937. It was a strange letter. He thanked her very much for her letter, which always gave him joy. 'I really need a bit of joy – I've been rather low-spirited lately, and try as I might, I can't seem to get out of it. There is so much work and so many duties. My only respite is the hunting hut. But I feel lonely there whenever I'm alone.' The day before, though, he'd been out hunting with friends. He went on to list his work days, saying he was free from the Friday. 'So of course I want to be with you on Saturday evening and Sunday.' He underlined the Sunday. He could meet her in Hanover or Frankfurt? He gave the times of the trains from Cologne as usual. His letters always ended with '*Heil Hitler!*'

The next letter, 13 November 1937, was written on five small sheets of paper from the hunting hut because he didn't have anything else with him. It was a recuperation being there, he wrote, so he was able to find himself again, away from the *Getrieb des Lebens*, the whirlwind of life. Struppi was with him. 'He's a good fellow.' He thought of her a lot, however much he liked to be alone. 'It's our secret.' The weather was cold. The quiet was doing him good. He listed his work commitments in detail again for the coming days. 'And how are you, little one? Do you think of me sometimes? As soon as I have a bit of time in the next weeks, we'll see each other.' Else thought of him all the time of course, as well he knew.

On 3 January 1938 he wrote from the Hotel Weisses Rössl in the Black Forest, where he was celebrating the New Year. Presumably he was there with his wife and children, but naturally he didn't mention that. 'Recuperating here for a week, and I really need it,' he wrote. 'I'm thinking of you, and want to wish you a Happy New Year. It comes a little late, I know, but nevertheless from the heart. I know I've upset you, and I know I've been unfair to you, but I don't want to excuse myself. At least not in writing. It's probably hard for you to understand me – I often can't even do it myself. I torture myself with all sorts of thoughts … In addition, my work, with all its duties and responsibilities, is a burden. And in my low moods, alcohol has been my saviour.' He was able to re-find himself in the beautiful winter landscape, he wrote. He'd been cross-country skiing that afternoon. There were some old couples staying in the hotel, celebrating New Year. He knew she often thought of him. As he did of her. How did she celebrate the New Year, he wondered. 'I leave here on 9 January. It would please me to meet you then. You too? I arrive in Frankfurt at 20.25. You could take the 15.02 from Cologne … otherwise I can't see how we can manage it. Please let me know by telegram. By Thursday if possible. Your Fried.'

By 22 February 1938 he was back in Brauschweig, back at work. 'My dear little one!' he wrote. 'The photograph arrived yesterday! I like it very much, and I thank you for it dear girl, and will look at it often till our next meeting.' He thanked her for her letter too, then moves on to a possible future meeting. 'Your plan is a good one, but it can't in fact happen in that way. The situation is: I received an invitation from the Führer yesterday to attend a gathering at his house in Munich on Friday. Of course I had to accept. And the *Reichsführer-SS* may need me on the Thursday. I could perhaps free myself on Sunday, but I'd have to be back in the office early Monday morning. As soon as I know the details I'll let you know.' He included the usual train timetables and the usual arrangement to meet in the station waiting room, second-class. 'Let me know by return of post. Otherwise let me know at the Hotel Four Seasons in Munich. I write in haste...'

He wrote in haste because 1938 was a very busy time, planning the top-secret invasion of the Sudetenland and preparing all those lies for the Allies, especially those naive appeasers in London. Big lies, never little ones, as the Führer liked to say. And it was especially busy for Fried and the *Führer*s of the future *Einsatzgruppen* troops, those SS units being formed to follow in the wake of the regular *Wehrmacht* in the planned war, exterminating any local resistance, mopping up.

But it didn't stop Fried writing to Else, his 'good' little one. He wrote sporadically, as and when he could see a free night coming up which they could spend together. The letters all followed the same pattern: he thanked her for her letters, he missed her, he felt warmly about her, the weather was good/bad, he wanted to see her soon, she should take the train from Cologne station and get to Hanover station by such-and-such. Wait for him in the second-class waiting room, round the back. He was finding it harder to take time off to see her.

The problem was: Else wasn't getting pregnant.

Once war broke out on 1 September 1939 with Germany's invasion of Poland, the letters became even more sporadic. But he knew she would understand, he wrote.

On 28 October 1939 Himmler issued an SS Order headed 'The *Reichsführer-SS* and Chief of the German Police in the Ministry of Interior, to the whole SS and police'. 'Every war is a loss of the best blood,' he wrote:

> Many a military victory was at the same time an extinguishing defeat of the *Volk*'s life-force and blood. But the sadly unavoidable loss of our best men, tragic though it is, is not the worst of matters. Much worse is the lost breeding of children by those men, living but away at war, or then, after the war is over, by the men who died during it. The old wisdom that only the man who has borne sons and children can die at peace is once again true in this war for our men of the SS ... Reaching beyond normal bourgeois laws and attitudes, it will be the highest duty for unmarried as well as married women and young girls of good blood to bear a child, not frivolously but in the deepest seriousness, with soldiers about to be sent to the Front, and of whom Fate alone can tell whether they will come home again or die in the field. For all legitimate and also illegitimate children of good Blood whose fathers fall in the war we take on, as personally ordered by myself, their guardianship in the name of the *Reichsführer-SS*. We will stand by the mothers, and will care for their offspring both in human and material terms till their coming of age, so the mothers and widows have no worries about need. The men and women who find their place remaining in the *Heimat* by order of the State, they too, men and women alike, have a duty to become fathers and mothers of (racially pure) children.

Over the next year Fried wrote when 'work' allowed, and they saw each other for a day/night here, a day/night there, as and when Fried had some leave from his mop-up duties. The *Reichsführer-SS* had posted him into an infantry division, he wrote on 25 February 1940, not the artillery, which he would have preferred. But he was in *sehr frohe Stimmung*, a very cheerful mood, looking forward to joining his troops. By 26 April he was writing that, unfortunately, there was absolutely no chance that they could meet at his hunting hut as planned. 'I think of you often, dear girl, and wish I could be with you. Heartfelt greetings. *Heil Hitler!* Your Fried.' By May he was in France. On 26 June he was back in the *Heimat*. His division had got as far as Lyons, he wrote. On the way home he travelled via Reims, Luxembourg, Trier, Cologne, then Braunschweig. Unfortunately Cologne was in the middle of the night, so he couldn't visit her. But he thought about her often. On 2 July he wrote to say he was trying to get her tickets to the Reich's Party Day. 'I believe, anyway, this war will be over very soon!' Seven days later he wrote again to tell her that the *Reichsführer-SS* had promoted him to Higher SS and Police Chief. He was probably being transferred to Norway. He thought he might manage a quick visit to Cologne. Then no letters for several weeks. He spent some time in Düsseldorf, not far from Cologne, so perhaps there were no letters because they were seeing each other. Who knows?

Then came the letter of 27 June 1941, with 'Braunschweig' already crossed out. 'My dear girl!' he wrote:

> I'm writing you these lines just a few hours before my departure. I'll set off tonight at 1 a.m. with my staff, and should be in Kraków by 15.00 hours. There I'll meet up with my troops, and then it's on to south Russia. More I do not know. I've talked to the *Reichsführer-SS* about our situation, and he also has a statement in writing about it, so everything is in order, just in case something bad happens to me. The *Reichsführer* was so nice about it, he gave me 2,000 marks to pay for everything. You can turn to him for help at any time. Your stay in the *Lebensborn* home at Steinhöring near Munich is fully arranged. You just have to make yourself known to them. You can go there two months before the big event. Meanwhile, I'm sending you 1,000 marks, and I'm putting a further 1,000 into your bank. You see, everything is perfectly organised.
>
> During these last few days of preparation I've had to see to all sorts of difficult matters, so I'm feeling rather nervy. The vehicles for me and my personal staff stand ready at the back of the house, together with all sorts of weapons. Once I give the signal for departure I'll feel more relaxed. I'm looking forward very much to the military engagement.
>
> I hope you are well. Hold your head high, and feel happy about what is to come, even if it is sometimes difficult. I'll write to you again soon.
>
> Heartfelt greetings and a loving kiss, your Fried.

So Else was pregnant with Renate. And Fried was off to Ukraine. By 27 August he was the SS general in charge of the *Einsatzgruppen* at Kamianets-Podilskyi, exterminating the Jews – a mass-murder of 23,600 men, women and children. By 29 September he was in Babi Yar near Kiev overseeing the massacre of an estimated 33,770 Jews, shooting them into pits outside the town. By November 1941, at the time of Renate's birth at the *Lebensborn* home at Steinhöring, he was in Riga, Latvia, continuing his work.

In a memo of 2 July from Reinhard Heydrich, Himmler's right-hand man, to the four *Höhere SS- und Polizeiführers*, police chiefs, including Friedrich Jeckeln (to name him in full), he summarised the 'basic instructions' which he'd already issued to his *Einsatzgruppen* in anticipation of Germany's invasion of Russia ten days earlier, on 21 June 1941:

> EXECUTIONS. The following will be executed: all officials of the Comintern. Officials of senior and middle rank and 'extremists' in the party, the central committee, and the provincial and district committees. The People's Commissars. Jews in the service of the Party or the State. Other extremist elements (saboteurs, propagandists, snipers, assassins, agitators etc.). No steps will be taken to interfere with any purges that may be initiated by anti-Communist or anti-Jewish elements in the newly occupied territories. On the contrary, they are to be secretly encouraged.

Those were the written instructions. In fact, the *Einsatzgruppen* had verbal orders to shoot all Jews. A report from *Einsatzgruppe A* on 15 October 1941 stated that security police were resolved 'in accordance with instructions received, to solve the Jewish problem decisively and by all available means'. And again, at beginning of 1942: 'Systematic cleansing operations are being carried out, in accordance with the principles laid down in orders concerning the relentless elimination of Judaism. Certain difficulties may be encountered in regard to the final and complete extermination of the Jews left in White Ruthenia after the German invasion.' Some had to be spared for essential work, apparently, and severe frost had impeded 'mass executions'. In spite of this, it had proved 'possible to shoot some 41,000 Jews'.

On 12 September 1941 Fried found time to write to Else, thanking her for her two letters and telling her that he'd acknowledged paternity for Renate with the *Reichsführer-SS*. 'You don't need to give my name at the *Lebensborn* home, just say that the father is a Higher SS officer who is away at war, and that the *Reichsführer-SS* has the details, and the paternity document.' He himself was in very good health, he wrote, though life was full of strife and difficulties. 'Are you a little happy anticipating the great event? Be proud, because you're giving your *Volk* the biggest and most valuable thing for its survival.' He ended with a buoyant '*Heil Hitler!*' But by 27 September his mood had changed and he only had time for a short note: 'I feel het up, somehow, and sometimes everything gets a bit too much. I have two separate tasks to complete, one in Kiev and the other in Kriwoj-Raj. Along with my military and police duties, there are other tasks to complete. My health is good, but if this goes on much longer it'll probably finish me. I fly to Kiev tomorrow. Kiev is a beautiful town, but very dangerous now...'

On 5 October came another short note thanking Else for the photographs and telling her 'Stay brave, little one!' By 1 December 1941 he was in Riga.

SS-Obergruppenführer und General der Polizei Ostland
Riga
1 December 1941

My dear girl! I've just come back to find your letter waiting in which you tell me that the stork brought baby Renate on 21 November. I am very happy, and congratulate you heartily, and hope that you managed everything successfully, and that you're already feeling well again. How I'd love to come and visit, both you and the little one. No, it's not at all the case that I'd prefer this not to have happened. I'm truly happy about it, and intend to help you in every way I can, and to look after the little one, so that she can one day become a healthy, dutiful German girl. We must see each other soon. It's such a shame you can't come here... with Renate too of course. Think about it...

What on earth was he talking about? There was no chance that Else, with or without baby Renate, could join him. Not to mention the fact that he was busy throughout November overseeing the killings in the Rumbula Forest, five miles outside Riga.

In fact, it was Friedrich Jeckeln himself who suggested to the *Reichsführer-SS* that shooting the Jews into deep pits in the forest was the most efficient manner of execution. Gas vans were too unreliable and messy. Shooting was quicker and easier. The pits could hold 30,000. The ground was suitable: sandy and soft. He'd devised a system to make the killing as easy as possible for his men, dividing the work among them so none of them had to take part in the whole thing. First, tell the Jews in the Riga ghetto that they were being resettled, and could each bring a piece of luggage, then march them out of the town along the country road to the forest in orderly fashion. There another team took over, ordering them to leave their luggage on the side of the road and undress. There were wooden boxes into which to put their valuables, rings and the like. By now the deception was over, replaced by terror and brutality – the Jews and their children harried to the pits with shooting and beatings and screaming and wailings. In November there was snow on the ground. As they moved towards the pits, naked, the mothers and fathers and grandparents held their children to themselves, soothing them. They were told to lie face-down, head to toe. There was a constant volley of rifle fire, with pistols to finish things off. The killing went on all day and into the night.

Once it was over Jeckeln phoned the *Reichsführer-SS* to tell him it was done and the Riga ghetto completely liquidated. Later he went to report to Himmler in person, who told him he was 'very satisfied'. So satisfied, in fact, that there would soon be more Jews arriving – from the Reich, to be held in Salaspils, the new concentration camp, first for slave labour, then for extermination. As per usual.

He'd had terrible blood poisoning on his right hand, he wrote in the same letter to Else, which made him feel very low. But he'd chosen a villa in the Kaiser Forest with ten rooms 'where I'm living quite *alone*...' and another equally lovely villa by the lake. He ended with 'Hearty congratulations once again! To both little girls, heartfelt greetings!' The Kaiser Forest is where the Salaspils concentration camp was being built.

Jeckeln
SS-Obergruppenführer und General der Polizei
Höhere SS- und Polizeiführer Ostland
Ritterhaus, Riga
17/12/1941

My dear girl!

Firstly, heartfelt thanks for your letter, in which you tell me, to my great pleasure, that little Renate is hale and hearty, and looks just like her father. You must forgive me if I don't ask all the questions, because I'm so taken up with my work here as never before that sometimes I'm not sure I'll be able to hold out. I'm sorry to hear you haven't been well, but I'm sure you'll feel better after some time recuperating in Munich. It was probably hard for you to part from little Renate, but I'm sure there'll be a solution. Of course I'd love to see the little one sometime, to see our handiwork. Hopefully I'll have that pleasure soon. [Unfortunately his home leave had been withdrawn for the duration.]

How is your work? . . . Hopefully your relationship with your *Mutti* will get better. In my case, my nerves are holding up well. I don't often manage to get to my villa with ten rooms in the Kaiser Forest. But I have a very good working together with my men. And since late October the winter weather here, with snow and ice, has been very beautiful. Many other things, to do with my work, can't be put in writing. But hopefully I'll be able to tell you about them personally soon.

I wish you, dear girl, a very Happy New Year!

Heartfelt greetings and a loving kiss, Your Fried

A month went by with no further news. Then came a short letter explaining that life in Riga was full of difficulties. Fried had been to the *Reichsführer-SS*'s HQ at the Front 'to report back and discuss the way forward'. He often had recourse to schnapps. It helped him feel better. But his belief remained whole, though he sometimes had doubts about himself.

A month later he wrote again, thanking his 'dear girl' for the charming photographs. 'Little Renate really is delightful, and strong too, so you're quite surprised. I'm really happy about the sweet one!' He told her to stop worrying. 'I am so pleased you want to have Renate living with you, and of course you'll be able to get a job if you want. Meanwhile, I'm happy to send you some money. Believe me when I say I often think of you, and don't think of little Renate in any way as a burden but as a beautiful and dear thing.' Then there was more news about a new division he was building up called *Kampfgruppe* (fighting group) Jeckeln. 'So I'll be very busy, but I'm very happy about it. A soldier's life.'

Happy, because he could finally get away from Riga. His next letter, dated 23 March 1942, came from a *Gefechtsstand* (command postbunker), who knows where? But evidently he'd been allowed a transfer, if only temporarily. He thanked her for her letter, and said he would be able to have some home leave soon. 'What's more, the *Reichsführer-SS* was here for a few hours three days ago, and I talked to him about our situation. He'll do everything, and tells me to tell you this. What's more, he'll look after you if anything happens to me. Renate is surely developing well. I look forward to hearing more about you and her soon. Myself, I'm really well. We have enough to eat, a good soup with peas and beans, but no potatoes. My troops are in excellent health, and their mood too. Everything here is to my taste. Even though it's still 30 degrees below zero.' The sun had been been shining for weeks, with masses of snow. But they all kept warm because there was masses of wood. The Bolsheviks hadn't made any inroads yet. He hadn't had such a good time in years. 'The war against the Reds will surely be decided this year, and then transform itself into a colonial one,' he wrote, evidently still convinced by Nazi ideology – the Thousand-Year German Reich. 'Be a little happy,' he admonished Else, 'in the belief that your worries will soon have a happy solution. I think of you often and dearly. Heartfelt greetings. *Heil Hitler!* Your Fried.'

A month later he was still happy as a lark. 'The times are so great, and the task so big that our own fate is quite unimportant.' Else should be proud of the task and duty she had taken on, the great joy of motherhood! 'Here spring has arrived!' The nights were cold, the days warm. He'd swum in snowy waters and he hadn't had the slightest illness in the last six months. The field kitchen supplied good food. In the evenings they got bread and a sausage or cheese. All very nourishing. 'I'm really well. I have a Messerschmitt 108 at my disposal.' He still didn't know about home leave. They'd celebrated the Führer's birthday, about 150 of them. Then it was back to their duties. 'I hope the enclosed photos make you happy. And so, dear girl, stay well and happy, *Heil Hitler!* Your Fried.'

Two months later, on 10 June, he was writing from an unknown place, not knowing if he'd have time to finish the letter because the times were dramatic and his duties heavy. But he was still full of optimism. Why? Simply because he knew he had children he could call his own, and they could achieve this for the German *Volk*. He thanked Else for her letter from Steinhöring, happy that she'd been able to spend some time with Renate. 'The little *Spatz* [sparrow] is very lively. So should she be, given she comes from two such excellent origins of parents. You know how much I'd like to be with you...' The next day he found time to continue the letter, going on for another six pages, so presumably the fighting at the Front was not quite as busy as he claimed. It turned out he'd been in Germany for a few days from 5 to 7 June because a meeting in Poznań had been postponed due to the death of Heydrich. He was worried about the bombing of Cologne. 'I am looking forward to a letter from you. *Heil Hitler!*'

By 18 July Fried wasn't sounding quite so optimistic. The Battle of Stalingrad wasn't going well for the Germans. 'Yes, the war requires sacrifices of everyone!' he wrote. 'But what do personal sacrifices matter when beating the enemy of the German *Volk* is at stake. Nothing but victory to complete extermination counts. England will be next.' The weather wasn't too good. Lots of rain. But his troops, his *Kamaraden*, were in good heart. 'Unfortunately, when we can meet isn't clear...'

There followed a gap of four months, either because he was too caught up in the fighting or Else subsequently destroyed the letters, or he'd finally got some home leave and they were able to meet. Who knows? He'd certainly spent 'a short stay' in Berlin, because he mentions seeing two of his children, Klaus and Ilse. Klaus was joining the Luftwaffe as a trainee. Ilse was 'a sweet girl.' So no more secrets there. But unfortunately he wasn't able to make a quick detour from Berlin to Cologne. The rest of his holidays went by well, he wrote, though his flight back was delayed.

Four months later, in November, he wrote that he was happy to think of their last meeting, so finally there had been some home leave. 'Don't take things so hard,' he told Else. 'I do have a nerviness in me which probably affects our togetherness, which always has to be grabbed here and there, so I'm not as free and carefree as before.' He thanked Else for her letters, and noted that although little Renate was still not with her, she would be soon. 'Maybe I'll come to Berlin for a quick visit soon . . .' It was the same pattern as before the war: Fried came briefly to Berlin on war business, Else took the train to meet him for a snatched night, waiting for him in the station waiting room. Perhaps they were hoping to produce another child for Hitler?

There were no more letters till June 1943. The war was taking its toll. There was another big gap till 7/11/1943, from another *Gefechtsstand*. 'Apparently today is Sunday, according to the calendar,' he wrote. 'I'm in a warm but dirty former Russian bunker.' It was the winter there. He was happy to hear Else was well, and that she could spend some time in Badenweiler with Renate. 'Everything is uncertain here, we can't look ahead.' They were fighting the partisans, with great success. The morale and belief of his troops was very good, and he was in excellent health. 'I wonder where you are now, and where little Renate? Write soon! I think of you often . . .'

Everything was uncertain, he wrote. It was definitely uncertain for Else, braving the air raids and the bombings and the endless travel delays just to have a day here and there with baby Renate. She was a bonny toddler now, and (joy!) unmistakably Fried's child. Same eyes, very blue. Same thick hair, light blond. Same sturdy build, quite unlike Else herself. Luckily there was no trouble from her boss at the bank when she took time off to see Renate. Fried had seen to that. Her annual week's holiday was stretched every now and again, it being in a good cause, and known to the *Reichsführer-SS* himself, who was Renate's godfather. Else, like many other German civilians fed on Goebbels's fake propaganda week in week out, never even considered Germany might be defeated. Fried had reassured her of final victory and she was happy to believe him. Anyway, 'defeatism' was a crime which could get you sentenced by the *Volksgericht* or People's Court, which was part of the Nazis' own judicial system running alongside the official courts. On the whole Else thought that understandable. Defeatism was something the Reich could do without in these difficult times. Had she known that some defeatists were sentenced to death, she might have though differently. Who knows?

'My dear girl, you haven't heard from me for very long time, but don't be cross,' Fried wrote on 25 April 1944, after a gap of five months, thanking her very much for her letters. 'Unfortunately your visit to Riga didn't work out. And now I'm back in a dirty Soviet nest, fighting the bandits again.' He went to Riga every now and again, where lots of work always awaited him and where in fact his wife and younger children were living, though he didn't mention that. He'd also been at HQ and in Munich, but unfortunately wasn't able to see little Renate. 'I desperately need some rest.' He hadn't heard a word for months from either of his eldest sons, who were both in the marines. The other children were well. His house in Braunschweig was still standing. 'We must see each other if I get leave … Even if I don't write, I think of you. *Heil Hitler!* PS I am flying to Berlin today and will post from there …'

There were three more letters in 1944, just notes really, as he moved from place to place. They were scrappy, rushed letters. But still, he wrote.

His last letter to her was dated 26 February 1945, HQ, Riga crossed out, with an FP No. 58200 added. And on the left: Jeckeln, *Waffen-SS* (added in his own handwriting) then the usual *SS-Obergruppenführer und General der Polizei. Höhere SS- und Polizeiführer Ostland* was also crossed out.

> *Mein liebes Mädelein!* My dear little girl!
>
> This isn't a voice from the other side speaking to you. I'm alive, and in spite of all that's happened to me I'm even quite well. Moreover, I've just realised that it was seven years ago today that we were first together. What carefree, beautiful days those were. I got out of Kurland [Latvia] in January, spent some days with the *Reichsführer-SS* preparing to take over a front line in my *Heimat* on the borders of the Reich. Then Stalin caught up with us, and within twenty-four hours I found myself with my troops stuck between Breslau and Oppeln. Then there was hard fighting. Four weeks later I was promoted to General of an SS Mountain Corps, though I remained in the Reich, not the mountains, hardly 300

kilometres from my *Heimat*. Then the Bolsheviks attacked again and there was hard fighting at the Front again. In spite of all this, we are in good heart and full of determination. Sooner or later the crisis will dispel.

My family were able to get out in time and are temporarily living in the hunting hut. A small apartment is being prepared in Braunschweig, which will solve the problem. I haven't had any news for a long time.

So, you and little Renate. I don't know if you got my last letter, which I wrote sometime mid-December. I got your letters of 15/12/44 and 3/1/45, both arrived in Upper Silesia on the same day, 10 February. I got your letter with the photo of little Renate when I was still in Latvia. What a fine sweet child! How I hope to see you and the little *Spatz* soon. I think of you both so often. Most of all, I remember our happy times together. Happier days will come again, and then we'll be able to see each other often again. But I only hope it will be *soon*, though to get away from here is completely impossible at the moment. More possible might be if you could get yourself to Berlin, and from there to a small town near B, which I can't name at the moment due to security concerns. I wouldn't be able to help you to get here. But think it over.

Thank you for your letter describing Christmas and the New Year, and I'm happy to hear that despite the hard times, they were pleasant. Little Renate must be quite a handful. But children are often hard work for their *Muttis*!

Otherwise, the demands of war in my daily life are very heavy. But it can't be changed, and each of us has our burden to carry. The most important thing is that we can battle through the storm!

I'm happy you're not in Cologne any more, and hopefully your *Mutti* has got used to the new life a bit.

I forgot to tell you that while I was with the *Reichsführer-SS* during those days, I managed to get away to Freiburg for a few hours to see my mother. The city looks shocking, but my mother hasn't been bombed out. She's prepared to put up with everything, but she refuses to leave Freiburg.

So my dear girl, now you know more or less how I am. I hope this letter gets to you soon, and finds you in good health. You should know that I think of you.

Best greetings to your *Mutti*, and for you and little Renate, loving kisses,

From your Fried.

In all there were eighty-three letters. Else read them again and again, secretly, filled with longing for what had been. But these days the letters were hidden under a floorboard in her bedroom. Because that was then. And this was now.

CHAPTER TWO

HEINRICH HIMMLER: THE GREAT ARYAN

So who was this Heinrich Himmler, Friedrich Jeckeln's SS chief, who visited terror and extermination on millions of lives? What was he? His first biographer, Willi Frischauer, called him an 'evil genius'. Evil, certainly. Genius? Well, judge for yourselves. Meet Heini, writing his daily journal up in the Austrian Alps on the annual Himmler family holiday in 1915:

> 1/8/15 Sunday, we swam for 3rd time… *Vati*, Ernsti and I swam a 4th time (!) after boating
> 2/8/15 Monday evening, we swam for the 5th time
> 3/8 Tuesday… swam for the 6th time
> 6/8 Friday… swam for the 7th time… and the 8th time
> 7/8 Saturday, morning, swam for the 9th time… swam for the 10th time
> 9/8 morning… swam for the 11th time
> later… swam for the 12th time
> 12/8 played, then swam for the 13th time
> 13/8 played, then swam for the 14th time
> 16/8 swam for the 15th and last time…

He was fifteen at the time.

Heini's two brothers, Gebhard, two years older, Ernsti, five years younger, weren't much better, all getting extra lessons and homework from their *Vati* (father) to keep up with schoolwork. *Vati* was deputy head at their local grammar school in Landshut, forty kilometres from Munich in Bavaria. Some teaching, mostly administration. Attention to detail, that was *Herr Professor* Himmler's thing, imparted daily to his three boys. He'd helped Heini with his first diary entry, to show him how to do it: exact times of departure, exact times of arrival, exact descriptions of places, using simple phrases as in 'very pretty' – all corrected by *Vati*. '13th wedding anniversary of my dear parents' wrote Heini in July 1910, showing a proper affection for his mother as well as his father. Perhaps it was *Mutti* who encouraged the boys to learn the piano, a socially useful accomplishment as the parents agreed. Gebhard was quite good, but try as he might Heini couldn't master it.

Vati read aloud to them most evenings while *Mutti* sat on the canapé doing her sewing and knitting. History, mostly. Germany had only unified into a nation forty years earlier, in 1871, so it was all about Bismarck and Emperor Wilhelm I, back to Friedrich the Great and Ludwig II. The favourite was military history. By the time he was ten Heini could recite all the famous battles by heart. Back and back he went, way back to the ancient Germanic race and the Teutonic myths. He had a good memory, did Heini. It would stand him in excellent stead later in life when he was busy collecting and collating incriminating evidence against any opponents of the Nazi regime.

The Himmler family apartment came with the job. It was spacious and comfortable in a Biedermeier petit-bourgeois way: dark upholstered furniture, large dining table for family meals, and plenty of shelves for Professor Himmler's books and collection of coins and for *Frau* Himmler's knick-knacks. Photographs show 'antique' *objets d'art* everywhere, and the walls crammed with small framed silhouettes of the Himmler ancestors, real or imagined, going back to the eighteenth century, because Professor Himmler was extremely keen on ancestry, that of his own family in particular. Accordingly, one room in the apartment was kept as a shrine to the family, called the *Ahnenzimmer*, the ancestors' room, for family documents and treasures and souvenirs. Professor Himmler liked to suggest there was some noble blood, way back, lost in the mists of time. He was very keen on noble German families in general, and one school friend of Heini's remembered that pupils laughed at him behind his back for being so 'pushy and fawning towards the upper classes'. He even asked one of his former pupils, Prince Heinrich of Bavaria, to be Heini's godfather. The family was strongly Catholic, typical of many in the southern Germany of those times: church every Sunday, prayers every night.

School was difficult for Heini. The only subject he was any good at was history. But his worst problem was the bullying, because Heini was known as a physical weakling. His body was podgy, his skin

pasty, his chest sunken, his shoulders sloping, his chin weak. He wore thick-lens gold-rimmed glasses. He was useless at sport, and this at a time when the young German Reich was on the march and everything military and athletic was admired. A classmate remembered exercises in the school gymnasium when the muscled, athletic boys were swinging on parallel bars and leaping over horse-boxes, perhaps doing a flip or two in the air, and Heini would be cowering at the end of the line hoping the bell would ring in time to save him from humiliation. Many a time he'd land in the middle of the horse-box and the bully sports master would laugh at him, shouting, 'Get off, Himmler!' but Heini was stuck, unable to budge without help. The same classmate noted that over the years Himmler adopted a sardonic smile and a superior manner to compensate – podgy Heini's way of survival. It didn't make him popular with his classmates, especially given his mediocre academic performance. Worse, he was known as a notorious informer, because he regularly snitched on classmates to the deputy headmaster – his *Vati*. Net result: whenever he approached a group of boys they would immediately disperse and meet up elsewhere, out of Heini's earshot. Heini fell back more and more on to his aloof manner.

During the First World War Heini listed every German advance meticulously in his diary. 'Now it's going along famously,' he wrote. 'I'm pleased about these victories, the more so because the French and especially the English are angry about them and the anger is not exactly insignificant. Falk and I would like best of all to be fighting it out with them. An English cavalry brigade has been thrashed (I'm glad! Hurrah!).' Falk was Heini's only school friend. They couldn't wait to fight for the *Vaterland*, as Heini noted again and again.

Perhaps Falk could expect to 'fight it out' before the war was over, but for Heini it was pure fantasy. No army or navy would recruit someone as short-sighted and sickly as Himmler. Nor did they. Not that anyone would know, listening him talk about his part in the war once he was *Reichsführer-SS*, right at the top of the Nazi tree, way above the truth and reality.

Heini didn't manage to get into Munich University. Instead he went to the Technical High School or *Hochschule* to study agriculture, specialising in fertilisers. He left with a basic diploma, then hung about at home at a loss as to what to do with his life. Gebhard and Falk had both been accepted for officer training with the 2nd Bavarian Infantry in 1917. But not Heini. His father tried every other Bavarian regiment on his behalf, in vain. Heini had to be content with unpaid voluntary work for the local War Welfare Office. Finally, in 1918, with German losses at the Front rising into their hundreds of thousands, he was accepted for training by the 11th Bavarian Infantry Regiment. But he was soon back home, unable to cope with the physical side of the training and the homesickness. No doubt there was bullying too. The reality of army life didn't fit Heini's bravura fantasies.

Back home, he changed tack. If he couldn't be a superhero in reality, he could in theory. He began to read every book he could find on the superiority of the Nordic race. There were plenty. Eugenics championed the survival of the fittest, the sterilisation of the 'unfit', and selective marriage to protect the purity of the race – all often accompanied by a nasty anti-Semitism. But while for most readers these theories were part of a varied whole, for Heini it became the whole. Nietzsche, Darwin, Francis Galton, Alfred Ploetz's *The Fitness of Our Race* – any theory to do with creating a superior race was music to Heini. Not just any race: the white Aryan race, his own Germanic race. Never mind that he didn't remotely resemble the idealised vision of that Master Race as described in Hans Günther's *Ritter, Tod und Teufel* (Knight, Death and the Devil): the men slim, narrow-hipped, broad-shouldered, with chiselled features, the women softer and more curved, 'both with shining skin flushed with blood, blond hair, clear conquering eyes, with the perfect movements of a perfect body – a royal species among men!' To which Heini commented: 'A book that expresses in wise, considered words and sentences what I have felt and thought since first I thought.'

By 1919 Heini had joined the Bavarian branch of the Ultima Thule Society. Their motto: 'Remember that you are German! Keep your blood pure!' Their symbol: the swastika. Anti-Semitic and anti-Communist, its aim was to unify a racially pure Europe under the leadership of the German Reich. Never mind that Germany had just suffered a humiliating defeat in the First World War. Their newspaper was the *Völkischer Beobachter*, later the paper of the Nazi Party. Soon Heini had joined the extreme right-wing *Freikorps Oberland*, fighting the Communists in the violent street battles which bedevilled the Weimar Republic. And joy! the *Freikorps* had a uniform – not a real one, and not very smart, but a uniform nevertheless. All his life Himmler loved a uniform. It offered him the persona he craved but could never achieve in reality. Heini was beginning to find his way at last.

But there was one problem which proved insurmountable: women didn't like him. Whether it was his podgy frame and weak chin or his increasingly odd ideas and supercilious manner, he just wasn't attractive to them. His cousin Lu had a girlfriend. So did Gebhard. But not Heini. He hid his humiliation behind his aloof smile and opted for another fantasy. It was a very developed fantasy, neatly dove-tailing with the one about his own superiority: his future wife would be racially pure, blond and blue-eyed, producing many beautiful Nordic Germanic children, and she would be happy to forge a life with Heini in the east, perhaps in Poland, where he meant to make his life on a large farm, colonising the territory lost in the 1914–18 war. Because Germany would soon be needing vast tracts of land to house future generations of the Greater German Reich. Heini would be a racial pioneer, with his wife standing steadfastly beside him. Never mind the reality – that he hadn't lasted more than a few weeks working on a farm for his year of practical experience during his diploma, after which he fell ill and went back home again. 'I work because it is my duty, because I find my peace in work,' he wrote in his diary, head way up in the clouds. 'And I work for my ideal of German womanhood with whom, some day, I will live my life in the east and fight my battles as a German far from beautiful Germany.'

But for the time being he was single, and unemployed. The 'work' he referred to was voluntary and unpaid, with Ultima Thule and *Freikorps Oberland*. Vaguely political. He'd had a job briefly, with a local business, Stickstoff GmbH (Nitrogen Ltd), as a lab technician, conducting tests on fertilisers. But his employer appears to have let him go after a few months. Heini didn't mind. Employed work was all well and good but it wasn't the same as political work, striving for a higher ideal.

After several months of listlessness, his father pointed out that Heini needed to earn a living. The economy in Weimar Germany was in a desperate state following the disaster of defeat in the war and the harsh terms of the Versailles Treaty. Extreme levels of unemployment and homelessness were creating a dangerous mood of despair and anger. The country was in a state of virtual civil war. By 1923 the price of foodstuffs was doubling in one day. The Reichsmark wasn't worth the paper it was printed on. In June it was 1,800 to the US dollar. By July it was 160,000. By August, a million. Foreign investors were taking their money out of the country as fast as they could. Like the rest of the German bourgeoisie, the Himmler family were finding it hard to make ends meet.

But Heini wasn't minded to find a steady job. Because he was busy with his voluntary work, and through it he was getting to know people with the same political views as his own, powerful people, gathering around a charismatic man called Adolf Hitler, leader of a new political party known as the Nazi Party. Heini joined in 1923. It caused trouble between father and son. Professor Himmler was a member of the Bavarian People's Party. Heini felt nothing but disdain for them, boringly conservative and useless as they were, stuck in all their old, passive ways. It was time for him to leave home. Get involved in political action.

Fortunately for Heini, one of the people he got to know was a man called Gregor Strasser, who owned the local chemist's shop in Landshut. Strasser had fought in the 1914–18 war, then joined a *Freikorps* to fight the Communists in the streets of Munich. When the Weimar government banned all extremist political groups, including the *Freikorps*, he became an early member of the Nazi Party, believing in the 'S' of NSDAP, which stood for Socialist, because he believed that the new post-war society should be more equal than the pre-war one, albeit in no sense Communist. He also believed that Germany needed a strong leader, and this Adolf Hitler was a great orator with the strength of a real Führer. He had some odd racial ideas, but he was gathering supporters around him, including a powerful paramilitary arm of SA – *Sturmabteilung* – Storm Troopers under the leadership of an 'old comrade', Ernst Röhm.

By the time Heini met Strasser in 1925, Strasser was the regional SA leader of the Nazi Party. He was a brilliant organiser, but he needed an assistant to do all the boring office work for which he had no time or interest. He quickly saw that this Himmler was the perfect man for the job, interested in every detail, especially any inside information gathered from secret informers about political opponents. 'He was like a schoolmaster who graded the lessons of his pupils with finicky exactitude,' remembered Walter Schellenberg, a later SS colleague, 'and for each answer would have liked to enter a mark in a class-book.' The new Rentenmark currency recently introduced by the Weimar government had finally brought hyperinflation under control, so Strasser was even able to pay his new assistant a small wage. The office was a room above Strasser's chemist shop.

Heini was as happy as a lark in that small room, his desk laden with papers and files plus a card index to keep tabs on local Communists and Socialists, or anyone else whose actions gave him cause for suspicion – clergy, teachers, factory workers, wives and mothers, farmers, trade unionists. Heini's card index grew and grew. Lists, how he loved them, always had. And now he had the perfect tool for it: a typewriter which made the work so much easier. 'A remarkable fellow,' Strasser told his brother Otto about his new assistant, laughing, referring to the extra work Heini was doing, chasing around the region, checking up on people and hidden arms depots – hidden because they were forbidden by the terms of the Versailles Treaty. 'Looks like a half-starved shrew. But keen I tell you. Incredibly keen. He has a motorbike. He is under way the whole day – from one farm to another, from one village to the next. Since I've had him, our weapons have really been put into shape. I tell you, he's a perfect NCO. He visits all the secret depots.'

Now Heini made it known he wasn't Heini any more. He was Heinrich Himmler. And with it, he took his first step into history.

And this first step into history was most gratifying. Discussing their views about the great Germanic past and the glorious future of the Third Reich, the Nazis began to coin their own terminology. They decided to use *Gau* to describe a region – an ancient word with fine Germanic roots. Now each region had a leader or *Gauleiter*. Gregor Strasser became the *Gauleiter* of Lower Bavaria. And who better to

be his deputy than Heinrich Himmler? Or *treue*, slavishly devoted, Heinrich, as he was known by Strasser behind his back. From the start, *treue* Heinrich showed a willingness to stop at nothing in fulfilling his devotion to the Nazi Party in general and to Führer Adolf Hitler in particular.

One of the first matters the deputy *Gauleiter* concerned himself with was to contact rich donors: industrialists like the Krupp and Thyssen families who bankrolled the Nazi Party from early on. Another early donor was the independently wealthy Kurt Lüdecke. Lüdecke later became disillusioned with the Nazi Party, writing an exposé of Adolf Hitler in 1938 titled *I Knew Hitler*. But for the time being he was an ardent supporter, part of the 'Socialist' wing of the Party led by Strasser. Lüdecke showed Strasser a 1925 letter Himmler had sent him in which he mentioned 'a project he'd been working on for some time now, namely to publish the names of all Jews, as well as all Jew-friendly Christians living in Lower Bavaria'. Strasser laughed: 'That's just like him,' he said. 'He sees in every creature who doesn't "think" Nazi a Jew or a Jew serf, a Jesuit or a Freemason.' But Himmler was still useful to Strasser. 'He's devoted to me and I use him as a secretary. He's very ambitious, but I won't take him along with me – he's no world-beater, you know.' Sure enough, within the year Strasser found another secretary: Joseph Goebbels. Who really was a world-beater.

The May 1928 election didn't go well for the Nazi Party. With the economy steadied now, the Social Democratic Party were the outstanding winners, gaining 29.76 per cent of the vote and 153 seats in the Reichstag, up twenty-two seats from the previous election. The Communists, led by their charismatic leader Ernst Thälmann, also did well, gaining 10.6 per cent of the vote and nine extra seats in the Reichstag. It was the centre parties who lost their seats. And the Nazis, who only got 2.63 per cent of the vote and lost two seats, ending up with no more than twelve seats, which included Gregor Strasser. And Adolf Hitler.

For Himmler things were nevertheless looking good. Power can make up for any number of weaknesses, and the deputy *Gauleiter* was quietly acquiring quite a lot of it, racing about the region on his motorbike, canvassing, getting to know high-ups, collecting all sorts of incriminating evidence, with every detail noted in his mounting files and his card index. What's more, with the donations from top industrialists like Krupp and Thyssen, the Party afforded him decent expenses now, so he was able to stay in nice *Gasthof*s on his travels. One fine day, a winter's day by all accounts with snow heavy on the ground, Heinrich entered the lobby of a *Gasthof* and bumped straight into a young woman, showering her with snow. She was called Margarete Concerzowo, from Bromberg in the West Prussian region of Germany, which was, after the Versailles Treaty, the Polish province of Pomorze. Marga was seven years older than Heinrich, divorced, a former nurse, now the owner of a successful health clinic. That is, Marga was a woman of independent means. Humourless and narrow-minded is how Lina, the wife of Reinhard Heydrich, Himmler's later right-hand-man, described Marga. 'Size 50 knickers, that's all there was to her.' It didn't put Himmler off. Nor even the fact that she came from a predominantly Polish province and hardly looked more Aryan than he did himself. The fact is, Himmler was in need of a wife and money. They were married within the year, in July 1928. That same year Marga sold her clinic and joined the Nazi Party. And they started a chicken farm.

By now Heinrich Himmler had moved office from Landshut to Party HQ in Munich. And he had a new post: Deputy Chief of Propaganda. There had been a brief meeting with Adolf Hitler the previous year – momentous for Himmler but not for Hitler, who had greater matters on his mind and hardly noticed Strasser's 'glorified office boy'. But by 1928 Hitler was beginning to take notice of this keen assistant of Strasser's, who was happy to work all hours and had a fine nose for sniffing out information about political opponents and traitors. And Jews. Himmler was always on the job. Did *Haupsturmbannführer* so-and-so really have a Jewish or half-Jewish wife?, he asked Albert Krebs, the *Gauleiter* of Hamburg, on a train journey from Elberfeld to Hamburg in 1929, doing the election rounds. And how did their colleague Conn come by his strange name? Might it be a cover for Cohen? And what about *Gauleiter* Lohse and the bank he used to work for? Wasn't it Jewish? Krebs said he tried to change the subject, in vain. But when Hitler heard of all this, he was suitably impressed. So when he promoted Strasser to Chief of Propaganda, Himmler was made his deputy and moved into Party HQ. And when Hitler needed someone to assist Erhard Heiden in running the nascent SS, the Führer's security unit, he again chose Himmler. The SS was a ragtag group of about 200 men at that time and needed someone to take it in hand. Himmler secretly let it be known that Heiden wasn't up to the job. On 6 January 1929 Hitler replaced Heiden with Himmler, awarding him the title of *Reichsführer-SS*. It had taken Himmler ten years to reach the shining pinnacle, and he wasn't letting go of it ever again.

The SS would become Himmler's route to power. But now, in Munich with his new job, just starting out, he got to know two men in the Nazi Party who would shape his woolly racial ideas into something much more systematic: Alfred Rosenberg and Walther Darré.

Rosenberg wrote books so opaque and convoluted that it was hard to know what he was saying – other than proving the superiority of the Germanic race. Stemming from the Baltic, Rosenberg hated all Slavs. The battle of survival was a battle of blood against blood. Blood was the image of the soul. The Nordic race was white and blond, going back thousands of years. Blond, beautiful and aristocratic. Like Queen Medintet-Garub of Egypt (2633–2564 BC). 'Remember the call of blood!' Rosenberg wrote in his book *Der Mythus des 20. Jahrhunderts*, which impressed Hitler and Himmler deeply. As to Jesus Christ and his apostles: they were contemptible, spouting 'typical Jewish arrogance and intolerance'.

Walther Darré was an agriculturalist who began his rise within the Nazi Party as a member of the Committee of Experts for Population and Racial Policy, becoming Reich Peasant *Führer.* He was a practical man who liked to put theories to practical use. He suggested to Himmler, busy breeding his chickens, that he apply his techniques to human beings – a kind of human experiment to similarly breed the Aryan Master Race. Where to find such specimens? Surely the *Reichsführer-SS* already had them to hand, said Darré. Among his SS. Here were 200 men, tested by racial experts, able to trace their ancestry back to 1800, and the officers back to 1750. And they were ready and willing to produce an even stronger strain of the race by procreating with equally racially pure women. With one eye on puny Himmler, Darré added that leadership wasn't just a matter of physical superiority. The *Reichsführer-SS* had to give moral leadership. He referred him to Heinrich the First, who lived in the tenth century. A fine leader of men. And wasn't Himmler a Heinrich too?

Gregor Strasser just laughed. What a crackpot! That Himmler wouldn't last long!

But it was Strasser whose days were numbered. The Night of the Long Knives of 30 June 1934 got rid of him and any other Socialist-leaning Strasser supporters, as well as Ernst Röhm, head of the SA, and his supporters – all carried out by Himmler's SS with the help of the *Geheime Staatspolizei*, the Gestapo, the Nazis' secret police formed by Hermann Göring within weeks of the Nazis' seizure of power in January 1933. For Himmler, it was his first foray into cold-blooded murder. The outcome was highly favourable: two rivals eliminated in one single action. Strasser, Himmler's former mentor, was gone. So was Röhm, one of the Führer's favourites. Outwardly Himmler expressed his deepest sorrow and regret, with sincere humility. Moral. Inwardly it was a different story, presaging his modus operandi from then on: the outer manner revealing nothing of the inner reality.

'For us as Secret State Police and as members of the SS, 30 June was not – as several believe – a day of victory or a day of triumph, but it was the hardest day that can be visited on a soldier in his lifetime,' as Himmler would tell a group of Gestapo officials on 11 October 1934, quite forgetting he'd never actually been a soldier. 'To have to shoot one's own comrades, with whom one has stood side by side for eight to ten years in the struggle for an ideal, and who had then failed, is the bitterest thing that can happen to a man.' There would be criticism from all sides, he warned. 'The attack of the Jews and all secret enemies occurs, as it has for centuries, via seeds of discord, via lies, calumny, via shameless intrigue.'

But for the time being, back in 1929, Himmler was still waiting in the wings. And one of his first concerns, as *Reichsführer-SS*, was to order a new uniform for himself and his men. SS Order No. 1 had already dealt with general matters concerning training, behaviour, intelligence gathering, smoking (none), attendance at Party speeches (obligatory) and at military parades and drill and singing sessions (bring your SS pass and SS songbook). Now to the uniform. Uniform is what gave a man authority. For the purpose he engaged a designer, Karl Diebitsch, and a graphic designer, Walter Heck, to produce something stylish and imposing. Black. Black tunic and breeches, black jackboots, black military cap, black tie. Plus a dagger and a belt buckle inscribed *SS-Mann deine Ehre heist Treue* (SS-Man Your Honour Means Loyalty). Only the shirts were brown in a nod to Ernst Röhm's SA, because for the time being Röhm was still alive and kicking and the SS still nominally part of and subordinate to his SA.

Himmler applied himself to every detail, entailing endless meetings and fittings. Apart from the basic uniform, there were armbands and epaulettes and badges designating the numerous ranks, all called *Führer* – *Gruppenführer*, *Obergruppenführer*, *Sturmbannnführer* – all black except for the white Death's Head skull on the cap, and plenty of silver detailing on the collars, oak leaves and the like, plus the swastika armband, which was red. A nice touch. Blood.

At the newly instituted SS Race and Settlement Main Office new applicants for the SS were being tested by the racial experts. *SS-Mann* had to be at least 1.7 metres in height, the *Reichsführer-SS* himself being no taller. Then they were graded into one of five racial groups: Pure Nordic, Predominantly Nordic, Light Alpine with Dinaric (Mediterranean), Predominantly Eastern, and lastly Mongrels of non-European origin. Only men in the first three groups would be considered. The lucky ones were then graded again, on a scale of one to nine according to their physical attributes. By 1932 the SS had expanded from 5,000 to 50,000 as big money flowed into its coffers from big industry. Soon after came the *Waffen-SS*, a parallel army to the regular *Wehrmacht*, with some forty regiments, battalions, brigades and divisions. Later came the invisible *V-men*, who wore plain clothes and spied on the population, reporting every detail back to the *Reichsführer-SS*. Because sometimes it was just that small detail which told you everything you needed to know.

It is almost impossible to imagine that elsewhere in Germany, under the liberal Weimar Republic, a completely different life was flourishing. Berlin especially was vibrant, exciting, free. Cosmopolitan. The cabaret culture was world-famous. The arts were at the forefront of the modern movement. Intellectual life – authors, poets, theatre critics, artists, musicians, social reformers, journalists – all noisily debating the latest news in the crammed, smoke-filled cafés and restaurants. But not for much longer.

The Nazis were on the move. By 1932 Himmler had met Reinhard Heydrich, a man as ambitious and cold-blooded as himself, but sharper and more intelligent, unencumbered by Himmler's woolly, romantic ideas about race and the mythical Germanic past. To these Heydrich paid dutiful lip service, as he did to Himmler himself, always issuing instructions, usually his own, 'by order of the *Reichsführer-SS*'. Heydrich, as it later turned out, was Himmler's nemesis. But there was no knowing it in 1932, at the beginning of their murderous relationship. Only high regard, and a silent recognition that the best place to carry out your 'Actions' large and small was in the dark, never committing anything to paper for the benefit of posterity.

Heydrich had applied to join the SS in 1931 after being dismissed from the *Kriegsmarine*, the German Navy, where he served in a communications unit, otherwise known as Intelligence. Always a ladies' man, he was dismissed for making a young woman pregnant and then refusing to marry her. (Typically, he thought he'd get away with it.) So he applied to the Hamburg branch of the SS instead and was taken on immediately – just the kind of man they were looking for: over six feet tall, blond, pale-blue eyes. And clever – rare among the membership in those early days. He was soon introduced to the *Reichsführer-SS*, who took him on to his own staff. What the SS needed, Himmler explained to his new recruit, was better Intelligence: a *Sicherheitsdienst* – SD, Security Service – staffed by their most intelligent men. Heydrich took on the task keenly, quickly organising the new department and adding several others while he was at it: an Administrative Office, a Recruitment Department, a Justice Department, a further Race Office, a Medical Office to assist, a Training Office, a Supply Office, all within his own SD – nominally answerable to the Main Office under the *Reichsführer-SS*.

Felix Kersten, Himmler's personal masseur, who treated his master several days a week trying to get rid of his constant stomach cramps and headaches and was thus in his confidence, noted that Heydrich knew just how to flatter his chief, always addressing him with a smart salute: '*Jawohl, Herr Reichsführer!*' Yes indeed! Himmler was mediocre in comparison to clever Heydrich, Kersten wrote in his memoirs. Not in the same class. Lena, Heydrich's wife, could only agree. Himmler was 'the schoolmasterly type', she wrote, 'who never looked like a soldier and always wanted to be what he was not'. Quite unlike her husband, she added, who was truly 'soldierly'. Walter Schellenberg, his SS colleague, noted that Heydrich was 'far superior to all his political colleagues and controlled them as he controlled the vast Intelligence machine of the SD'.

But the *Reichsführer-SS* was too preoccupied to notice. He was busy with the talented Walther Darré, now Chief of the SS Race and Settlement Main Office, thrashing out the ten key points of Himmler's 'Engagement and Marriage Decree':

> Point 1: the SS is an association of German men of Nordic determination selected on special criteria. Point 2: the future of our people depends on the selection and retention of racially and hereditarily sound good blood, and I establish with effect from 1 January 1932 the 'marriage consent' for all unmarried members of the SS. Points 3 and 4: marriage consent would be granted and/or denied exclusively on the criteria of race and hereditary health. Points 5 and 6: every *SS-Mann* to apply for consent, and if he persisted in marrying despite being denied the consent, would be dismissed from the SS – though he would be given the option to resign. Points 7, 8 and 9: restated the role of the SS Race Office, should there be any confusion. Point 10 summed up: the SS is clear that with this Order it has taken a step of great significance. Derision, scorn and misunderstanding do not affect us. The future belongs to us.
>
> Signed, Heinrich Himmler.

Derision, scorn and misunderstanding: all that was in Himmler's past. The future belonged to him, and his SS. 'What we must fight for is to safeguard the existence and reproduction of our race and our Volk, the sustenance of our children and the purity of our blood,' as Hitler had already written in *Mein Kampf* way back in 1924. And he never veered or wavered from it. Even in his last will and testament, written in his Berlin bunker on 30 April 1945 as the Russians were flattening to rubble the city all around him, he declared his creed one last time: 'Above all I enjoin the leadership of the Reich to adhere to scrupulous observance of the race laws and merciless resistance to the world-poisoner of all peoples, international Jewry.'

Himmler spent most of 1932 campaigning for the July election, swiftly followed by the November election, because the July one had produced a stalemate. What a puzzle the results of the November election were to the Nazi leadership. In July they were getting over 37 per cent of the vote and 230 of the 584 seats in the Reichstag. This time they were expecting to get the 293 seats needed for an outright win. Instead they lost thirty-four, leaving them with a shortfall of ninety-seven seats to get the majority they needed. Astonishingly, the DNVP party gained fourteen seats. More astonishingly still, the left-wing parties did extremely well, the Social Democrats gaining twelve seats and the Communists, under their charismatic leader Ernst Thälmann, gaining eleven. The turnout was an incredible 80 per cent. What in heaven's name was going on?

In fact it wasn't too hard to work out, had Hitler and his Nazis looked more closely at the economy. It had gone into freefall following Germany's disastrous defeat in the 1914–18 war and the punishing terms of the Versailles Treaty. Things were just beginning to recover when the 1929 Wall Street Crash threw everything into chaos again, giving the Nazis, thriving as they did in times of political conflict, their chance. But by late 1932, with renewed financial support from America through the Young Plan and Germany's crippling war reparation repayments massively reduced, the economic situation was looking healthier again. And the Nazi Party lost its shine.

Clearly democracy wasn't working, thought Hitler. But what to do? Lie was the answer. Lie about everything. What they needed was a coalition, Hitler explained to the centre parties, against the Communists and the Social Democrats who were bent on destroying Germany. He gave his word that he could be trusted to honour their decision, whatever that might be. And they believed him and brokered a coalition, because in the end the centre parties were more frightened of the Communists and the Socialists than of the Nazis. So the Nazis never actually won an election in their own right at all.

The result of that fateful coalition on the Right was the Nazi *Machtergreifung* in January 1933. President Paul von Hindenburg, the great First World War hero, thought the 'little corporal' Adolf

Hitler wouldn't last long. It was Hindenburg who didn't last: he was dead by August 1934. And Hitler was Chancellor of the German Reich, to do with it as he pleased, regardless of the fact that two-thirds of Germans had never actually voted for the Nazis. Now they were subjected to six years of a brutal terror regime, followed by a war that had been planned all along and which, in the end, killed over 40 million.

Once Hitler had his *Machtergreifung* everything changed. Overnight. Now the Nazis unleashed their terror, arresting thousands of their political opponents, incarcerating them in prisons and 'wild' concentration camps till the first proper camps were ready. Better still, just shoot them on the spot 'while trying to escape'. Within six months they had banned all political parties, the free press, the independent civil service, the trade unions and introduced the Enabling Act, which transformed the democratic system into an effective dictatorship by giving the regime 'emergency' powers. Then came *Gleichschaltung* for anyone of influence – lawyers, teachers, businessmen, doctors, civil servants – or else they lost their jobs. Next came an alternative legal system in the form of the People's Court, specifically for acts of treason, large and small – including the crime of not giving the *Heil Hitler!* greeting with sufficient zeal when entering an office, classroom or bar. The court was up and running by April 1934.

Power in the wrong hands. There you have it. Once power gets into the wrong hands there is virtually nothing the small individual can do about it.

Now Joseph Goebbels and his Ministry of Propaganda and Enlightenment came into its own, deluging the German people with lies and disinformation and fake news in the press, on the wireless and in the newsreels shown weekly in local *Kino* cinemas across the land. The streets, it seemed, were thronged with hysterical crowds screaming, '*Sieg Heil! Sieg Heil!*' wherever the Führer passed in his black Mercedes, accepting their adulation with his limp salute, in one of his new uniforms, because from now on Hitler was never seen in public in anything but a uniform. So powerful was that image, so convincing, that no one worked out that a few thousand people were enough to create a crowd. No one wondered where the other two-thirds of Germans who'd never voted for Hitler were hiding. 'Like a blazing fire the news spreads across Germany! Adolf Hitler is

Chancellor of the Reich! A million hearts are aflame! Rejoicing and gratitude pour forth,' blared the wireless into every home. 'They are joyously shouting *Sieg Heil! Sieg Heil!* into the night!'

Lies were embedded in the language. People were not arrested, they were taken into 'protective custody'. They weren't killed, they were 'shot while trying to escape'. Adolf Hitler was the 'Führer' of the Great German Reich, soon to become the Greater German Reich through *Lebensraum*, the invasion and occupation of foreign territory. The Aryan race was superior to all others. Jews were an inferior race, non-Germanic, responsible for the stab-in-the-back defeat in the 1914–18 war. There was a 'traitor' round every corner, in every tenement block and every local *Gasthof*. It was the duty of every loyal citizen to report them. Local Gestapo offices were soon inundated with denouncements – neighbours with long-held petty grudges settling scores.

On 5 March 1933, after two months of terror 'Actions' against any political opponents – Communists, trade unionists, Social Democrats – and a relentless propaganda campaign, Hitler called a plebiscite to legitimise the regime. Should there be any waverers, there had been the shock of the Reichstag fire to persuade them. This was the perfect example of lies and fake news: a put-up event organised by the Nazis themselves, blamed on an innocent Communist, which allowed the Nazis, spearheaded by Himmler's SS, to immediately arrest and incarcerate 10,000 Communists, including Ernst Thälmann, who began eleven years of solitary confinement, after which he was executed. The Nazis won the 'election' with a happy majority. Watch out Germany!

Within days of the so-called plebiscite there were 'Actions' against the Jews. In Braunschweig, where Renate Röder's unknown father was based, an SS unit dressed up as robbers broke into and looted Jewish warehouses in the sure knowledge there would be no police patrols for the duration. In Dresden the synagogue was ransacked. In Göttingen and Breslau Jewish lawyers were forbidden entrance to the courts. By mid-March Jews were being dismissed from local government and colleges across the Reich. Jewish judges were banned from the courts by the end of March. On 1 April there was an official boycott of Jewish shops, doctors and lawyers. By 7 April Jews were being dismissed from the civil service, including people with just one Jewish grandparent. Then came the scientists and the university professors. Then the Jewish children, who were no longer welcome in their schools. By 1934 most of the Jews had lost their jobs. Later their homes and assets. Later still, their lives.

Himmler was poised to act, his racially pure SS already well established by the time of the *Machtergreifung*. He was the main architect of two of the first laws passed by the Nazis, ably assisted by Walther Darré, the race expert now promoted to the Minister of Agriculture. First came the Hereditary Homestead Law. Second, the Law for the New Formation of the German Farmer Stock. *Lebensraum* is what they were both about: to provide homesteads and subsidies for the farming families who would furnish the racial stock in the lands to the east conquered in the coming war. Handy too for wheat and oil. 'We are dependent on the import of raw materials,' as Hitler told Otto Strasser, Gregor's brother, discussing the economy. 'Our task is to take in hand a great organisation of the whole world so that each country produces what is most suitable to it; it is for the white race, the Nordic race, to carry through this gigantic plan. Believe me, all National Socialism would be worth nothing if it were limited to only Germany, and did not seal for one or two thousand years the mastery of the superior race over the whole world...' After which Strasser left the Nazi Party.

1934 saw the rise and rise of Heinrich Himmler. Gone were the miseries and humiliations of his youth, replaced by a seemingly confident *Reichsführer-SS*, always in his black uniform and jackboots with a military cap hiding his oddly shaped head. He travelled the country to address his *SS-Führer*s in long, schoolmasterly speeches to which they listened with rapt attention, given it was forbidden to slip out in the middle. That same year he opened the first of his *SS-Junker-Schulen* officer-training schools at Bad Tölz in Bavaria – *Junker* being the term for landed gentry, because Himmler was minded to create his own SS aristocracy. The following year he opened another, in Braunschweig, presumably with the help of Renate Röder's father. Applicants didn't need any academic qualifications. It was more important they were blond, more or less, and blue-eyed, more or less, athletic, and at least five foot seven tall. Their curriculum, devised by Himmler, concentrated on the National Socialist *Weltanschauung* ideology, comprising Germanic history and myth, with special attention to Alfred Rosenberg's *Der Mythus des 20. Jahrhunderts* and Hitler's *Mein Kampf*, accompanied by the study of military tactics, the handling of weapons from bow and arrow to sub-machine gun, and the dark secrets of intelligence-gathering. The afternoons were dedicated to sport. So excited was Himmler with this fulfilment of a long-held dream that he sometimes woke his chauffeur at 5 a.m. to be driven to Bad Tölz in time to see his *Jungen* (youths) get up, bleary-eyed, and make their way naked to cold showers and the start of their day. One *Junge* remembered how the *Reichsführer-SS* was almost in tears just watching them.

Once the youths qualified as SS officers they passed out by way of a pseudo-military ceremony at which they spoke the SS oath: 'I swear to you, Adolf Hitler, as Führer and Chancellor of the German Reich, that I will be loyal and brave. I pledge obedience unto death to you and those you appoint to lead. So help me God.' They were used to oaths. As Hitler Youths they'd stood before the *Blutfahne* (Blood Banner) to commemorate the blood of the heroes who'd died during the Beer Hall Putsch in 1923 and sworn: 'In the presence of this blood banner which represents our Führer I swear to devote all my energies and my strength to the saviour of our country, Adolf Hitler. I am willing and ready to give up my life for him. So help me God.'

To celebrate the Führer becoming President of the German Reich in 1934, new wording was written for the *Führer Eid*, the Hitler oath, to be sworn by all military personnel:

> I swear to God by this Holy Oath
> That I shall render unconditional obedience
> To the Führer of the German Reich and people,
> Adolf Hitler, supreme commander of the armed forces
> And that, as a brave soldier, I shall at all times be prepared
> To give my life for this oath.

While they were at it, the Nazis introduced another oath for the civil service and all public servants, swearing obedience and allegiance to Adolf Hitler, the ceremony rounded off with rousing renderings of 'Deutschland, Deutschland über Alles', and the 'Horst Wessel Lied', the Nazis' favourite. What was a public servant to do? Swear the oath, or lose his job and his livelihood?

By now Himmler had a new adjutant, Karl Wolff. They'd met in May 1932 when Wolff, an *SS-Sturmführer*, was attending an officer-training session in Munich. Himmler was thrilled. Here was a young officer, good-looking, six feet tall, blond, blue-eyed and, most importantly, from a different background to the usual intake – haute-bourgeois, *Gymnasium-* (high school) educated, his father a lawyer – who had all the social polish which Himmler, try as he might, never possessed. Wolff could smooth relations with businessmen, wealthy industrialists, Prussian nobility, army generals, bishops and anyone else who made Himmler feel uncomfortable. Just leave it to Wolff. And so it remained, right up to the end of the war. Except that Wolff lived to tell the tale. 'My first impression of Himmler was a great disappointment,' he wrote in his self-serving post-war memoirs. 'I was considerably taller than him and had already been awarded the Iron Cross First and Second Class and been an officer in one of the best and oldest regiments in the German Army – the Hessian Lifeguard Infantry Regiment in Darmstadt. Himmler on the other hand had no war decorations and had nothing in common with the soldier at the Front. His whole bearing was rather sly and unmilitary. But he was well read and tried to engage our interest in his knowledge, and enthuse us with the tasks of the SS.' But Wolff was at his master's side to the last, contributing to Himmler's rapid rise to terrifying power as he eliminated his Party rivals one by one.

The mid-1930s were Himmler's best years, riding high, travelling the Reich with Wolffie, as Himmler liked to call his adjutant in private – two cheerful fellows in smart black uniforms, seated side by side in the back of the black Maybach tourer, roof down whenever the weather permitted, chauffeur up front, heading for a meeting with *SS-Führer*s, a secret armaments depot or concentration camp. Together they found Wewelsburg – an ancient, abandoned medieval castle, towers, turrets, moat and all, near Paderborn in northern Germany – the perfect setting for Himmler's new Order of SS Knights and their chivalrous deeds. Over the next years Himmler spent a small fortune restoring the castle and acquiring 'medieval' furniture, produced by the finest craftsmen in the Reich, including a King Alfred Round table for his twelve Knights, each with their own coat of arms. Later there were flags and banners and swastikas. And SS runes carved into the walls and the oak doors and throne-like seats. And a library with 12,000 books on ancient German history and myths. But first and foremost they needed a crypt for the secret meetings of the Chosen. It can still be visited, that crypt, with its stone bench-seat running in a circle round the thick walls, and urns on pillars and swastika runes carved into the stone floor – an eerie place filled with a gloomy light and a strange, unholy atmosphere. Himmler's own quarters in the castle were dedicated to the tenth-century King Heinrich I. *Gruppenführer-SS* Taubert was in charge of the renovations. He was told to find a Gobelin tapestry featuring 'a fully developed virginal girl, a future mother' and a stone sculpture of a mother and young boy, much like the one at the Steinhöring *Lebensborn* home where Renate was born.

Himmler had a mistress by now, another of the perks of power. She was called Hedwig Potthast, twelve years younger than him, and although no beauty, prettier and blonder than Marga. She was working at Prinz Albrecht Strasse, the notorious Gestapo HQ, when they met in 1936. She soon became Himmler's private secretary and then his mistress. He called her *Häschen*, 'little bunny'. By 1941 *Häschen* was pregnant. She bore him two children, a boy and a girl. He bought her a nice house in Berlin, but during the chaos of the last year of war Himmler moved them to the safety of Berchtesgaden, Hitler's alpine retreat, guarded by a triple ring of SS security. In 1945, with the defeat and total collapse of Germany, *Häschen* and her two children went into hiding, then disappeared forever into the mists of history.

In November 1935 came the Nuremberg Laws, with the Law for the Protection of German Blood and German Honour and the Reich Citizenship Law, stating that only true Germans, pure-blood Germans, could be Reich citizens. Himmler could hardly have been happier. Now he founded his SS 'charity', *Lebensborn*, the pinnacle of all his dreams. 'My first aim in setting up *Lebensborn* was to meet a crying need to give unmarried women, who were racially pure, the chance to have children free of cost,' as he put it to his masseur Kersten during one of their sessions, quite carried away with his own version of the truth. 'You can hardly imagine how much it means to a woman who used to be cold-shouldered and insulted because her child was illegitimate, to enter a home where she can relax spiritually and physically, receive medical attention and feel that everybody is glad about the child she's going to have.' Renate's mother must have passed all the racial tests, though that was one thing she wasn't prepared to admit.

Blond and blue-eyed and racially pure. 'The ideal German,' joked the man in the street as long as no one was listening, 'should be as blond as Hitler, as tall as Goebbels, and as slim as Göring.' Not to mention Himmler.

'In my opinion, a much greater selection process called forth by National Socialism will take place and make itself felt,' Himmler told a group of Hitler Youth in May 1936, looking ahead. Racial selection had been known a long time in animal-breeding, he explained to his dutiful listeners, going on and on. But with humans it was more complicated. 'Because the body and each movement of the hand or foot, the stride, the gait – all of that represents a value. It is not inconsequential. Like the ear, like the structure of the skeleton, and, as every soldier knows, like a man's eyes. They can be blue, and despite that we will not take the man with blue eyes if you see that, when you look at him, when you speak with him, his eyes flicker or his eyes, locked in deepest introspection, are weak-willed, declare to you: I am not willing to endure the battle of life.' No, no! In spite of his blue eyes, the SS would not take him. 'We, who took part in the war... as soldiers, as Front fighters... we know all this,' he said. What on earth was he talking about? He had never been a soldier and never been anywhere near the war.

During those early years of Nazi rule foreigners flooded to Germany to admire their great achievements, culminating in the spectacle of the 1936 Olympic Games. The new motorways, the zero unemployment, the splendid public works. No sign of concentration camps. No unhappy Jews. But once the Games were over the terror regime was back. Up till then, Hitler had been careful not to alienate the average German, offering them all sorts of cheap holidays and sports facilities and entertainments to keep them happy. Because he knew well enough that two-thirds of them hadn't voted for him. But now that all changed. 'After the Olympics we'll get ruthless,' as Joseph Goebbels had written in his diary on 7 August 1936, anticipating the success of the Olympic Games propaganda coup. 'Then there will be some shooting.'

By 1938 the Nazi terror regime had such a brutal hold on Germany that Hitler and his cronies were confident of planning an 'Action' which would announce the way they meant to proceed with the Jews from then on. It came to be known as *Kristallnacht*, the Night of Broken Glass – smashed shop windows, looted homes, glass everywhere. Officially, it was a spontaneous outpouring of pent-up resentment by the German public, provoked by the 'murder' of Ernst vom Rath, a junior German diplomat in Paris, by a Jew two weeks earlier. Secretly it had been weeks in the planning. '*Geheim!*' – secret – went the final instruction to all Gestapo offices at five minutes to midnight on 9 November. 'Actions against the Jews, especially against their synagogues, will take place throughout the Reich shortly.' Between 20,000 and 30,000 Jews were to be arrested, 'above all well-to-do Jews'. Detailed instructions would follow. As they duly did, from Heydrich: 'LIGHTNING, URGENT, IMMEDIATE ATTENTION!' it was headed. 'The German police have received the following instructions from the *Reichsführer-SS* and Chief of Police: only such measures should be taken as will not endanger German life or property, that is, synagogue-burning only if there is no fire danger to the surroundings.' Special care was to be taken that non-Jewish businesses were secured against damage.

Apart from anything else, *Kristallnacht* was an excellent way to raise money. Göring suggested the Jews contribute one billion Reichsmarks to repair the damage caused by all that burning and destruction. Jewish businesses would be 'Aryanised', that is, confiscated. This was backed up by an order from Heydrich/Himmler that any Jew in possession of emigration papers should leave the country within three weeks. Heydrich wrote a report adding up the total benefit: 7,500 Jewish businesses had been destroyed, plus 177 synagogues; 25,000 Jews had been taken to concentration camps in order to encourage the others to flee Germany, leaving everything behind. It caused an international outcry. But no action was taken. The *Reichsführer-SS* took himself off for a well-deserved holiday in Italy.

'He is modest in manner,' wrote the British author Stephen Roberts about Himmler after visiting him in 1938 – not the only foreign visitor to be duped by the *Reichsführer-SS*. 'He sets an example of quiet dignity and simplicity of life that is often lacking in Nazi Germany, and remains entirely unspoilt, living like a clerk in a simple Berlin flat.' Evidently it had never entered Mr Roberts's imagination that the *Reichsführer-SS* might be lying. Far from living 'like a simple clerk' Himmler now owned a splendid villa in Dahlem, the most fashionable district of Berlin, and a holiday villa at the equally fashionable lake of Tegernsee in Bavaria. But how was Mr Roberts to know? All Himmler's properties were registered in Martin Bormann's name. Never tell, never write anything down. That was the *Reichsführer-SS*.

Things were on the move in Nazi Germany in 1938. A thorough cleansing of the ranks was in order. First came the *Wehrmacht*. It was positively stuffed with officers and generals who were anti everything the Führer was trying to achieve. Generals von Fritsch and von Blomberg were dismissed on dubious charges, swiftly followed by sixteen others. Forty more were transferred and effectively demoted. Loyal General Keitel took over at the Ministry of War, responsible only to Hitler himself. Next it was the turn of the Foreign Office, where charming von Ribbentrop replaced Konstantin von Neurath, another troublesome pest. Ambassadors to Rome, Vienna and Tokyo were removed. At the Ministry of Economics and Finance the banker Hjalmar Schacht handed in his resignation quoting 'fundamental differences in our economics policies'. And all this because, by 1938, the time had come to prepare for war.

Himmler did his bit, setting up a new department: the *SS-Erganzungsamt* (Replenishment Office) to acquire new racially pure blood from any conquered areas. In May he and Wolffie accompanied the Führer on a state visit to Mussolini in Italy, travelling with an entourage of 500. Apparently Friedrich Jeckeln, Renate's father, was one of them. The main purpose of the visit was to secure Mussolini's compliance with the Nazis' plan for the annexation of the Sudetenland and later Austria, as a first undeclared step to war. By September Himmler and Wolffie were goose-stepping at the head of their SS units in their black uniforms, arms outstretched, at the Nuremberg Party Rally to rousing music from military bands. On 8 November Himmler gave one of his interminable, convoluted speeches to his *SS-Gruppenführers*. 'It is not only the battle of the nations,' he explained, 'but it is the *weltanschauliche* battle of the entire Jewry, freemasonry, Marxism and Churches of the world. These forces – of which I assume the Jews to be the driving spirit, the origin of all the negatives – are clear [they know] that if Germany and Italy are not eradicated, *they* will be *vernichtet*, exterminated. That is an elementary conclusion. In Germany the Jew cannot hold out.' On and on he went. The SS had to be without pity, said the *Reichsführer-SS*. 'It is a matter of indifference if in a town of 1,000 people have to be put down. I would do it, and I would expect you to carry it out. About that there is no doubt.' The Jews would be *ausgehungert und abgeschlachtet*, starved out and slaughtered.

Nineteen thirty-eight was the year of great gambles. There had already been one, in 1936. At 5 a.m. on 7 March 1936 German troops marched across the Rhine bridges, *Marsch! Marsch!*, to retake that part of the Rhineland which had been allotted to the French following Germany's defeat in the 1914–18 war. It later transpired that the *Wehrmacht* had strict instructions to retreat immediately if the French or the British intervened, because Germany was in fact nowhere near ready for war at that time. But there was no intervention. Hitler and his cronies could hardly believe their luck.'We make no further demands for territory in Europe,' broadcast the Führer that same day on Goebbels's wireless, in full lie mode, knowing that most Germans had no wish for war. 'Germany will never break the terms of Peace!' he declared.

So in March 1938, emboldened by that unbelievable success and much better prepared for war now, came the next big gamble: the *Anschluss*, the annexation of Austria, to 'restore order'. There was no order to restore, but no matter. Kurt Schuschnigg, the Chancellor, and 76,000 other opponents of the Nazis were arrested and transported to Dachau. A plebiscite was held on 10 April which the Nazis won, fear being a useful political tool. The next day Jews were ordered out of their homes and into the streets to wipe Schuschnigg's election slogans off the walls and scrub the pavements on their hands and knees, with crowds of local Nazis looking on, jeering and spitting, caught on camera for Goebbels's newsreels to celebrate this first step in the creation of the Greater German Reich. The non-Nazi Austrians were nowhere to be seen. No doubt hiding in their homes.

Next step, Czechoslovakia. 'In Berlin the best opinion is that Hitler has made up his mind for war if it is necessary in order to get back his Sudetens,' wrote William Shirer, the American newspaper correspondent, on 9 September 1938, perhaps not realising that Hitler had in fact been planning for war since the early 1920s. 'The radio has been saying all day that Great Britain has told Germany she will fight if Czechoslovakia is invaded. Perhaps so. But you cannot forget *The Times* leader of three days ago inviting the Czechs to become a more "homogenous state" by handing the Sudetens over to Germany.'

So that was another gamble which paid off, because the appeasers in England and France were persuaded that Hitler would keep his word and avoid war, as long as he got back that small part of Czechoslovakia which was rightfully his in the first place. Neville Chamberlain in his bowler hat and umbrella came and went from his meeting with Herr Hitler, emerging from his biplane back in London waving his piece of paper, signed by the Führer, assuring the world that all Germany wanted was peace.

Everything was going beautifully to plan, thought the *Reichsführer-SS*. Who would have thought, back in 1928 when he was still struggling to be someone of significance, that he would find himself in such jubilant circumstances? What a difference ten years can make. Who held the power now!

'*Sehr geehrter Herr Minister!*' Himmler wrote to Franz Gürtner, the Justice Minister, on 16 May 1938. 'For some two months you have been telling me that in your view too many people in the concentrations camps have been shot while attempting escape.' Poor Dr Gürtner was evidently still labouring under the illusion that he might uphold a last vestige of the rule of law. But he soon found out. 'The day before yesterday I was in Camp Buchenwald and was shown the body of a worthy twenty-four-year-old SS man whose skull had been smashed in by two criminals with shovels . . .' Two criminals? Who actually was the criminal, Dr Gürtner might have asked himself. 'Both the criminals escaped,' the *Reichsführer-SS* continued, quite beside himself. 'Because of too great leniency one of my decent men has had to lose his life. Two further criminals, who patently knew of the break-out attempt, were shot in flight.' Apparently two further criminals had also assisted the breakout. 'I can tell you now that the death sentence on the [other] two will be carried out, in the camp before the assembled 3,000 prisoners – preferably with the rope on the gallows. *Heil Hitler!* Yours H. Himmler.' Dr Gürtner had better watch out.

By 1939, unbeknown to the German public and the rest of the world, preparations for war were well under way in the Reich ministries, all by now infiltrated by a parallel staff and administration – a state within a state – headed by Nazi Party members in the Ministry of War along with the fighting force of Himmler's *Waffen-SS*. Having occupied Czechoslovakia without any serious outcry from the international community, it was time to take Poland. But what to do about Russia? Lie was the answer. The bigger the lie the better, as the Führer always said. The result was the Molotov-Ribbentrop Pact, a non-aggression pact signed between Germany and Russia on 23 August 1939, effectively agreeing to carve up Poland between them, Germany occupying the west, Russia the east. Hitler's true purpose:

to keep the Russians happy while Germany continued to rearm in preparation for its ultimate war, the racial war, with Russia. Apparently even the great liar Stalin was taken in. Poor Poland.

At 4.30 a.m. on 1 September, German Panzer tank columns crossed the border into Poland without any formal declaration of war. An hour later Hitler addressed the German *Volk* on the wireless. There had been fourteen border incidents in the night, he said. 'In order to put an end to this lunacy I have no choice but to meet force with force.' Two days later the British government finally understood what was happening and delivered an ultimatum. Sir Nevile Henderson, the British Ambassador in Berlin, reported that the German people were 'horror-struck at the whole idea of war which was being thrust upon them'. Presumably he was referring to those Germans who'd never voted for the Nazi Party in the first place. There was 'utter gloom and depression', he wrote. When the ultimatum expired, it was war.

CHAPTER THREE

LONIA, MENDEL AND JOE

On 1 September 1939 Lonia Goldfeld was in the family apartment at 22 Nalewki Street in Warsaw, giving the maid and cook their instructions for the day. She was twenty, dark-haired and dark-eyed, with an attractive, lively way about her. Her older sister Frania was married to a doctor, Marcel Celmeister, and lived nearby. Her younger sister Yadzia was fourteen and out on a trip. Her brother Sevek was away in Montpellier in France, studying medicine. Her other brother Julek had joined the Polish Army, stationed somewhere near a border, preparing to fight the Russians or the Germans, take your pick.

'This is the Polish rebel force!' had come the announcement on the wireless at the border town of Gleiwitz on the night of 31 August 1939. 'Radio station Gleiwitz is in our hands. The hour of freedom has struck!' How were the Polish listeners to know it was a lie, perpetrated by one of Reinhard Heydrich's 'provocation' units, as ordered by *Reichsführer-SS* Heinrich Himmler? The SS unit wore Polish uniforms and a prisoner was shot and left lying there to be photographed as evidence. There had been a secret dress rehearsal five days earlier, and now everything went without a hitch. That the 'Polish' announcer on the wireless had a German accent didn't raise much suspicion – many ethnic Germans had accents. Another SS unit, again in Polish uniforms, attacked the customs post. Another, in customs uniforms, counter-attacked. Earlier some Sachsenhausen prisoners had been shot, then dressed in Polish uniforms and left for dead in the 'battle'. Ox blood was splattered on the walls and floor of a forestry station at Pitschen. At 4.30 the next morning, German Panzer columns crossed the border into Poland.

The reason Lonia was at home running the household was that their mother Nicha had died suddenly of a heart attack two years earlier, so now it fell to Lonia to keep family life going, look after their father, Josef, and Yadzia, and help with the family business – a prosperous leather goods one, the factory taking up the ground floor of the large apartment block where they lived and which the family owned. The Goldfelds also owned several other properties and businesses across Warsaw – in other words, theirs was a well-off, assimilated Jewish family, typical of many in their circle: doctors, lawyers, business people, academics, all Polish as much as Jewish, speaking only Polish at home. But by now, in 1939, they were holding their breath, not knowing what might happen next. Nothing good, anyway, if what was happening to the Jews in the German Reich was anything to go by.

Lonia's mother Nicha had taken the precaution of buying a large bag of $20 US gold coins early on as news of what was happening in Nazi Germany filtered out of the Reich and into Poland, knowing they were the safest currency in those troubled times, and hiding them away in the apartment. Typical, said the family, smiling at Nicha's pessimism. Didn't they already have enough money and property – enough even for a rainy day? But Nicha was the businesswoman in the family. And she knew her husband, Lonia's father Josef, was no good at business. He was a craftsman – a fine leather craftsman, which is how the couple met in the first place. But never a businessman. Nicha bought those gold coins because she could sense what was coming. Though her darkest fears came nowhere near the reality.

So there was no one at home on that day, 1 September 1939, except Lonia. It was still the school summer vacation, and her father and Yadzia and Frania were away on a trip to the countryside outside Warsaw. Lonia had just finished giving the maid and the cook their instructions for the day when the bomb came through the ceiling. Their apartment was on the fourth floor, the top floor, and the bomb fell straight through into the living room with no warning, setting it and the kitchen next door on fire. The cook and maid raced down the stairs to the basement, shouting at Lonia to follow. But Lonia was looking for her mother's ring. She couldn't leave without it. By some miracle the bomb didn't explode, she found the ring, and she joined the others in the basement of the building. It turned out that it was a German bomb from Göring's Luftwaffe, delivered on the very first day of the German invasion of Poland. That night they stayed with Lonia's uncle and his two children. Her aunt had been killed in the raid.

Things moved fast after that. On 17 September the Russians invaded and annexed eastern Poland during that brief period of time when Stalin and Hitler were allies, carving Poland up between them. By 27 September Warsaw had surrendered to the Germans. Fifty thousand people from the surrounding countryside, fleeing the fighting, came pouring into the city seeking refuge. Sevek came back from France. Julek came back from eastern Poland – a civilian now that the Polish Army had been defeated. On 29 September Lonia watched from the window of their apartment as German Army trucks appeared in Nalewki Street. German *Wehrmacht* soldiers broke into the Goldfeld factory below and removed all the equipment and goods, shouting '*Raus!*' at anyone who got in their way, pistols and rifles at the ready. Then they banged up the stairs in their heavy army boots, searching through every apartment in the block, plundering furniture, paintings, rugs, china – anything of value; the place was stripped bare. By 12 October the newly established administration announced the creation of a ghetto for the Jews of Warsaw, to be run by a twelve-person *Judenrat* or Jewish Council, many of whom Lonia knew well. Nalewki Street became part of the ghetto. The cook and the maid fled in tears to live with their Polish families.

The first Jewish ghetto had been established at Piotrków Trybunalski, only weeks after the Germans crossed the Polish border with all that fake news, fanfare and brutality. Then came Łódź and Warsaw, quickly followed by Cracowa, now renamed Krakau. In the end there were over 300 ghettos in Poland, large and small, all run by Himmler's SS. Their stated aim: killing the Jew, sooner or later, in one way or another. In the Warsaw ghetto 400,000 Jews, a third of Warsaw's population, were crammed into an area of less than 3 per cent of the city. Then 100,000 more were added, 'resettled' from elsewhere in Poland.

On 26 October the forced labour of the Jews began, herding them into the factories and workshops already existing in the area, now 'Aryanised'. By 20 November Jewish bank accounts were frozen. By 23 November Jewish businesses had to display the Star of David, quickly followed by all Jews having to do the same. Jewish property and assets were confiscated by 5 December. By 11 December Jews were barred from all public transport, and the resettlement of the new arrivals began. The Goldfelds had to accommodate another family in their apartment. It was a deeply religious Hasidic family, and it was terrible for both sides. Lonia used her influence with the *Judenrat* to exchange them for another, more assimilated, family. But sharing the apartment with strangers was hard. Lonia had to learn to cook and clean. Josef, their father, was suddenly old and defeated. For the time being Yadzia was still able to attend school – an exclusively Jewish school within the ghetto.

You can't say they weren't warned. As *Reichsführer-SS* Heinrich Himmler put it in his April 1936 pamphlet for the new recruits to his SS: 'Why do you in the SS have to learn about the Jews? Because they are the most dangerous enemy of the German *Volk*.' History showed that the Jew worked as a parasite in all countries and peoples, he wrote. It was a deliberate and planned destruction of the host *Volk* by infiltration of their race-pride, their thought and their feeling, their ways, their rights and their culture. 'The Jew is a *Schmarotzer*, just like the parasites which live off the productive work and strengths of animals and plants. The Jew is the bloodsucker of the world. Judas Ischkariot, the traitor.'

Or, as Hitler had already expressed it in a letter of 16 September 1919, years before the Nazis came to power: 'Anti-Semitism as a political movement neither can nor should be based on fleeting emotions, but on the acceptance of fact – and that fact is that Judaism is a matter of race and not of religion. The final aim of such anti-Semitism must be, unquestionably, the expulsion of the Jews.' He followed it up later in *Mein Kampf* with: 'If, at the beginning and during [the First World War] someone had only subjected about twelve or fifteen thousand of these Hebrew enemies of the people to poison gas – as was suffered by hundreds of thousands of our best workers from all walks of life and callings on the battlefield – then the sacrifice of millions at the Front would not have been in vain.' Hitler could hold forth on the subject for hours of an evening among his cronies during his Table Talks, confident that it would remain within the four walls. Wrongly, as it turned out. 'As soon as I have the power,' he confided in one of his early talks, in happy anticipation, 'I shall have gallows after gallows erected, for example in Munich on the Marienplatz. Then the Jews will be hanged, one after another, and they will stay hanging until they stink. They will stay hanging as long as hygienically possible. As soon as they are untied, then the next group will follow, and that will continue until the last Jew in Munich is exterminated.'

As soon as he had the power, Hitler put *Reichsführer-SS* Heinrich Himmler in charge of the extermination of the Jews, knowing that Himmler would stop at nothing to please his master, and anyway shared his views on the parasitic Jew. So it was Himmler's SS who manned the exterminating *Einsatzgruppen*, and it was his SS who guarded the ghettos and ran the concentration camps. And, until the 'Final Solution' provided by the gas chambers, it was they who ran the units which rounded up the Jews, marched them along roads leading out of their towns and villages into the dark forests beyond and ordered them to undress, leaving their clothes in neat bundles by the wayside, then harried them naked to the edge of deep pits where they shot them one by one.

Himmler called it a *Harte Reinigung*, a hard purification of Nordic blood. Again and again he told his new SS recruits that they had to be 'hard' to fulfil their destiny. Especially with the best of the Jews, the strongest fighters, including the children, because 'one day these children will grow up. And do we want to be so stupid as to say – no, no, no – we're too weak to do it, so we're leaving it to our children to deal with in their turn? By which time the Jewish hate would have grown bigger, the today smaller but later bigger wish for revenge would be visited on our children, so they have to once again sort out the problem. No, we can't be responsible for that! That would be cowardly. And that's why we have drawn up a clear solution – as hard as it might be, but we will do it, because it is necessary.'

To his *SS-Gruppenführers* in Poznań, now renamed Posen, he further explained:

> The *Ausrottung* [extermination] of the Jewish people belongs to those subjects which can be spoken of lightly: 'the Jew must be exterminated,' as every Party member back home might say, and then up they come, one after another, these fine 80 million Germans, and each one has his decent Jew; all the others are *Schweine*, pigs, of course, but this one, this one is a decent fellow. Not one of them has had to go through with it. Most of you, here, you know what it means when 100 corpses lie there, when 500 lie there, when 1,000 do. To have held up strong through it, and, apart from a few weaklings, have managed to remain decent fellows, that's what's made us hard.

And then he added that key thing: 'This is something never to be written down, and never to be part of our recorded history...'

By 21 September 1939, hardly three weeks after the Germans invaded Poland, Reinhard Heydrich, Himmler's right-hand man in the SS in charge of the *Ausrottung*, had already issued instructions to the *Einsatzgruppen*: 1. Jews to be moved out of Reich, into Poland, using cattle trucks. 2. The Jews of Poland and other occupied territories to be moved out of the countryside into towns, and into ghettos. 3. *Judenräte* to be created to see that all future instructions were scrupulously obeyed on pain of 'the most severe penalties if sabotage should occur'.

By 15 November 1940 a high brick wall round the Warsaw ghetto was finished, watchtowers and all, built by the Jews themselves, overseen by SS guards. Now the ghetto was completely sealed off from the rest of Warsaw. Lonia watched from her window, weeping. Even so, in those early days people made desperate efforts to continue as much of their normal lives as possible: teachers set up impromptu schools for the children, doctors treated their patients, there were social gatherings and musical evenings, and those who were young and fit enough went to work long hours in one of the factories and businesses set up in the ghetto by the Germans, making up for their loss of manpower now that their own workers were away at war. The Goldfelds' leather goods factory was 'Aryanised' by a German company, along with the rest. Lonia's father went on working there, at least for the time being. Julek worked there for a while, then disappeared into the Warsaw underground. Sevek disappeared altogether. Yadzia went to school, while it was still possible. She was plump and pretty and blond and could easily pass for a Polish girl. Soon someone had furnished her with false papers and she began smuggling food in and out of the ghetto for the family. Sometimes she smuggled out some of the leather goods stolen from the Goldfeld factory too. She got very good at doing deals with the SS guards, who liked the leather goods. At other times she used the cash converted from those gold coins of Nicha's as bribes. She grew up fast. But as conditions in the ghetto got worse and worse, the family agreed she should disappear altogether. One night she slipped out of the ghetto and never returned. She was hidden in another part of Warsaw by the Polish family of one of her old school friends. She was never found out. Nor was the family. Which was just as well, as it would have meant certain death for all of them.

There is a heart-rending photograph taken of a New Year's Eve 'party' in 1941 when it was still just possible to celebrate New Year – some musicians playing in the background, Lonia in the foreground on the left, Julek bottom-right. They are all smiling brightly at the camera, defying the present. It is likely the photograph was taken by Mendel Albek. Mendel was Lonia's betrothed. They'd met a year earlier, in the ghetto, introduced by the lawyer of the family sharing the Goldfeld apartment. Mendel was exceptionally handsome. Kind too. And decent. And Lonia fell for him, wholly and for ever. But her father was not pleased. Mendel came from a religious Hasidic Orthodox background and was uneducated in any sense recognised by Josef. What on earth did Lonia see in him?

Mendel was from Łowicz, a town thirty-five kilometres west of Warsaw, the population half-Polish, half-Jewish, with some ethnic Germans thrown in. The family spoke Yiddish at home. They went to the synagogue every Friday evening and every Saturday morning. When he was a boy Mendel longed to be permitted to attend public school along with the Polish boys of the town, but in Hasidic communities that wasn't allowed. His sisters were allowed, but not Mendel, the boy. Mendel had to attend *Cheder*. He begged and begged his parents to let him go to the public school, because he longed for a better education and a wider knowledge of the world, but they were too traditionally religious to agree. The Albeks ran a small general store in the town – that is, his mother ran it. In Hasidic families the men studied the sacred texts and prayed, the women worked and earned the money. The family lived in rooms above the store. All their neighbours were Jews like themselves. Next door lived Nathan the Slaughterer, so called because he slaughtered animals for the Jewish community: chickens, geese, whatever came his way. He was a huge man, six foot five, and a great storyteller. In the attic lived an old man who eked out a living making paper bags. In the back courtyard lived a *melamed*, a rabbi for children. In addition to his teaching the *melamed* would sort out any young man who didn't want to join the army, by crippling him – not too much, just enough to keep him safe. Their landlord was an anti-Semitic Pole, but otherwise life was safe and fine.

It was a happy childhood, not poor, not rich, but somewhere in between. Neighbours were always in and out of the Albek store, passing the time of day. There was plenty of local gossip to keep things lively, and plenty of boys for Mendel to play with in the cobbled street. In the heat of the long summer days they swam in the river, in the cold of the short winter days they took the horse-drawn sledge and raced across the snow and ice, whooping and shouting. And Mendel's life might have continued in that safe, lost-in-time way, except that on 1 September 1939 war broke out, and the German Army immediately set about removing the Poles into the *Generalgouvernement* area in the centre of Poland and the Jews into their ghettos. By early 1940 the Albek family were living in two rooms in the Warsaw ghetto. And Mendel met Lonia, introduced by the lawyer. What did Mendel see in Lonia? Everything, really: her strength, her vitality, her deep dark eyes, her educated, cultured background which he'd always wanted for himself but hadn't been allowed. Her determination to survive.

By 1941 things were turning from bad to worse in the Warsaw ghetto. The official food ration for Germans was 2,613 calories a day; for Poles it was 699; for Jews, 184. It became normal to step over dead bodies on the pavements. The *Judenrat* recorded 44,630 deaths in 1941. Thousands of orphaned children roamed the streets begging and stealing, or crouching in doorways, half-dead from starvation and grief. 'The children in the ghettos were swollen with hunger, some were unable to walk, and most had their bodies covered with sores and ulcers,' one witness later reported. 'They were without shelter, without food, without shoes and clothes, in rags.' They were often beaten up. If they were caught smuggling they were shot on the spot. Now there were 'selections' every morning at the *Umschlagplatz* (Assembly Square) to separate the sick, old and dying from those young and strong enough to work. The sick and dying went one way – to the cattle trucks for 'transportation' – the others went back to their ghetto factories and workshops.

Himmler was highly satisfied with the 'hard' brutality shown by his SS men in the Warsaw ghetto and rewarded them richly with extra rations – schnapps, cigarettes, cash. Later there were specially struck ghetto medals, freely distributed to what the *Reichsführer-SS* liked to call his *Ghetto Liquidatoren*. 'I saw a little girl trying to slip past at the ghetto crossing post,' remembered yet another witness at the post-war Nuremberg Trials. 'The guards spotted her and shouted to her to stop. Slowly one SS man took his rifle off his shoulder. The child fell over and begged for mercy. The guard laughed: 'You won't die, but you won't do any more smuggling either,' and shot her feet, which later had to be amputated.'

Only those who could work for one of the German-run ghetto enterprises were spared. The Goldfeld leather goods factory now had 3,000 workers producing shoes and bags for the Reich as well as boots and belts and leather gloves for the *Wehrmacht*. The Schultz branch of the business was the textile and manufacturing side, again with several factories in the ghetto, large and small, contributing to the German war effort by making uniforms for the German Army, including the greatcoats needed for the freezing Russian winters. Unless they were leather, in which case it was over to Többens.

By 1942 Mendel had the necessary papers from the *Judenrat* to be employed by Többens. They employed 15,000 workers in their various ghetto factories, all unpaid slave labour, but at least they were protected from the daily selections and 'transportations'. Lonia was meanwhile working at a fish factory, cleaning fish. But she lost the job when she got some fish bile in her eyes and went blind. Luckily her brother-in-law, the doctor, knew how to treat it and she recovered after a month. But she'd lost her job. She and Mendel went in panic to the *Judenrat* and she managed to get a job at Többens along with Mendel, saved, dear God, for the time being at least, from transportation.

On 28 June 1942 there was a happy event: the marriage, in the ghetto, of Lonia and Mendel. At least, it would have been happy, but for the two fathers. For Mendel's father the Goldfeld family were so assimilated they hardly featured as Jews. For Lonia's father the Albeks were backwoods Hasidic Jews with no education or culture of any sort. Even as father and daughter made their way to the *Cuppa*, the marriage tent, he was still trying to persuade Lonia to change her mind. A lost cause, of course. Because Lonia was set on Mendel from the start. And he on her. So there was no changing either of them, and the fathers finally had to give way. Luckily the newlyweds, with their contacts on the *Judenrat* and their protected jobs at Többens, were able to find a room of their own in the ghetto, away from the frowning fathers. And it was in one of the rooms that they managed to build a false wall behind which the Albek family hid during the bad times when SS guards marched through the ghetto in their hob-nailed boots, rifles cocked, kicking down doors searching for anyone trying to avoid transportation. Mother Albek had died by then, of cancer but more likely of pure terror. So it was just father Albek and Mendel's two sisters who had to be hidden. Even so, it was almost impossible for them to fit into the small space, making not a sound, hardly daring to breathe.

By then Lonia's other uncle and his wife had already died from starvation and despair, so Lonia and Mendel were looking after their five-year-old son, Henek. But as things got worse and worse they decided the safest place for Henek was in the orphanage run by Dr Janusz Korczak. Dr Korczak had been a famous educator in Warsaw before the war, writing children's books and textbooks, and he'd run an orphanage for Jewish children. In 1940 he moved all the children into a building within the ghetto walls so the orphanage could continue, gathering more and more as time went on, now including Henek. Korczak and his staff tried to maintain some kind of normality for his orphans with lessons every day, some sport and art, and even putting on shows from time to time. But on 7 August 1942 SS guards and soldiers stormed the orphanage and took the children to the *Umschlagplatz* for transportation. One hundred and ninety-six children walked two by two, hand in hand, to the square, led through the streets by Dr Korczak, who refused to leave them, though he'd been offered a chance to secure his own survival by the Polish underground, who were aware of his pre-war reputation and knew he wasn't Jewish. People stood on the pavement in silence, weeping, watching them go. Korczak had told the children they were going out to the countryside where there were fields and fresh air, so much better than the ghetto. They each had a small rucksack and were allowed to take one favourite book or toy. The orphanage staff went with them, singing songs on the way. They were bound for Treblinka.

Perhaps it was the worst moment of all for Lonia and Mendel, watching Henek go, hand in hand with another little boy, in his short trousers, with his knobbly knees, each with their little rucksacks, Henek waving gaily to them standing on the pavement, happy to be off to the fields and the fresh air.

Lonia and Mendel went on working at the Többens factory. Their boss, Walter Többens, came from Hamburg and he saw the war in general and his factories in the Warsaw ghetto as a once-in-a-lifetime chance to make his fortune. Apart from the big 'Aryanised' Goldfeld factory he also had factories in Prosta and Leszno Streets, and various smaller 'cottage' industries. He was an opportunist, plain and simple. Ideology didn't come into it for Többens. As far as he was concerned, the Warsaw ghetto Jews were good workers. As such, he was minded to protect them from the authorities and from transportation. He made sure their working conditions were reasonable. The factory was clean and fairly sanitary. The hours were long but manageable. There was a canteen where the food was better than anyone else could secure in the ghetto. He turned a blind eye to a bit of food-smuggling. Not surprisingly, the Többens employees were envied by all the other ghetto workers enduring inhuman conditions week after week, month after month.

But time was running out, and not just for the Jews. By early 1943 every German soldier on the Russian Front knew the war was lost. The Battle of Stalingrad during that winter of 1942–3 had been the turning point, and now the only question remained why was the Führer still exhorting them to die for Germany? The Thousand-Year German Reich was done for, everyone knew it. They called the medals distributed more and more freely by the Führer to his brave troops on the Eastern Front the Order of the Frozen Meat.

Only a few held on to their illusions, unable to let go. Including *Reichsführer-SS* Heinrich Himmler, busy with transportations of every sort – partisans, Polish underground, Jews. On 20 January 1943 he sent a memo to Dr Ganzenmüller, the Reich State Secretary for Transport, about the recently occupied territories in the Soviet Union: 'In this connexion the transportation of the Jews is of the first importance. The transportation of Jews from the west is likewise essential, or we shall have to reckon with an increase in terrorist activities. I need your help and cooperation in this matter. It is absolutely necessary that additional goods trains should be placed at my disposal if I am to carry out these tasks with the speed required. I am well aware of the strain at present being placed on the transport system, and of the many demands with which you are faced. Nevertheless, I must ask you to come to my assistance and provide me with more trains.'

Having organised the Wannsee Conference of 20 January 1942 for the Final Solution of the extermination of the Jews, the *Reichsführer-SS* couldn't very well let up now. True, most of the organisation had been done by his sidekick Reinhard Heydrich, but he was the one to shoulder the responsibility. Fifteen Party leaders had attended, including Göring, Bormann, von Ribbentrop, the racial expert Albert Rosenberg and Hans Frank, who travelled from Krakau to Berlin for the purpose. *Obersturmbannführer* Adolf Eichmann was also present, sitting quietly in a corner with a stenotypist, taking the minutes. Dr Rudolf Lange, commander of the SS Security Police in Riga, was there too, though not the overall SS Chief of Northern Russia, Friedrich Jeckeln, Renate Röder's father; he was too busy dealing with the Jews of Riga by mass-shooting them in pits, the gas chamber method not yet having been perfected – which was the whole point of the Wannsee Conference in the first place. Apparently there were some 5 million Jews in need of extermination in Russia. About 2,300,000 in Poland. Over a million in Western Europe. And 742,800 in Hungary. A total of 11 million if one included Britain and Turkey. No wonder Himmler was pressing Dr Ganzenmüller for more trains.

It was Heydrich who explained the details of the Final Solution to the Wannsee Conference, adding that it had been sanctioned by the Führer. In a word, the Jews would be gathered into transit ghettos, as was already under way, and thence 'transported' further east. Coded language was used throughout and nothing incriminating written down, as Himmler had long since instructed his underlings. The able-bodied would be put to work. 'Undoubtedly a large percentage of these will be eliminated by natural attrition. Those who remain alive, certainly the most resistant group, will be treated accordingly since they would constitute a natural selection of the fittest who would form a new cell from which the Jewish race could again develop,' explained Heydrich. And what might 'treated accordingly' mean, Eichmann was asked at his trial in 1961. 'Killed. Killed. Undoubtedly killed,' he answered. The methods for keeping the people calm on their way to the gas chambers were discussed too, always avoiding anything incriminating. Someone wondered whether half-Jews might be included? Eichmann was despatched to report on the effectiveness of the gas vans. He admitted at his trial that he could hardly look inside a van, so shaken was he. When the corpses were tipped into the pits the limbs were still supple, 'as if they'd been alive. Just thrown in the trench. I can still see the civilian with pliers pulling out the gold teeth.'

On 9 January 1943 Heinrich Himmler himself came to see how matters were progressing in the Warsaw ghetto. The final phase of liquidation began ten days later, on 18 January. On 19 January there was an uprising in the ghetto, many Jews feeling there was nothing to lose. They were going to die one way or the other. News of the German retreat at Stalingrad gave them hope that the war would end soon, and that their deaths would not have been in vain. Himmler was likewise affected by the news from Stalingrad. The Führer was raging. The Jews would pay. The uprising was brutally put down.

By April 1943 there were only 50,000 people left in the Warsaw ghetto. The rest had died from starvation, typhoid and cholera, or been transported. Rumours abounded that the remaining 50,000 would soon be transported. Panic spread through the ghetto from Leszno to Karmelicka Street. At Többens and Schultz the two bosses, Többens and Stehman, tried to calm their workers, promising to protect them. They held a meeting on the factory floor and once all the workers were assembled Herr Stehman walked up to the front and stood on a chair so that everyone could see and hear him. His voice was full of emotion, like a father talking to his children. They were not going to be transported, he assured them, but they would be taken further east to a work camp called Poniatowa, and carry on working there much as before, only in greater safety and better conditions. 'What is keeping you here, after all?' he challenged them. 'What kind of life do you have? You don't have fresh air. You don't have trees. But in Poniatowa the situation is completely different. There are large living quarters without bugs, with good air, not heavy work. Beautiful things are waiting for you there.' The assembled workers, including Lonia and Mendel, could hardly believe it. Many clapped and cheered and thanked Herr Stehman. But then a voice rose from the crowd, a woman's voice. 'We expect death there,' she said. 'I don't want you dead,' Herr Stehman replied. Which was no more than the truth, because both Herr Többens and Herr Stehman needed their workers. But the woman didn't believe him. 'Where are our sisters and brothers and parents and children?' she asked bravely.

The workers dispersed, some hopeful, others in despair. Mendel and Lonia were among the optimists. They decided to believe Herr Stehman, hoping and praying he wasn't lying. Two days later it was confirmed: they were being 'transported' to Poniatowa.

The following Tuesday, at eleven at night, Mendel heard a great commotion in the street below. He went down the four flights of stairs to have a look, then hid in the shadow of the building. SS guards were surrounding the Többens factory, flushing out any workers hiding there and breaking up the machinery. Three boys about eighteen years old had fled the building and were hiding close to Mendel, trying to make a run for it. 'Don't do it,' Mendel whispered. 'Come upstairs with me and we'll hide you till it's over.' They wouldn't. They'd already decided that their only hope of survival was to get to the corner post of Leszno and Karmelicka Street and run for freedom. Which they did, minutes later. A few shots were fired, and the three boys lay dead on the ground.

Mendel went upstairs and told Lonia what had happened. They sat late into the night, talking quietly so as not to wake his father and sisters, trying to decide what to do. Mendel thought they couldn't escape, seeing what had happened to those poor boys. Lonia thought they might survive, given they were in good health. 'They won't kill us. They need us to work,' was her view. Good health was relative of course. But in comparison to most, Lonia and Mendel were indeed in good health, helped by extra rations from the Többens canteen and Yadzia's smuggling. 'What about Papa and the sisters?' said Mendel. There was no answer to that.

The next morning they started to prepare for the transportation. They were only allowed to take one rucksack or small case each, but Többens promised that if they packed the rest up it would be delivered to Poniatowa by truck. They packed three big bags bound with string and Mendel delivered them to the factory. His sisters

Frania and Genia helped, but his father hardly moved, unable to take in what was happening. Too old, too sick, too defeated. He just sat and rocked on his chair and prayed. For Lonia and Mendel there was so much to do and so little time: deciding what to take and what to leave, visiting the *Judenrat* to join the desperate queues all trying to get more information about what was going on, contacting Yadzia to tell her what was happening. Többens said they were needed for work at Poniatowa, they told her. They needed workers to carry on making the clothing and equipment for the German troops in Russia. She didn't believe them.

All the rumours seeping through the walls of the Warsaw ghetto made it clear that the war couldn't last much longer. The German troops on the Russian Front were as good as done for. The fierce winter had killed hundreds of thousands again, as it had the previous winter. Their winter clothing was nothing like warm enough to deal with thirty-five degrees below zero, which it could be in the depth of a Russian winter. Apparently, when the soldiers got out of their Panzer tanks to relieve themselves they could freeze to death on the spot, left standing in the landscape like ice statues. The Russians, meanwhile, accustomed to those conditions, were clothed in furs and felt-lined boots. And although their T-tanks were smaller and more basic than the German Panzers, they were strong and could manage any kind of terrain: mud, swamps, snow drifts, ice, you name it. The only way for the German soldier to escape was to dig a foxhole in the ground as soon as he saw a line of T-tanks coming over the horizon, curl up in the hole till the tank had driven over him, then throw a grenade as it turned, before making a run for it. The German Panzers meanwhile, so big and technically advanced, got completely bogged down – first in the muds and swamps of autumn, then in the deep snows of winter. What's more, they couldn't get the spare parts needed to mend them, because the factories were too far away. And their fuel was running out. And the extreme bravery of the Russian soldiers, who attacked the Germans in wave after wave, the first wave dropping their rifles for the next wave to pick up and advance fearlessly. And imagine, apparently there were women fighters among them! Hundreds of thousands of Germans were being taken into Russian captivity. Someone had seen a newsreel somewhere on the other side of the Ghetto wall – lines of German POWs as far as the eye could see, shuffling along over the pale land of the Russian spring.

'No. The war can't last much longer, Yadzia,' said Lonia firmly, like the older sister she'd always been. 'We'll soon be liberated by the Russians.' It was Yadzia's last visit to the ghetto. They wept as they bade each other goodbye – father, daughter, sister. Then she crept out into the night and through her secret crossing, helped by who knows who, for who knows what bribe. After the war it was estimated that the Poles had saved between 100,000 and 120,000 Polish Jews, including children.

On 19 April 1943 another ghetto revolt broke out, the Polish Resistance having furnished the Jewish fighters with some rifles and grenades, though nothing like enough to overcome the SS guards. Perhaps Julek was among them. They never saw him again. Nor Sevek, who'd fled to the eastern borders of Poland with his wife Inge. On 21 April Többens confirmed to its workers that they were being transported to Poniatowa. The Schultz workers were going to another 'work camp' near Poniatowa, named Trawniki. The Goldfelds and Albeks went down the stairs to the street below for the last time on 23 April 1943, each carrying one small case, and made their way to the *Umschlagplatz* with everyone else, dodging the gunfire and the fighting which had been raging for the past two days. Jürgen Stroop, the Police Chief of the Warsaw Ghetto, received an order on that same day from *Reichsführer-SS* Heinrich Himmler. He was to suppress the Warsaw uprising with '*grösster Härte*', the most extreme hardness. It was a familiar term to Stroop, who'd been a member of the Nazi Party since 1932 and an early member of the SS. Hardness, he understood, was the only way to deal with this kind of resistance. He ordered his men to torch the ghetto, thereby flushing the last fighters and resisters out on to the street. 'Each building was systematically cleared and subsequently burned to the ground,' he later recalled. 'Nearly always the Jews then came out of their hidden places and bunkers. But quite often they stayed in their buildings so long, till they came out from the sheer heat and terror, leaping out, first throwing mattresses and bedding on to the street from their burning houses. With broken bones, they still tried to crawl across the street into other buildings which were not yet on fire. Again and again you could see they would prefer to go back into the fire than hand themselves over to us.' To Friedrich Krüger, the Higher SS and Police Chief of the *Generalgouvernement*, he wrote four weeks after the outbreak, on 16 May 1943, to confirm: 'The former Jewish quarter in Warsaw no longer exists. With the blowing-up of the Synagogue, our Great Action ended at 20.15 hours. The grand total of Jews killed is 56,065.'

Himmler later said that this had indeed been the final moment to clear the Warsaw ghetto of the remains of its original 500,000 Jews. He was delighted, he added, at an additional bonus of the clearing: finding hidden caches of gold in the rubble. He'd never seen such a pile of gold in his life, he exclaimed, beaming. It was unbelievable: American dollars, twenty-Reichsmark pieces, Austrian crowns, Russian roubles, 'all out of one single ghetto!'

But not Nicha's gold US dollars, as it happens. Because they were safely stashed away with Yadzia on the other side of the ghetto walls. As for Jürgen Stroop, he was executed as a war criminal in Warsaw in 1952. Friedrich Krüger committed suicide in May 1945.

There was a final selection at the *Umschlagplatz* that fateful day of 23 April 1943. Goodness knows, Stroop didn't want to displease his chiefs and let old and infirm Jews on to the trains bound for the 'work camps' after all the good work done clearing the ghetto. No, they were bound for the other trains, cattle trucks, going in the other direction.

At that final selection on the *Umschlagplatz* that day, both fathers, Goldfeld and Albek, as well as Mendel's two sisters Frania and Genia Albek, and the other Frania, Lonia's aunt, and her husband Marcel Celmeister the doctor, all sick by now, were among those selected for transportation to the Treblinka death camp. Lonia tried to hide her father behind her, but it was no use. They were hounded and harried off, amid shouting and rifle butts, towards the railway station and the waiting cattle trucks, and no one ever saw them again. The rest, the survivors, returned to their factories for a final headcount and whatever else needed to be done before their own departure. Later that evening, under cover of darkness, Mendel went back to the *Umschlagplatz* and called out his father's name, again and again. 'Father, where are you? Answer me! Where are you? Hanoch! I, Joseph. I, Mendel!'

Now everyone was standing in line, being counted and listed. Mendel slipped into the line beside Lonia. Lonia had meanwhile noticed that the SS guards were separating the husbands from the wives. Who knew why? She took off her wedding ring and gave the guards her maiden name, Goldfeld, not Albek. Mendel also took off his wedding ring. Then the line was marched to the opening in the ghetto wall at Leszno and Karmelicka Streets and out into Zamenhofa Street. Ah, how heartbreaking was that, seeing Zamenhofa Street again after all that time. How many memories? How many friends? How many aunts and uncles, fathers and mothers, sisters, brothers? All lost. Now the pavements were lined with the Poles of Warsaw, their former neighbours, some silent, heads bowed in shame, others shouting abuse and spitting.

The Jews were marched to the railway station by the SS guards, shouting: '*Los! Los! Schnell! Schnell!*' Move, move! Faster! Faster! There were snipers on the roofs of the buildings taking potshots as they scurried along. Good sport it was. Once they reached the trains, many Jews threw their so-carefully packed bundles away in sheer panic as they scrambled and shoved to get into the safety of the goods wagons. The night was filled with screaming and crying, the guards standing about on the platforms, smoking and laughing.

Lonia and Mendel had to wait hours before they could get on a train. They lay on the cold ground and watched the dawn turn into pale morning. Finally another goods train arrived and they were able to squeeze into a wagon already filled with people, some sitting on the floor, some standing, so tight they could hardly breathe. There were moans and complaints, but in the end they found a space just big enough for the two of them. At three o'clock they were finally on the move, perhaps to Poniatowa, who knew, stopping and starting and jolting all the way. It was evening when they reached Valshewansaka station, where, astonishingly, they were let out for a while to stretch their legs and walk up and down the platform. It must have been Többens and Stehman interceding for their workers, wanting them ready and fit for work. A courageous few even managed to barter some food from a stall. Then it was on to Otwock and Dęblin, arriving at Nałęczów at six the next morning. At every station there were some good Poles giving them water. The train was halted in Nałęczów for the whole day. The air inside the wagons became putrid, even with the doors open. Lonia and Mendel kept to themselves, avoiding the quarrels and fights which broke out here and there. Finally, they were shunted to a branch line and on to a narrow-gauge local train.

They arrived at Poniatowa at eleven at night and scrambled off the train into the darkness. SS guards awaited them with flash torches, but no shouting or harassment. The Jews of Warsaw felt a mixture of fear and hope as they were marched through the concentration camp gates and into their new place of work. The Jewish police, already installed, took them to a makeshift canteen for some soup and coffee. They were told to wash up the bowls before going to find somewhere to sleep. But Többens had prepared nothing in the way of accommodation, so that first night was slept out in the open, on the hard ground. At least they were together, whispered Lonia and Mendel. And alive. That alone was a miracle. They kept their thoughts away from their families.

Early next morning, before roll call on the *Appelplatz*, Lonia and Mendel looked around. No one stopped them – a strange and thrilling experience after life in the ghetto. They gathered information about their surroundings from people they met, piecemeal. Poniatowa was thirty-five kilometres from Lublin, which was part of the *Generalgouvernement* and deep in the countryside, surrounded by forest. Apparently it had previously been a prisoner-of-war camp for Russian soldiers captured on the Eastern Front during Operation Barbarossa – those heady early days for the Germans, long since gone.

The camp was surrounded by high barbed wire and watchtowers manned by SS guards with machine guns. The conditions had been brutal, apparently, with the SS guards treating the Russians like animals. Many local ethnic Germans had joined the SS to become guards too – all Himmler's racial standards were forgotten now. They were trained at Trawniki, the nearby SS camp – the camp the Schultz workers were now bound for. Twenty thousand Russians had died there, either from starvation or execution. Later Poniatowa turned into a forced-labour work camp for the German war effort. Some pre-war factory buildings were adapted and basic barracks built for Többens workers still producing German Army uniforms and clothing for the increasingly desperate German population back in the Reich – shirts, blouses, coats. The first Jewish workers, about 1,500, had arrived in late 1942, along with a new set of camp guards. Then 15,000 more arrived, from the Warsaw ghetto. Including Lonia and Mendel.

As they walked around Lonia and Mendel discovered the workshops and the factory, and a fenced-in road lined with barbed wire and watchtowers which led to the administrative block some two kilometres away. Then they found the accommodation barracks, which were like every other concentration camp, arranged in rows, about thirty-five huts in all. Except that here husbands and wives were allowed to live together. They went into one of the huts, saw the tight rows of four-tiered bunk beds and noted a basic kitchen and table at the far end. And a pot-bellied stove too, fed by wood from the forest, which gave off a bit of warmth. They managed to find two bunks together. They were amazed by it all – amazed they were allowed to wear their own clothes and not the usual concentration camp stripes, amazed that clogs were provided. And that the food was quite good. Perhaps Herr Stehman had been telling the truth after all.

How could they know this was all part of Himmler's last-ditch plan – desperate to increase productivity? Productivity in the Reich had been low all along due to resistance and sabotage by the former Communist and Socialist workers, but it was even lower now, in the fourth year of the war, because the workers, well informed by numerous secret networks, could see the war would soon be over. 'There have been complaints for several months about inadequate production of the armaments of "Middle German Steel Works" in Groeditz, district Grossenheim, which has a workforce of about 6,000 people. Absence from work without good reason and unnaturally high reports of sickness led to a situation where temporarily up to 1,200 workers were missing. In several cases damage to machinery caused suspicion of sabotage,' went one typical report by the Dresden police to the local Gestapo in June 1939. But by 1943 matters were considerably worse. Himmler's concentration camps and slave-labour camps were the only answer. The German war effort was increasingly desperate for clothing, uniforms, shells, grenades, rifles and anti-aircraft guns. And construction materials – stones from quarries, bricks, cement, timber. Himmler, in overall charge of production from the concentration camps, promised the Führer he could do it. The Führer really wasn't interested in the how. Just give him good news. He raged if you gave him bad news.

The *Reichsführer-SS* hastily applied himself to the problem. First, he had to get his camp workers better nourished or they wouldn't be able to work at all. 'Try to obtain for nourishment of the prisoners the greatest quantity of raw vegetables and onions. In the vegetable season issue carrots, kohlrabi, white turnips and whatever such vegetables are there in large quantity and store up sufficiently for the prisoners in the winter so that they have sufficient quantity every day. I believe we will raise the state of health substantially thereby,' he wrote to Oswald Pohl, Chief of the SS Main Economic and Administrative Office, in December 1942. Most camps were surrounded by fields and forest, so that shouldn't be a problem. But it wasn't enough. The workers needed inducements. Himmler came up with three, on a rising scale: first, cigarettes; second, a small wage; lastly, and only for the most skilled workers, a weekly visit to the camp brothel. Himmler was a great believer in camp brothels. Originally they were for his SS guards. But now, as things got worse and worse, he extended them to a few privileged inmates. Roll call at Poniatowa was at 6 a.m. Work started at seven and ended at five in the evening, with a half-hour break at midday. Their job was sorting and reusing clothes brought in by rail from elsewhere. The tailors of Warsaw were kept busy, whirring and stitching at their sewing machines. Lonia was amazed at the quantity and the quality of the clothes.

'Where do they come from?' she whispered to one of the other women working beside her at the wooden bench on that first day.

'Us,' came the short answer.

At first Lonia didn't understand – couldn't take it in.

'Auschwitz,' said her work neighbour. 'Concentration camps.'

So the rumours of gas chambers were true, Lonia finally realised. Before, when the woman at the Többens meeting had shouted out about Jews being killed, she hadn't really believed it. Because it was unbelievable.

That evening she started to tell Mendel. He already knew.

By spring 1944 it was clear to everyone that Germany was defeated – to the German troops on the Western as well as the Eastern Front. That is, everyone except Hitler and a few of his closest cronies, including Himmler. When the Allies stated at the Casablanca Conference in January 1943 they would accept nothing but an unconditional surrender, Hitler's reaction had been first to rage, then to send a Führer Order to his army generals, naval commanders and Göring's Luftwaffe to fight on to the death. In point of fact, there was little left of Göring's famous Luftwaffe. And the German troops taken prisoner in Egypt by Montgomery's 8th Army at the Second Battle of El Alamein and then in Tunisia in May 1943 had already given themselves up in their hundreds of thousands – long lines of them straggling across the desert into captivity, most of them relieved not to be forced to die for the Führer any longer, all ideas of the Master Race lost in the sand. Then came the Allied invasion of Sicily and

Italy. And now the Allies were planning the invasion of mainland Europe for the summer of 1944. German Intelligence knew this. Only they didn't know exactly where or when.

None of it was admitted by *Reichsführer-SS* Heinrich Himmler, head way up in the clouds. He was busy as ever with his concentration camp regulations and his vicious reprisals against opponents to the Nazi regime at home and abroad. But none of it distracted him from what had always been his main concern: his insistence that SS officers produce racially pure children for the Master Race in his *Lebensborn* homes, now stretching way into the German-occupied countries, especially Norway, that land of blue eyes and blond hair, which now had eight *Lebensborn* homes. As late as spring 1945 Himmler was still writing memos to the *Lebensborn* administration in Munich, and still urging his SS officers to do their racial duty. As though the Reich, on the very verge of collapse, still had a thousand years to go.

No more than seven months after Lonia and Mendel arrived in Poniatowa, Himmler let loose *Aktion Erntefest*, Operation Harvest Festival, a sentimental euphemism for an act of unimaginable horror and revenge. With the end of the war in sight there had been more and more instances of resistance and uprising in some of the concentration and work camps, including Poniatowa. Added to the uprisings in the ghettos, Himmler's patience abruptly ran out. He ordered his SS and police, keenly assisted by their local Special Forces, to liquidate the camps in the Lublin area, including Majdanek, Trawniki and Poniatowa. He was especially annoyed with *Untersturmbannführer-SS* Gottlieb Hering, the *Kommandant* at Poniatowa, for running such an ill-disciplined, almost pleasant, camp. What on earth was Hering thinking? Was it a holiday camp?

The date set for the *Aktion* was 3 November 1943, starting at Majdanek, the main camp, then bringing the SS guards over to Poniatowa the following day to help with the next mass-killing. Then on to Trawniki. The first sign of what was to come was in August. There had been an inspection of the camp by *Obergruppenführer-SS* Odilo Globocnik, a man already known for his liking for sadistic torture, after which rumours spread like wildfire that Hering had been severely reprimanded for his 'soft' regime and ordered to execute any resisters from then on. He was also ordered to build a crematorium. Globocnik informed Hering that there was a lot to do in a very short time. The 43,000 Jews left in the Lublin camps had to be exterminated by 5 November, as ordered by the *Reichsführer-SS*.

In September a new unit of guards under Globocnik arrived to run the camp in preparation for the *Aktion*. Globocnik's guards were terrifying in their brutality, taking open pleasure in killings and torture, lost in their own depravity. A work-detail of 300 inmates were told to dig trenches by the edge of the forest, apparently for anti-tank warfare. Few were fooled. Lonia and Mendel knew that the only solution was to try and escape. They'd already been making secret preparations under Hering's 'soft' regime. Thanks to Nicha's gold dollars, Yadzia had managed to find a man who was prepared to help. He was an ethnic German called Eduard, living in Yadzia's local district in Warsaw. Eduardo had a motorcycle, and he agreed to hide in the forest close to Poniatowa camp, at an agreed spot, and provide the getaway. He was well paid but it was still a huge risk, meaning certain death if caught. The motorcycle was a two-cylinder one, so he could only take one escapee at a time. Lonia first. One day she disappeared into the forest with eight others while out in the fields beyond the barbed-wire fence, digging those vegetables. Someone spoke for each of them at roll call and it was hours before their disappearance was found out. All but Lonia were recaptured over the next days, and each day thereafter Mendel was speechless with terror when guards brought back another escapee, bound and beaten. Would it be Lonia? It never was.

A miracle, it was. Most of the Jews at Poniatowa, some 14,000 by then, knew they had no chance of escape. The camp was too far out in the countryside, too isolated from human habitation, utterly lost to the rest of the world. Licensed by the *Reichsführer-SS* to do their worst, the new rota of SS guards had a free hand to commit any horror they pleased, though what pleased them next, by way of an alternative to the daily executions, was unimaginable to the rest of humanity. Once power gets into the wrong hands it inevitably promotes those in its own image: sadists, torturers, killers.

As soon as any escapees were recaptured they were brought back to the *Appelplatz*, and the workers were ordered out of their workshops and barracks to witness what happened to them by way of the newly devised punishment. As described by one of only six survivors of Poniatowa camp, as later testified by the British War Crimes Investigator, there was a kind of giant frying pan in the middle of the

Appelplatz, filled with boiling oil. Into this they threw the escapee. The terror and the screams of the dying would stay with those few survivors of Poniatowa for the rest of their lives, filling their nights with nightmares and their days with sudden, black panic. It was not possible to recover from the knowledge of such depravity.

Mendel had to wait six weeks for his own escape, also on the back of Eduard's motorcycle. During all this time he had no proof that Lonia was safe with Yadzia, so day for day for six weeks he stood in speechless panic on the *Appelplatz*, watching those horrors, terrified that Lonia had perhaps been recaptured and was being held somewhere, and that she would be one of those dragged on to the *Appelplatz* and thrown into the boiling oil. In his head he knew it was unlikely, but his heart was petrified.

Still, the day came when Eduard was waiting for him with his motorcycle, at the same spot in the forest as he'd waited for Lonia. Mendel had been out of the camp with a work-detail felling trees to be transported to the Eastern Front. Who knows how long Eduard had been waiting for him. But there he was, risking his life for some gold coins, or, perhaps, for humanity. He took Mendel as far as a railway station distant enough from Poniatowa not to cause suspicion – the same station he'd used for Lonia. Taking them all the way to Warsaw on the back of his motorcycle would have been too dangerous. Somehow Mendel made it back to the house where Yadzia and Lonia were hiding – still with the same Polish family. It was another miracle. But Lonia and Mendel couldn't speak to one another. Because Mendel was completely mute. It took months for his mental and physical functions to return.

But he'd escaped the camp. And the massacre at Poniatowa and Trawniki, which took place over two days, on 4 and 5 November 1943. The trenches had already been dug. The Jews were told to undress and went naked to the edge of the pits, where they were shot, one by one, with music playing on loudspeakers to cover the sound of the shootings. Some were spared for a few days so they could remove the corpses from the pits and incinerate them in the recently constructed crematorium. Then they too were killed. Many of the *Waffen-SS* soldiers brought in for the task were blind-drunk. In all, there were 40,000 dead from Himmler's *Erntefest*.

Lonia and Mendel, reunited by some miracle in Warsaw, knew they couldn't stay with the Polish family hiding Yadzia for long. They moved from one secret apartment to another every few days, hidden by local Polish families they'd known long ago, in another time and another world. Some were old school friends of Lonia's, some had worked for the Goldfelds, some were devout Catholics who refused to bow to the Germans and the evil which surrounded them. Others were paid by Yadzia with the last of Nicha's gold dollars. They all knew hiding Jews was punishable by death. There were many narrow escapes. Once, when Lonia and Mendel were hiding with Stephania Przesnyska, a former Goldfeld worker, German soldiers banged on her door and forced their way into the apartment, searching for Jews or members of the Polish Resistance. Lonia and Mendel only had time to hide under a bed. Luckily, Wiesław, Stephania's twelve-year-old son, who was ill, was lying in it. Or perhaps he wasn't ill, just pretending. Either way, the soldiers came so close to the bed that Lonia could see their boots. But seeing a sick boy – perhaps typhoid or cholera, who could know – they quickly retreated.

Lonia and Mendel, on the run again, found a concrete bunker buried under rubble. There were a dozen Jews already hiding there, freezing in the dark, snowbound winter days, only emerging at night to scavenge for food. That place lasted for several weeks – till someone informed on them. Informing was a lucrative business in those days, and it offered the double bonus of securing your safety with the German police. Once again, Lonia and Mendel were forced to run for their lives and find a new hiding place. Finally, it was down into the sewers of Warsaw with the rats and the criminals and the fearful stench. But by then they'd met up with other survivors and they were armed. Some of them, including Mendel, emerged at night to take part in the second Warsaw Uprising which continued through August to October 1944, led by the Polish Resistance, anticipating the imminent German retreat and the arrival of the Russians. They knew Soviet troops were stationed on the far side of the Vistula. Why weren't they crossing the river? It was beyond understanding. The reason was brutally simple: the Russians were waiting for the Germans to destroy Warsaw brick by brick and the Polish Resistance with it, before making their move. Let the Germans do the dirty work. The Russians didn't enter Warsaw till 17 January 1945. It was Mendel's thirty-third birthday.

When they finally emerged from the sewers into the daylight, Lonia and Mendel saw nothing but rubble. Warsaw was flattened.

The Russians provided the survivors with food and water, then sent them on their way to manage as best they could. There was nothing left: no administration, no transport, no postal service, no housing. It was bitterly cold. The streets were filled with people scavenging and searching. Feral, orphaned children roamed about, stealing and begging. Many survivors died during those first days of freedom: too weak, too defeated, too despairing. Or they ate too much too fast, so their starved stomachs couldn't cope. There had been a lot of shooting down in the sewers during the last days of war and many of Lonia and Mendel's friends had been killed. The Germans had filled the sewers with gas before they left. The survivors were sick as dogs.

But there was Yadzia, safe and sound with her Polish protectors. It was unbelievable – almost impossible to take in really. She was twenty now. 'A woman!' as Lonia exclaimed, thinking back to the young girl she'd looked after when their mother died. The three of them held each other, weeping. They were the only survivors of the Albek and Goldfeld families. Together they found one of the apartment blocks which had been built by the Goldfeld parents as an investment property before the war: Grajewska 21, in the Praga neighbourhood. It was badly damaged and there were people living there. Some of the Polish tenants recognised Lonia when she appeared at their door. They were not pleased. But they couldn't stop Lonia and Mendel and Yadzia moving into one of the apartments.

It only had two rooms, and at one point there were thirty people there – all Jews who had nowhere else to live, all with their own stories of horror and miraculous survival, all searching for lost relatives, lost lives, trying to imagine a future for themselves somewhere, somehow. They possessed nothing but the clothes they stood up in, and even these were sometimes shared – shoes, especially, which were needed by those going out to find food, or find a job. Because to obtain legal residence under the new administration of Warsaw you had to have a registered job. Lonia's was to collect the rent off the other tenants of Grajewska 21 on behalf of the provisional Communist authorities. That made the Goldfelds and the Albeks and their Jewish friends even less popular. Past resentments were revived. Past anti-Semitism too. Mendel slept with a pistol under his pillow.

But not all was bad. They were free. And one day Lonia came back to the apartment with some wonderful news for Mendel: she was pregnant.

Some weeks later Mendel was returning from one of his scavenges when he found Lonia in the inner courtyard of the apartment block, arguing with a Russian Army officer who had just commandeered the garages for his company's jeeps. Lonia was objecting loudly, insisting on compensation. Mendel ran straight up to the Russian, almost jumping on him. And kissed him. Lonia was speechless. What on earth had got into him?

It turned out the officer was Sevek Duzenman, Mendel's best friend from his home town of Łowicz, who had enlisted in the Russian Army in order to fight the Germans. Upstairs to the apartment the three of them went, talking and laughing. They just couldn't believe the happy coincidence. There was so much to talk about they hardly knew where to begin. Eventually Lonia and Mendel told Sevek about the lawsuit which the Polish tenants were trying to bring against them to oust them. 'We'll soon change that!' said Sevek. 'I'm a captain in the Russian Army! It's a Russian military tribunal, isn't it? I'll say I'm the father of your child.'

It worked. The military judge dismissed the tenant's lawsuit forthwith.

It was September before they were able to contact Lonia's uncle Simon Goldfeld in America – the same uncle to whom Sevek had written in 1939, hoping to leave Poland and continue his medical studies over there. Too late, as it turned out. Now Lonia and Mendel and Yadzia were planning the same, only this time it was to get away from Communist Poland, not the Nazis. First, though, they had to reach the safety of the American Zone in Germany.

They set off in late November 1945, on foot, with as much luggage as each could carry, including the last of Nicha's gold coins. The snow was deep, the ground treacherous, the temperature freezing, but they knew they couldn't wait any longer. Sevek Duzenman and a group of others went too, over the Sudeten mountains into Czechoslovakia – weeks of trekking higher and higher, through snow drifts, across frozen streams, skirting isolated farmsteads with barking dogs and mountain villages with suspicious inhabitants, bartering food, sleeping wherever they could, the men armed, watching out for any lurking dangers. And Lonia heavily pregnant.

They arrived in Germany in the early days of January 1946. Another miracle. It seemed the gods meant them to survive.

First they stayed in a Displaced Persons camp at Schwandorf in

Bavaria. That is where their child was born, on 6 February 1946, in the US Army field hospital. They called him Joseph, after both fathers. Joseph Heinrich Albek. His birth certificate was in German. Soon everyone was calling him Heinele, an affectionate German nickname. The past was the dark past, Heinele was the golden future. Soon after the birth Lonia and Mendel moved to nearby Schwarzenfeld which, in the past, had been declared Jew-free, following Joseph Goebbels's designation. They rented a room in the house of an elderly couple – former Nazi Party members, though you wouldn't know it now. They doted on baby Heinele, Jewish on both sides of the family.

CHAPTER FOUR

HEINRICH HIMMLER: RISE AND FALL

How can such a horror happen? How can men hate so much? Kill so much? Destroy so much? Power in the wrong hands is surely the answer. And ideology. In this case Nazi racial ideology.

So here we have Heinrich Himmler, the one who was no one, until he became someone, finding his nasty niche in the Nazi Party, now rising higher and higher. Without the opportunity, Himmler remains a crank. With it, he's murderous. All that 'mopping up' by his SS: Communists, Socialists, academics, civil servants, shopkeepers, secretaries, doctors, housewives. All that extermination of the Jews. Which went hand in hand with another horror: the breeding of the pure Aryan. Yes, hand in hand they went, breeding and extermination, like two evil twins, a perfect twosome, just made for one another: blond and blue-eyed one half, dark and black-eyed the other.

'Obviously it is possible in the east with the trains – that a train freezes up and people freeze,' said the *Reichsführer-SS*, addressing a group of newly appointed *Gauleiter* regional leaders in Poland. 'You cannot blame the train or anyone. That is just the climate. It is regrettable for Germans, it is regrettable for Poles, if you like. It is even regrettable for Jews, if anyone wants to pity them. But it is neither intended, nor is it preventable. I consider it wrong to make a great *Lamento* about it.' On and on he went, quite carried away, soon turning to the subject closest to his heart: 'I propose that we be pitiless in the settlement policy because these new provinces must become Germanic, blond provinces of Germany – must become National Socialist provinces. They must really be a Germanic blood-wall, a wall within which there is no blood-question, no children-question, but where one day we will again become a *Volk* of abundant children. That I see as the task, and here I request all help from you.'

So there you have it. Head way up in the clouds, dizzy with success. How was Himmler to know that the *Götterdämmerung*, downfall, was waiting in the wings. But we know. And we can watch him rise and rise, before he falls and falls.

In 1940 Himmler was busy organising another *Lebensborn* home near Posnań, now renamed Posen, German-style, concerning himself with every detail of the building and administration as usual, just as he had at the first *Lebensborn* home at Steinhöring, spending staggering sums of money on his pet project in spite of the pressing demands of war. But he was worried that not all his SS officers were doing their duty, producing the pure Aryan for the future Thousand-Year German Reich. The problem was, even when his SS officers were given special leave from the Front and went to spend some happy leave at one of the *Lebensborn* homes, they didn't always provide. If only they could follow the example of Friedrich Jeckeln, Renate's father. The east should become 'a breeding ground for sound German stock', he told his officers again. 'Unless the blood of leadership in German veins, by which alone we stand or fall, can be increased by the admixture of good blood from elsewhere, we shall never achieve world mastery.'

And then there was the war. 'The sadly unavoidable loss of our best men, tragic though it is, is not the worst of it. Much worse is the lost breeding of children by those men, living but away at war, and then, after the war is over, by the men who died during it. The old wisdom that only the man who has borne sons and children can die at peace is once again true in this war for our men of the SS...'

Luckily there were some good replacements to be found in occupied Poland.

In most small towns and villages of western Poland the population was roughly divided: one-third Polish, one-third ethnic German, one-third Jewish. It was a simple rural life quite different to the highly cultured life in a city like Warsaw. The land was flat, the farmhouses old with pitched roofs and small windows against the snowbound winters, the yards cobbled, with geese and hens and barking dogs on chains, fields stretching in either direction as far as the eye could see under a wide sky, the narrow irrigation canals lined with weeping willow trees – an ordinary sort of landscape until the sun came out, when everything lit up, becoming beautiful as a painting.

The people got on well enough until the Germans came. Soon there were no more Jews. Ethnic Germans were safe. The remaining Poles were moved out of their villages and small towns into the

Generalgouvernement. But what about their children? That was a key question for *Reichsführer-SS* Heinrich Himmler, because among those Polish children there were some good racial specimens. And these good specimens, if not taken – stolen – would certainly be the ones to cause trouble for the Reich in the future.

It was the Great Task. Under Himmler's instruction the SS Race and Settlement Main Office had already prepared a questionnaire for the schoolchildren of Czechoslovakia, and now it was Poland's turn. It started with innocent medical questions about the state of the children's teeth, the strength of their legs, plus any history of tuberculosis or measles, then upped in a *getarnten Fragebogen* ('disguised' curve) to the important questions. 'The questions that really interest us,' as Himmler wrote to *SS-Brigadeführer* Hoffmann, the Chief of the Race and Settlement Main Office in Poland: 'Exact height and weight, then the colour of eyes, in three categories: blue/grey/green, brown/dark brown, and black, and then the colour of hair in two categories: blond/dark blond, brown/dark brown/black.' While he was at it, Himmler wondered whether Crakow, now spelt Krakau in the German way, might not be renamed *Himmler Stadt*, because it was such a beautiful town, filled with charming Renaissance buildings, exactly as he, who appreciated beauty, liked it.

Beautiful too was Himmler's personal train, which he loved so much he named it 'Heinrich' after himself. It had offices, sleeping accommodation, a central communications unit, a galley kitchen, a plush dining car and his own bureau. On 28 May 1940 Himmler sat down at his desk on 'Heinrich' and wrote a memo of the meeting he'd had with Hitler about the Polish question. It was headed *Geheim!* (Top Secret). 'On Sunday 25 May I showed the Führer my paper on the Handling of Foreign Races in the East. The Führer read the six pages through, and found them good and correct. He nevertheless gave the instruction that only a very few copies should be distributed, to be handled in the strictest secrecy.'

A month earlier a letter had arrived on Himmler's desk – a desk covered in lists and notes and card indexes just as it had been in his first office above Strasser's chemist's shop in Landshut, all those long, long years ago. The letter was addressed to *Hochverehrter*, highly esteemed, *Reichsführer*. It came from *Untersturmführer-SS* Dr Sigmund Rascher, who was involved in medical research at Dachau concentration camp. He was attending a specialised course, he wrote. 'During this course, where research on high-altitude flying plays a prominent part, determined by the somewhat higher ceiling of the English fighter planes, considerable regret was expressed that no experiments on human beings have so far been possible for us because such experiments are very dangerous and nobody is volunteering. I therefore put the serious question: is there any possibility that two or three professional criminals can be made available for these experiments? The experiments, in which the experimental subject may, of course, die, would take place with my collaboration. They are absolutely essential for the research on high-altitude flying, and cannot be carried out on monkeys. The Luftwaffe physician is also of the opinion that the problems in question can only be solved on human beings.' He signed off 'With my most hearty wishes, *Heil Hitler!* Your gratefully devoted, S. Rascher.'

It took the *Reichsführer-SS* no time at all to give his assent.

Just as well, because Operation Barbarossa, the invasion of the Soviet Union, began hardly a year later, on the night of 21 June 1941, apparently taking even the great fox Stalin by surprise. Success after success!

So by the time the Russian winter set in Rascher had to address another problem: how to resuscitate the many Luftwaffe pilots who were being shot down into the ice-cold sea. Freezing experiments took place in great baths filled with ice. Sometimes the subjects were dressed in flying-suits, sometimes not. 'Two Russian officers arrived at approximately four in the afternoon,' recalled a medical underling after the war at the Nuremberg Trials. 'Rascher had them undressed and they went into the water naked. Hour after hour passed, and while usually after a short time, sixty minutes, freezing set in, these two Russians were still conscious after two hours. All our appeals to Rascher asking him to give them an injection were to no avail.'

Regrettable, but there really was no point making a great *Lamento* about it. War was war. The Russian was the enemy. The racially inferior.

The Führer now spent much of his time at his field HQ, the *Wolfsschanze*, Wolf's Lair, at Rastenburg in East Prussia, near the Eastern Front, protected by a triple-ringed circle of SS guards which provided the kind of security Hitler needed in these dangerous times – not only from his Russian enemy but from his own, within the Reich. Ever since the invasion of Czechoslovakia in 1938 the official opposition to the Nazi regime, led by a top-secret group of army officers and generals, diplomats and politicians and men of the Church, had been plotting his removal by force, including assassination if necessary. But it was almost impossible to gain access to the Führer these days. He hardly went out except to provide Goebbels with enough film footage for his weekly newsreels, to convince the German public that all was well within the Reich and beyond, fighting the Russians. What with the newsreels and the reports on the *Volk*'s wireless, all produced by Goebbels's Ministry of Propaganda and Enlightenment, fake news was flourishing in the Reich.

Himmler, alarmed at the thought of losing touch with his Führer, swiftly set up his own 'field HQ' near Lötzen, some twenty kilometres from the Wolf's Lair. It didn't amount to much: a few wooden huts by a railway siding. But what matter? It existed, and anyway the railway line was the key, making it possible for him and Wolffie to come and go in 'Heinrich'. This is where his four *SS-Einsatzgruppen* generals, including Renate Röder's father Jeckeln, reported to the *Reichsführer-SS*. This is where he wrote his memos instructing mass-murder to his concentration camp *Kommandanten*. This is where he and Wolffie spent many cheerful hours with their *Waffen-SS* officer *Kamaraden*, drinking and talking late into the dark pine forest night.

In October 1941 Himmler and Heydrich spent two days at the Wolf's Lair discussing problems about the armaments industry with Hitler and Martin Bormann. How did podgy, weak-chinned Himmler feel, standing next to tall, blond, blue-eyed Heydrich, the perfect SS officer in his immaculate black uniform and shiny black jackboots? Work-slows and sabotage were holding things up, they explained to the Führer and his right-hand man, Bormann. Shockingly, it was happening within the Reich as well as in Poland and Czechoslovakia. The Führer was not pleased. Heydrich promised to increase 'discipline' at the concentration camps. Dr Erhard Wetzel, Chief of the SS Race Political Section, wrote: 'Camps for Jews will be set up in Riga and Minsk, where Jews from the Old Reich might also be sent. Jews are now being evacuated from the Old Reich to Litzmannstadt [formally Łódź] and other camps, from whence those fit for work will be transferred to workforces in the east. In the present state of affairs there are no objections to getting rid of those Jews with the Bracksian device, who are not capable of work.' The Old Reich referred to Germany, anticipating the New Reich in the east, which in turn anticipated the Thousand-Year German Reich. The Bracksian device referred to was the gas vans. Wetzel suggested sending one of his race experts to Riga, to give SS General Friedrich Jeckeln some technical advice. Himmler and Wolfie set off for Kiev for urgent talks with officers of the *Einsatzgruppen* C and D. News there wasn't good. Apparently, many of the *Waffen-SS* troops could only do their duty, that is, shooting Jews in mass-pits in the forest, when they were drunk. The *Reichsführer-SS* was obliged to give them one of his 'hard task' talks.

As often as possible Himmler, ever watchful, despatched Wolffie to the Wolf's Lair just to keep an eye on things. Not that he was involved in any military planning, but there were plenty of other matters for the *Reichsführer-SS* to organise. Top of the list was Auschwitz. Sometime that summer of 1941 he travelled back to Berlin from his field HQ in 'Heinrich' for a meeting with Rudolf Höss, a dedicated member of the *SS-Totenkopf* (Death's Head) unit who'd been ordered to convert a former Polish barracks at Auschwitz into a concentration camp, using the expertise he'd acquired first at Dachau then at Sachsenhausen. The Führer was planning the Final Solution to the Jewish problem, Himmler confided in top secret to Höss, and Auschwitz had been chosen 'first on account of the favourable position in regard to communications, secondly because the area lends itself to easy isolation and camouflage', as Höss would later explain from his cell in a British prison in June 1945, once all the hell and destruction was over and he himself was awaiting his death sentence.

But for the time being, in the summer of 1941, he was to be

Kommandant of the new and most technically efficient concentration camp at Auschwitz, and what's more, take on the task with loyal SS bravery. 'It is a hard, tough task which demands the commitment of the whole person without regard to any difficulties that might arise,' Himmler told him. 'You will receive more detailed instructions from *Sturmbannführer* Eichmann of RSHA [the Reich Security Office], who will shortly pay you a visit.' True to form Himmler ended his instructions: 'You have to maintain the strictest silence about this order, even to your superiors. After your meeting with Eichmann send me plans of your intended plant immediately. The Jews are the eternal enemy of the German people and must be exterminated. All Jews we can take now, during the war, are to be exterminated. If we do not succeed in destroying the biological basis of Jewry, someday the Jews will annihilate the German *Volk*.' When Eichmann turned up he made it clear to Höss that killing by gas vans, as had so far been used in the east, was out of the question for Auschwitz. The numbers of Jews due to arrive in mass-transports were far too high. Gas chambers were the answer. But before they were killed, the healthy Jews at Auschwitz had to provide slave labour for Himmler's various business enterprises, aimed at supporting the German war effort – foremost among them, working hand in hand with IG Farben, building a synthetic oil and rubber plant, using coal from Silesia. And an armaments factory, planned at nearby Birkenau.

But it was all so slow. Lack of materials. Lack of manpower. The war. Everything caused delays. Himmler wrote and telephoned and threatened. But by December 1941 the gas chambers at Auschwitz still weren't ready. Luckily the news from elsewhere was better. Renate's father, Friedrich Jeckeln, SS Chief of Northern Russia, phoned the *Reichsführer-SS* personally that month to confirm that the Riga ghetto had been totally liquidated. The pits in Rumbula Forest had been dug wide and deep enough to contain over 20,000 bodies – most shot in the back while standing naked at the edge of the pits. Jeckeln had plenty of killing practice by then, at Babi Yar and Kamianets-Podilskyi in Ukraine; and given that the more efficient method of gas chambers wasn't ready yet, there really was no other way. Later that month he reported in person to the *Reichsführer-SS* at his field HQ where Himmler was still playing at war. Himmler was satisfied with the results, as testified by Jeckeln at his trial in Riga in 1946. But Jeckeln's work wasn't done yet, the *Reichsführer-SS* apparently told him back in 1941. There were more transports due to arrive from elsewhere for liquidation, and he wasn't bothered which method of killing Jeckeln chose, whether shooting or just chasing the Jews into the swamps. He was only worried about his troops, his brave *Waffen-SS*, their morale and mental breakdowns, which were increasing by the day. It was a big problem for Jeckeln too, the morale of his men, as Fried confided in his letters to Else Röder. But what to do?

Elsewhere things were easier. In occupied northern Europe – that is Norway, Denmark, Holland, Belgium, albeit not England – Himmler was in close contact with Johann Albin Rauter, an early member of the Austrian Nazi Party and now the SS chief of the region, busily planning the 'new Europe' of the Greater German Reich. 'The new Europe is not a matter only for the present, but for a *grossartiger* [fabulous] future,' as Goebbels put it, filled with heady optimism. But should these newly acquired territories be referred to as a *Völkerbund*, based on one of the Nazis' favourite terms, the *Volk*, wondered Himmler, or should it be referred to as a kind of federation, thereby avoiding any trouble from those elements in the population who hadn't yet fallen into line? Decisions, decisions!

The *Reichsführer-SS* was so busy. Along with everything else, he had to keep a close eye on the work of the RKF, *Reichskommissar* for Consolidation of German Nationhood, keeping them up to scratch. Again, no detail was too small. 'Only girls of good blood who have been examined by RuSHA and who are really capable of Germanisation should be taken into service,' he wrote in a letter of 4 March 1942 about the employment of 'foreign' maids by favoured members of the Nazi Party, especially mothers of four or more children. And then there was the continued problem of homosexuals, some even within the ranks of the SS. It was probably best 'for them and us' to castrate them, as Himmler confided to his masseur Kersten. He duly wrote a confidential memo to the SS, following his decree that 'a member of the SS or police who commits an indecent act with a man will be punished by death'. True to his rule of silence, he added: 'This order is to be made known orally and confidentially to all members of the SS and police with the instruction that communications about this outside the SS and police are forbidden.'

On 27 May 1942 there occurred an event which put everything else in the shade. Reinhard Heydrich, Himmler's Chief of Staff, was assassinated in Prague, by Czech partisans. He wasn't killed outright, but died in hospital a week later. People close to Himmler noticed something strange: far from being downcast, he seemed in high good humour. Not outwardly of course, but you couldn't help noticing the spring in the *Reichsführer*'s step. There were even rumours that Karl Gebhardt, Himmler's personal physician, sent to help the local doctors look after Heydrich, actually did the opposite. Heydrich had been acquiring too much power recently, becoming more and more of a threat to Himmler; and although Himmler wasn't as clever as Heydrich, as everyone who knew them agreed, he was clever enough to spot a threat to his power when he saw it. He didn't visit Heydrich in hospital for five days, by which time his former Chief of Staff was as good as dead.

Either way, the revenge wreaked by the SS on the local community was devastating. The village of Lidice, suspected of harbouring the partisans, was razed to the ground. Some 420 men, women and children were murdered. Two children were spared. They were judged to be good Aryan specimens and taken away to be Germanised. The same happened in the villages of Ležáky and Pilsen. An SD Intelligence report described how the people of Pilsen came out of their homes with their arms raised in a Hitler salute, trying to show their 'German friendliness'. To no avail.

Heydrich's state funeral was held in Berlin on 9 June 1942, gun carriage drawn by six black horses, black *Waffen-SS* guard of honour and all. Hitler spoke first. Then came Himmler, delivering the eulogy, piously holding Heydrich's two sons by the hand. That evening he took the opportunity to address a large group of his *SS-Gruppenführers* gathered for the funeral, full of renewed vigour.

He spoke to them 'as a soldier', again completely forgetting he'd never been a soldier. Also apparently forgetting what every real soldier at the Front knew: that the war was already effectively lost. '*Meine Herren*,' spoke he, grandly, stating the obvious: 'Gentlemen! Should the war continue a year longer, the SS battalions will decrease somewhat.' The single most important task, therefore, he concluded, was 'never to allow the front line of the *Waffen-SS* and the police to die out in any way. And if at some time we have to put the sixteen-year-olds and the fifty-five-year-olds to arms, then we will do it. It is completely immaterial whether one year-entry bleeds more or bleeds less if it is a question of a whole *Volk* surviving... War is no matter of sentimentalities. The war will be won because we have the conflict between Europe and Asia. We have here the conflict between the Germanic Reich and the *Untermenschen*. This we have to win – and we will win it.'

For anyone else this might have been a good moment to end. Not the *Reichsführer-SS*, quite heady with his unfettered powers now that his Chief of Staff was dead. On and on he went. 'In the final analysis we have the thicker skull. We have the better blood, the stronger heart, the better nerves.' With an oblique reference to Stalingrad he reassured his apparently rapt listeners: 'Now the whole SS will march on with beating drums and helmets donned. And if another blow strikes us, we will march on.' An hour or so later he came to the future, once the war was won, lands conquered and peace declared: 'An increase of 30 million people "of Germanic blood" which added up to some 400 million people in the northern part of Europe would need to be "regulated" by "white Nordic races".' So remember to treat young Norwegians, Dutch and Flemings and so on well. Similarly, they had to think about the future settlement of conquered territories in the east. 'If we do not make the bricks here, if we do not fill up our [concentration] camps with work-slaves... to build our towns, our villages, our farmsteads... then after a long war we will simply not have the money to furnish the settlements so that really Germanic people can live there and take root in the first generation...' Nothing new here. It was Heini speaking, head still filled with ghastly fantasy.

But what on earth was Höss doing at Auschwitz? Why was it still not running to full capacity? Himmler set off with Wolfie and a phalanx of *SS-Gruppenführers* to find out for himself.

First they went to the SS officers' mess, then the works office, where Rudolf Höss explained some of the difficulties: shortage of materials, not enough strong and experienced workers, plus the problem of policing the farms and fields, which lay outside the camp. Himmler was not impressed. Onwards, for a guided tour of the camp itself. Further problems: extreme overcrowding and insufficient sanitation in the barracks, giving rise to sickness and a further shortage of workers. Himmler was thoroughly fed up. 'For the *SS-Führer* there are no problems – his task is continually to remove problems himself the moment they appear!' he told Höss. 'Over the how, YOU blow your brains out, not I!'

On to Birkenau, to see how the building works were getting on. Lastly it was the gas chamber of Bunker No. 1, disguised as a shower hut with a hidden crematorium underground. By 1943 the two large crematoria situated away from the main buildings at Birkenau were ready. They each had five ovens and could burn 2,000 corpses every twenty-four hours, working day and night, but for the time being they had to make do with small ovens. The problem here, Höss explained to Himmler, was that they couldn't keep up with the amount of corpses to be burned. And then there was the problem of the stench if the wind was in the wrong direction, leading locals to complain. Problems, problems!

Himmler decided to watch the process for himself, Höss said, using an observation window. It seems the *Reichsführer-SS* had got a taste for it, watching Dr Rascher's experiments. The first task was to get groups of Jews into the gas chamber without panic breaking out. The guards and *Sonderkommando* work parties, mostly concentration camp inmates, were told to say it was just a shower hut. There was to be no shouting or wielding of whips. No dogs. Friendly. Once the Jews, the old, the young, the sick, were safely inside, the doors were slammed shut and locked. Canisters of Zyklon B were quickly poured in from the roof and the screaming and wailing rose to a pitch as those inside struggled for air and for life itself. Speed was of the essence. 'Himmler viewed the extermination process in complete silence, saying nothing at all. Several times he watched me unobtrusively and the *Führer* and *Unterführer* taking part,' said Höss in his prison cell after the war. The whole process took about half an hour, he said, then the doors were opened, the ventilation plant switched on, and the *Sonderkommandos* went into the chamber to pull out the bodies. Gold teeth removed with pliers. Hair cut. Spectacles collected. Nothing wasted.

The VIP visitors went on to inspect the IG Farben synthetic oil plant, which was conveniently close, on the other side of the River Soła. Apparently it wasn't working efficiently. The Jews were too weak. Too slow. How many more excuses could Höss come up with?

After lunch they were invited to inspect the 'ramp' where the initial 'selections' took place, the old and infirm straight to the shower hut, the young and still strong into the barracks, rows and rows of huts as far as the eye could see. Men this way, women that, cases and bundles thrown on to the ramp to be 'sorted' later by the *Sonderkommandos* – keep fur coats, hidden jewels, bank notes sewn into hems of clothing, throw the rest. Two trains arrived that afternoon, each with some 1,000 German Jews who'd fled to Holland – to no avail. They emerged blinking and terrified after days crammed in cattle trucks, foul and stinking. SS guards were waiting for them, armed with whips, pistols and iron-tipped batons, baying dogs straining on leashes. '*Raus! Raus!*' It worked fast and efficiently. Most satisfactory to the *Reichsführer-SS*.

After that it was back to the officers' mess for something to eat. During the meal Höss took the opportunity to ask Himmler once again for an increase in camp guards, given the extreme shortage and wastage as former Hitler Youths who joined the *Waffen-SS* expecting to go to the Front to fight for the *Vaterland* found themselves working at Auschwitz and soon asked for transfers. Or had breakdowns. 'Impossible,' replied the *Reichsführer-SS*. Improve the technology, he suggested. Fritz Bracht, the *Gauleiter* of Upper Silesia, was present at the meal because Himmler was due to spend the night at his residence in Kattowitz, and he invited Höss and a few other high-ranking guests back to his home for an after-dinner drink. Himmler, in garrulous humour now, drank some wine, smoked a cigar and talked on and on about all sorts of things: books, Germanic history, the *Waffen-SS*, travels to the Front with the Führer – everything but the day they'd just had at Auschwitz. Apparently he was in 'best sparkling form' and stayed up so late that everyone was half-asleep and couldn't wait to get to bed.

The next morning Himmler had a stimulating discussion with Bracht about how the plans for resettlement of Aryan Germans eastwards were proceeding in his *Gau*. Then it was off for the second day of inspections at Auschwitz. This time it was all about the running of such a huge enterprise: the workshops, the kitchens, the butchery, the bakery. Höss had another go at discussing such matters as food shortage, overcrowding and the resulting hygiene problem, which was severe. Himmler was again not interested. Höss had to remember they were in the middle of a war, he said. Instead, according to Karl Wolff, giving evidence at his trial in Munich after the war, Himmler turned his attention to the corporal punishment of women, watching one being flogged with five strokes on her bare buttocks. Before Himmler and Wolffie and their entourage left, Himmler promoted Höss to *Obersturmbannführer* by way of encouragement.

But what of the other evil twin, the one going hand in hand with all that extermination? 'Germanisation of Children of Polish families and from former Polish orphanages' went a directive from the *Reichsführer-SS* to all *Höhere SS- und Polizeiführers*, SS and Police Chiefs, of occupied Poland in February 1942. The *Lebensborn* organisation no doubt had the original copy. Other copies went to the Race and Settlement Main Office, the Reich Security Office, the Ministry of the Interior and the Ministry of Education. The orphanages were full of children whose parents had 'disappeared'. Other children should simply be stolen from their homes – those who looked racially pure and healthy. Luckily they weren't hard to spot: blond hair and blue eyes, though sometimes a good specimen, although not strictly speaking blond, might be beautifully built, like one of Leni Riefenstahl's athletes. The local Race and Settlement Main Office officials should examine the children, said the directive, and if they passed the racial tests send them off to one of the designated children's homes for some weeks of Germanisation. Thereafter children between the ages of two and six should be shipped to the Reich and one of the *Lebensborn* homes, who would place them with a deserving childless family. Nazi Party members. The older children, who were less easy to assimilate, would be sent to boarding schools in the Reich and thence into slave labour, as farm boys and the like. 'The children are to be described as German orphans from the reconquered east.' Reconquered. Not conquered.

Rumours soon spread that the Nazis were searching the towns and villages for children. What could it mean? Perhaps it referred to the orphanages which were full of children who'd lost their parents, either from fighting during the early days of the war or because their parents had been liquidated for political reasons. How could they know that within days of the occupation of Poland rafts of Himmler's racial experts had moved into a vast office in Posen, with Walther Darré, Himmler's Chief of the SS Race and Settlement Main Office, in overall charge. Apart from RuSHA, there was VoMi, the Office for the Repatriation of Ethnic Germans, and RKFVD, the Office of the Reich Commissioner for Strengthening Germanism, each with numerous subsections. 'All the good blood in the world, all the Germanic blood which isn't on our side, can be our future destruction,' as Himmler had already said in 1938. 'I really mean to bring back German blood from anywhere in the world, to steal it and rob it from wherever I can.' In the journal *Deutsche Arbeit* he wrote: 'Our task is not to Germanise the east in the old way, that is, teaching those who live there how to speak German and about German laws. But, instead, to ensure that only people of pure Germanic blood live there at all.' By 24 October 1943 he was telling his SS officers that they had to make Poland 'their own', and that this could only be achieved through blood – lost blood to be retrieved. 'Wherever there is good German blood in the world, we have to take it for ourselves, and let no one else have it,' he was happy to repeat, again, adding: 'The most dangerous enemy for us is the one of our own Germanic blood who fights on the other side.'

Members of the NSV, National Socialist People's Welfare Organisation, including some so-called Brown Sisters, were seen walking up and down the village streets, peering through windows, knocking on doors. Their child had been chosen for a free holiday, they told the mothers, smiling in a friendly way. What kind of holiday, asked the doubtful mothers standing on their doorsteps in their aprons and headscarves, arms folded. Nothing to worry about, the Brown Sisters reassured them. Just bring the child to the local council offices tomorrow for testing. Testing? What kind of testing? Most mothers, becoming fearful, said no, their child didn't need a holiday. And why weren't the children next door being offered a holiday too? If the mothers persisted in their refusal a policeman or a member of the NSV soon called. Now it was an order, not an offer. The policemen were local, formerly decent men, now suddenly officious and self-important. At seven the next morning they came banging on the door: they could either bring the child to the council offices or the NSV would take them, the mothers were told, and the parents would be arrested. The mothers fell to their knees, begging and weeping. It was no use.'They always took the most beautiful children,' the villagers told the Polish Mission after the war. Those who were dark-haired, dark-eyed, disabled, sick or educationally subnormal were left behind. They were the lucky ones, it turned out.

The beautiful children were taken to requisitioned buildings like the one in Kalisz near Posen, once a convent, now occupied by the NSV for the Germanisation of Aryan Polish children. It was a large, beautiful building dating from the nineteenth century, white, with a steep red-tiled roof and turrets and an interior of long echoing corridors, lofty ceilings and white-tiled kitchens leading outside to an extensive, well-tended kitchen garden and an ornate chapel with a statue of the Virgin Mary, arms outstretched to the children of the world, the whole place surrounded by a high wall – a world of its own completely cut off from the everyday life of the town. The nuns had been forcibly removed and now the convent was filled with confused, frightened, weeping children, girls as well as boys, all more or less blond and blue-eyed, ranging from babies to toddlers to fourteen-year-olds, all strictly supervised by the NSV and the Brown Sisters with their Nazi Party badges pinned to their brown uniforms.

There were rafts of medical staff equipped with a variety of pseudo-medical equipment to further categorise the children, based on eleven racial categories, all meticulously noted on index cards, that favourite of the *Reichsführer-SS*. Apart from the usual weighing scales and wooden measuring tapes there were calipers and cranometers and endless colour charts – plus photographs of each child, front and profile, to be attached to the index card. The nose alone merited three measurements: length, width and shape. Eyelids, chin, lips, colour of skin (five categories from rosy to yellowish to 'darkish'), hair, eyes, shape of head, height, deportment, shape of face – on and on it went, all typed out on those beige index cards, duly filed away in locked metal cabinets.

Then came the form-filling, stamped by RuSHA, index card,

comments and photograph attached. Each child's card had a number but no name, plus the date on which they were 'transferred'. There were two extra sections, one headed 'Political Assessment', the other 'Behaviour in the Camp'. The Warsaw Institute for Nazi War Crimes is full of these forms and index cards, hundreds and hundreds of them – all nameless and anonymous, identities lost except for those haunting photographs stapled to the forms, because one of the first things the busy NSV administration at Kalisz did once the form-filling was done was to change the names of the children from their own Polish ones to new German ones.

In December 1942 Himmler had found it necessary to issue a directive from the Reich Ministry of the Interior concerning a certain problem which had arisen at Kalisz: 'It has been shown in the course of time that it must be expected that remaining Polish relatives and friends will attempt to find the location of the children. That however would endanger the children's Germanisation. Setbacks to their education, which may occur if the children come under the influence of their relatives, must be avoided at all costs. I therefore request that a separate police registration office be established for that home, to be known as Police/Registration Office II in Kalisz/Warthegau.' If it was ever possible to trace the stolen children before the directive was issued, now it became impossible. When the parents went, in despair, to see their local mayors they were greeted with '*Raus!* Get out!' They were new mayors, of course, because the Nazis had replaced all the old ones with loyal supporters of the regime.

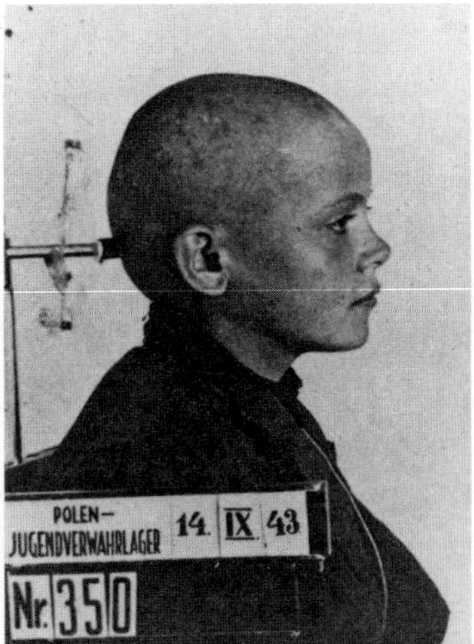

Once the Germanisation of the children was complete they were taken to Kalisz railway station bound for the Reich, the toddlers to be adopted by good Nazi families, the older boys to farms as slave labour, the girls as domestic help. The boys had first to join Hitler Youth camps to prepare them for the hard work ahead. The camps were often in pleasant environments, beside a lake or surrounded by meadows with shining Alps beyond. But that was the only pleasant thing about them. The parade ground stood in the middle, swastika banners and flags flying high. Hitler Youths in uniform lined up there every morning at six for reveille with bugles and drums, giving the Hitler salute. There were large communal tents and a field kitchen with wooden tables to one side. Each tent held twelve boys, ten German, two Polish. There was enmity between them from the start, given the knowledge the German boys had of the Poles – a subhuman, primitive race who lived in filthy hovels and were enemies of the Reich, killing their fathers and brothers.

The training was deliberately brutal. Sport was the main activity. The games were all team games, designed to toughen the boys up and make them 'hard' – one side German, the other the 'enemy' – war games, in preparation for the boys' future in the real war. Bullying was encouraged, because the strong should triumph over the weak, just as in Nature herself. There was shooting practice with air rifles, grenade-throwing with lumps of metal the same shape and weight as a real grenade, map-reading and orientation, and long marches through the countryside, singing those marching songs. 'What are we now! Hitler Youth! What do we want to be? Soldiers!'

'This youth will learn nothing other than German thinking, German behaviour,' announced Hitler during one of his Table Talks, this one at Reichenau in 1937. 'When these youths come into the Pimpfe aged ten, and feel, for the first time, some fresh ideas and fresh air, then we can, four years later, take them into the Hitler Youth and keep them there for another four years. And then we'll really have them, and won't ever give them back, but take them straight into our Nazi Party... thence to the *Wehrmacht*, into the SA or the SS... And they'll never be free again for the rest of their lives!' By 1934 the membership was over 2 million. By 1936 it was 5,400,000. By 1939 and the outbreak of war it was 8,700,000 out of a total of 8,870,000 eligible members. The wonder is that there were still

170,000 resisters. How were the *Volk* to know that within five years Germany would be defeated, the Nazi dream of the all-conquering Hitler Youth dead and buried in the ashes?

According to the Polish Mission set up after the war to try and find them, some 200,000 children were stolen from Poland during the war. Not to mention Czechoslovakia and all the other countries occupied by the Nazis. *Lebensborn*, the 'fount of life', turned out to be the fount of death. No more than 40,000, mostly the older ones who could remember what had happened to them and where they came from, managed to find their way back home after the war. The rest lived on in Germany with no idea that they were, once upon a time, in another world and another place, a Polish one.

By the summer of 1943 things were looking grim for the Thousand-Year German Reich. The German Army under General Rommel had surrendered to the Allies under General Montgomery in North Africa, which was almost as shocking as the German defeat at Stalingrad. Then the Allies landed in Sicily, beginning their invasion of mainland Europe. Meanwhile the bombing raids on German cities intensified, razing whole districts to rubble. There were SD reports that public opinion was turning against the Nazi regime, most people, civilian and military alike, now desperate for the war to end. Although the German public didn't know it, some high-up Nazis within the regime were beginning to put out feelers for a peace deal. It was a non-starter. At the Casablanca Conference in January 1943 Churchill and Roosevelt had made it clear: unconditional surrender or nothing. Stalin had been unable or unwilling to attend the conference. General de Gaulle was there to represent Free France, which was just as well bearing in mind how much death and destruction lay ahead for his country.

As for Himmler, his mind was occupied with higher matters. 'We have only one task,' he told his SS officers on 24 April 1943, head still way up in the clouds. 'To stand and pitilessly to lead the race battle. I say now once more what I have already said today to men at another position: the reputation of horror and terror which preceded us in the battle for Kharkov, this outstanding weapon we want never to allow to diminish, but only want to strengthen it.' On a practical level, the *Arbeitserziehungslager* (work camps) had to be kept at full capacity, producing the building materials for the colonisation of the east, including a good road and railway system from west to east. On 11 May 1943 he turned his attention to Riga and the Salaspils concentration camp, run by Friedrich Jeckeln. 'This camp is practically a concentration camp but it is under the command of the Security Police,' he wrote. Jeckeln had indeed been in the Security Police before the war. 'The inmates are occupied in digging turf, mining, quarrying, manufacturing cement. In no circumstances do I wish this to become a concentration camp of any *Oberabschnitt* [highest level] . . .' meaning the business of mass-extermination. Until more Jewish transports started arriving from elsewhere, after which everything changed again.

By the spring of 1944 everything was in chaos in Nazi Germany, the Russians advancing on the Reich from the east, the Allies preparing for D-Day in the west, the opposition to the Nazi regime within Germany itself preparing for the 20 July putsch, organised in top secret by General Ludwig Beck and Carl Goerdeler, one-time mayor of Leipzig, to be carried out by a group of army officers led by Count Claus von Stauffenberg. But you'd never know any of that at the *Verwaltungshauptamt* – the SS Main Economic and Administrative Office, based at Prinz Albrecht Strasse in Berlin, headed by Oswald Pohl – which was proceeding as it always did, maintaining the fiction of an imminent German victory in spite of the carpet-bombing of the city by the Allied Air Forces.

Oswald Pohl had a daily meeting with the *Reichsführer-SS* whenever Himmler was in his office, which was less and less frequently these days. But one day in May 1944 he was at his desk, surrounded by paperwork as usual, applying himself to the minutiae of administrating the concentration camps – some 1,000 by now including the sub-camps, stretching across Poland and beyond. So Pohl made his way along the wide corridors of Prinz Albrecht Strasse to the anteroom of the *Reichsführer*'s office, waiting to be called in. Two of Himmler's tallest, blondest SS adjutants stood either side of the high carved oak doors. Once inside, Pohl stood to attention till Himmler, head down, busy busy, was ready for him. '*Heil Hitler, Reichsführer!*' he said, clicking his heels and giving the Hitler salute.

The room was large and airy, panelled in the same oak as the doors, the floor covered in coconut matting. Beautiful, no expense spared. Himmler's desk was as big as a dining table, again oak, a bronze bust of Hitler on one side and a white porcelain figure of a drummer boy on the other. Pohl wore his usual black SS uniform and highly polished black jackboots. Himmler was immaculate in his field-grey uniform with laurel leaves and wreath on the lapel, black belt and tie; military style since he'd recently been promoted to General of the Army Reserve by the Führer, who had little choice. So few *alte Kamaraden* left. So Heini was a soldier at last. Just a shame it wasn't the real army. And a shame about the bearing – the sloping shoulders, the weak chest, the pudding-basin shaved head, the thick glasses and the small mousey moustache. However much he tried, Himmler remained 'the schoolmasterly type who never looked like a soldier and always wanted to be what he was not', as Heydrich's wife put it once the war was over and it was safe to say such things.

By the time Pohl arrived, Himmler had already had his daily session with his masseur Felix Kersten, still trying to conquer those stomach cramps and headaches which had plagued him all his life.

When he was good and ready the *Reichsführer-SS* got up and led Pohl to a round table in the far corner of the room by a large window. The table was also oak, with a nice vase of orchids in the middle. There were easy chairs either side. The two men sat down and made themselves comfortable. There was an unpleasant matter to discuss – an escape from Belsen some days earlier. Four men. Stupid, the two *SS-Kamaraden* agreed. The alarm had gone off instantly and a search party of SS guards had been despatched, aided by local police. The men were soon caught and brought back. The next morning at 7.15 they were dragged out into the middle of the barrack square in front of all the camp inmates, lined up to witness what happened. A wooden whipping block awaited. The men had already been badly beaten. After the whipping they were covered in blood and almost dead. Then they were hanged, publicly, Pohl confirmed. '*Gut*,' said the *Reichsführer-SS*, satisfied. 'Good.'

But nothing stands still. Hardly a week after the Führer had promoted Himmler to General of the Army Reserve, the Russian Army crossed the border into eastern Poland and reached Majdanek concentration camp, the first of many horrors to come. By spring 1945 they'd reached Silesia, capturing thousands of the one-time Master Race. By early March the American First Army had crossed the Rhine at Remagen. Two weeks later Field-Marshal Montgomery's 21st Army Group crossed the Lower Rhine. The Russian Army reached Gdańsk, onetime Danzig. By April they were close to Vienna. 'Attack!' raged the Führer from his Berlin bunker. 'Death not surrender!'

By May 1945 it was all over: Germany defeated, the Allies victorious. Himmler, more fixer than soldier, had been making moves to save his skin for months by then. Always in secret, always in the dark. First potential peace negotiators in neutral countries like Switzerland and Sweden. In Sweden he contacted the humanitarian Count Folke Bernadotte. The go-between was Walter Schellenberg, Chief of *Amt VI* (Foreign Intelligence), one-time SS, now peace-broker. They were offering, he and his onetime *Reichsführer-SS*, what they called 'a just peace'. A what? asked General Dwight Eisenhower, Supreme Commander of the Allied Expeditionary Force in Europe. Good God! When the offer reached Whitehall an encoded telegram was quickly despatched to Stalin via Sweden. 'The British and American Governments propose to reject it and to inform Himmler that unconditional surrender is the only acceptable offer.' When news reached Hitler of Himmler's betrayal, Martin Bormann, dog loyal as ever, sent a telegram to Admiral Karl Dönitz: 'New treason afoot. According to enemy broadcast the *Reichsführer-SS* has made capitulation offer via Sweden. Führer expects you to act against all traitors with speed of lightening and as hard as steel. Signed: Bormann.' Speed of lightening, hard as steel. Nazi language, as Himmler once knew it. Dönitz took no notice. Within days Hitler and his mistress, now wife, had committed suicide in their bunker. Joseph Goebbels followed soon after, poisoning his wife and six children.

It was time to go underground, strip off the beloved uniform, put on a nondescript one, shave the moustache, mingle with the crowd of terrified burghers, evacuees, escaped slave workers, soldiers on the run. Himmler had months earlier stolen the identity card of a country policeman who'd been sentenced to death by the Nazi People's Court for 'defeatism'. Hitzinger was his name. The real Himmler was left with two loyal SS adjutants, no one else. The three, in disguise, on the run like scared rats, were in Lübeck in northern Germany when there was another air raid, the bombers of the British Royal Air Force wreaking their final revenge for the early-war bombing of East London, Coventry, Portsmouth, Liverpool, Glasgow and more. In truth there was nothing much left of Lübeck, the first air raids having started way back in 1942. The three *SS-Kamaraden* ran for safety into a public air raid shelter. No one recognised them, Himmler as insignificant now as he'd always been in reality, under that black SS uniform.

Once the air raid was over the three decided it was time to make a run for it again. When they came to their first checkpoint they felt safe, mingling with the crowd. It was the British Army checkpoint at Bremervörde. Himmler/Hitzinger presented his identity card. He didn't know the sentry had orders to arrest anyone in uniform. The sentry called his sergeant to take them inside. And now, to the disgust of his two SS officers, Himmler, *Reichsführer-SS*, lost his nerve. His whole body shook. 'I am Heinrich Himmler,' he stated, perhaps thinking, even now, that the great name would save him.

On 21 May 1945 Sergeant-Major Edwin Austin was sitting in a cinema in Lüneburg in northern Germany watching a Bing Crosby film along with other men of Field Marshal Montgomery's Second Army HQ Company. Two weeks earlier, on 4 May, Montgomery had accepted the surrender of German forces in northern Germany in a tent on the Lüneburg Heath. Now they were there to bring some order and security to the post-war chaos. Before the war Edwin Austin had been a dustbin man in Barnes, South London. But the war had shown Austin to be a man of underrated talent. By the time he joined Montgomery's HQ Company he was in charge of guarding captured Nazis, most of whom had been on the run for days if not weeks, many in disguise. Now a notice appeared on the cinema screen interrupting the film to summon Sergeant-Major Austin to HQ at 33 Uelzener Strasse. Another one, thought Austin. A few days earlier it had been *SS-Obergruppenführer* Prützmann, commander of the 'Werewolf' Nazi resistance movement against the Allied occupation forces. Austin had searched him thoroughly and found the cyanide capsule, but he'd missed a second one hidden in Prützmann's mouth. It was a painful death – small consolation, because Austin's job was to keep valuable prisoners alive till the British Intelligence officers arrived to interrogate them. 'Curious that it should fall to me to handle this human rubbish!' he told the historian Willi Frischauer in 1953.

Frischauer was born in Vienna in 1906 and managed to escape to Britain before the *Anschluss* in 1938. It left him in the perfect position, post-war, to write biographies of various top Nazis, based on first-hand accounts, including that of Heinrich Himmler. 'I recognised him immediately,' Austin told Frischauer. Himmler had been on the run for days and was by now wearing only underpants and a khaki shirt with an army blanket to cover his bare legs. No moustache, and blinking half-blind for lack of his thick spectacles. So much for the great SS Commander and Chief of Police, thought Austin.

He decided his best plan, to avoid any further mishaps, was to knock Himmler out cold with a heavy sandbag which he'd brought along for the purpose. But Colonel Michael Murphy, Chief of Intelligence at the HQ of the Second Army, refused. 'So I grabbed him and I shoved him into the room,' Austin told Frischauer. 'That's your bed. *Ausziehen!* Undress!' Himmler, still wafting in his superior cloud, was affronted by his treatment. 'You don't know who I am!' he said in English, albeit with a strong German accent. The dustbin man and the great Aryan confronted each other. 'Oh yes I do!' said Austin. 'You're Himmler! So undress!' Himmler stood in the middle of the room, naked, puny, receding chin, unshaven. Captain C. J. Wells, the army medical officer, came in to check for the inevitable hidden cyanide capsule – examining toes, ears, hair. He found nothing. 'Come closer to the light!' he ordered, to check Himmler's mouth. He'd just inserted his fingers when Himmler clamped down hard with his teeth and crushed the capsule. Austin grabbed him by the throat, but it was too late. Himmler took a quarter of an hour to die, writhing in pain. Austin stood by, disgusted. Then he threw a blanket over the naked body and left the room.

What does it take to be a murderer like Himmler, an exterminator of millions? Nothing much really. Just brutality, plain brutality. No need for intelligence, education or culture, though those attributes are not excluded. Just a preparedness to kill people, shoot them in their beds at night, or arrest them and bundle them into waiting cars to be murdered 'while trying to escape', or torture them to death under interrogation, or transport them in cattle trucks to concentration camps. Or to Siberia for that matter, or a desert somewhere. Equally you can starve people to death, which is cheaper. Or gas them. Or beat them to death. Or blow them up with a bomb. They might be political opponents, they might be the wrong ethnic or tribal group, they might be racial subhumans. What matter? They need to be killed – to solve the problem once and for all. The dead can't fight, organise revolts and revolutions, assassinate you or depose you. Best to deal with their children at the same time, because these are just the kind to rise up and make trouble for you a few years on. Yes, killing's the thing. Some even like it. For most, it's just a means to an end.

For Himmler it was ideological. Racial. You don't have to simplify it, it's already simple enough: breed the pure Aryan in SS *Lebensborn* homes, in secret, to produce the Master Race and take over the world in the Thousand-Year German Reich. Or enter a village in Poland and remove all the Jews to a concentration camp, then steal the children with blond hair and blue eyes and take them to the German Reich. Don't bother about the rest.

So Willi Frischauer, writing the first biography of Heinrich Himmler in 1953, was wrong. *Himmler: The Evil Genius of the Third Reich* was the title. Evil, yes. Genius, never.

PART TWO

THREE FUTURES

CHAPTER FIVE

RENATE TELLS HER STORY

Sometime after Germany's defeat, formally declared in May 1945, Else Röder arrived at Kohren with her mother to reclaim her child, Fried's child, and take her back home. Perhaps *Tante* Hilde had been part of the plan all along, just taking care of Renate on the *Reichsführer-SS*'s instructions, till Else could come and collect her. It was Else's one consolation for Germany's defeat: she was able to find and claim her child.

For Renate, now aged almost four, it was very different. This was the third parting from someone she loved in her short life, first from Steinhöring, then from her next *Lebensborn* home, then from *Tante* Hilde, and she resisted it with all her might. But Else took her firmly by the hand and dragged her wailing all the way to the railway station. That's how Renate told it years later, adding that *Grossmutter* held her other hand even tighter. She never loved *Grossmutter*.

They didn't go back to Cologne, which had been so badly bombed there was nowhere to live. Instead they tried to survive in the countryside, near a place called Straubing in Bavaria, joining an ad hoc community in an abandoned house, foraging for food on the land and in the forests – left-over potatoes and cabbages in the fields, mushrooms and berries in the woods, the occasional chicken donated, flapping and squawking, by the local farmer's wife. It was a flotsam community of mostly women and children and a few old men, because the younger ones, the husbands and sons and fathers, were either prisoners of war in England, or worse, in Russia. Or dead. Millions of dead. No one really knew where their men were, and Else Röder later recalled that this is what made it possible for them to survive: they were all in the same boat, all helping each other out. Someone might have a bicycle, someone else might have a wooden cart. The women took turns cleaning and looking after the children and cooking on an old iron stove. As the weather turned cold that autumn they chopped down trees for firewood. In the evenings they sat round the fire talking and sometimes, when the mood was good, singing the old German songs. Renate loved it, soon forgetting all about *Tante* Hilde. When the weather was fine the children raced about outside all day long. When it rained they played inside, drawing and making puppets, dressing up and putting on shows for the grown-ups. Years later she still remembered that when it snowed during the winter of 1945 they sledged down the slopes on planks of wood, screaming and shouting – hordes of children, wild as hawks.

Germany was full of such communities trying to survive in the post-war chaos, before the Allied occupying forces had time to set up proper local administrations again. But by the spring of 1946 things were gradually returning to normal. Else Röder found a small flat in Cologne, on Neue Strasse, a busy road not far from the centre, and the three of them, Else, her mother and Renate, took leave of their new friends and joined the steady flow of humanity making their way back home. Renate vividly remembered the trek from the countryside because they had to cross the bridge over the River Rhine, avoiding the gaping holes in the shattered iron girders – the bridge badly bombed in the last months of the war as the Allies made their final push into Germany. The gaps were temporarily covered with wood, but you could see the river flowing fast far below. It was terrifying. '*Schau nicht runter!*' Don't look down! '*Heb meine hand*!' Hold my hand! Else held Renate with one hand and pulled a wooden cart with her bundle of possessions in the other. Plenty of people lost their nerve halfway across, frozen with fear, and had to be forced on by soldiers with rifles.

Cologne was in the British Zone. Else Röder's first reaction was relief. Thank God it wasn't the Russians! But as time went on, instead of relief she became unsure of herself – unsure of all her previous certainties. Contrary to dire warnings from neighbours who'd once been keen Nazi supporters, it soon became clear that the British administration was reasonably efficient and, for the most part, fair. Of course there were exceptions, but on the whole the occupying forces behaved well. They helped clear the rubble from the bomb sites, they gave the children sweets and bars of Cadbury's chocolate, they smiled as they passed you in the street. Public transport was re-established. One day a Tommy offered to carry Else's bundle of foraged wood. In her confusion, she refused. Soon she had her job back at the savings bank. She couldn't afford the tram so it was an hour's walk there and an hour back, but she didn't mind. Renate started Kindergarten. Renate's *Grossmutter* ran the household.

But there was something else, something Else couldn't quite put her finger on: things felt different, and not just because the war was over. There were no more Hitler Youths strutting about in their uniforms, no more *Sieg Heils!* No more blaring military bands, no more swastika banners. No more photographs of Hitler on sideboards and above mantelpieces or hanging on classroom and office walls. No more Jews hounded in the streets. No more Friedrich. Where was Fried? Alive or dead? In Russian captivity? She thought about his letters from a place called Riga in Latvia where he'd been personally posted by *Reichsführer-SS* Heinrich Himmler in 1941 as the SS Kommandant of the recently conquered Northern Russian region. She knew he was there with his wife and children, but it hadn't stopped him writing her loving letters. And then, quite suddenly: silence. Where was he now? Years earlier, in the good Riga days, he'd sent her a photograph of himself in full SS general's uniform, looking spelendid. Now it was hidden under the bedroom floorboards with his letters.

The Nuremberg Trials, running from 20 November 1945 to 1 October 1946, were a profound shock to the Germans. Hitler was already dead of course. So was Himmler. So was Goebbels. So, apparently, was Martin Bormann, Hitler's right-hand man at Berchtesgaden, which had been bombed to smithereens by the US Air Force, though some said he'd escaped to South America. But there they were, all the rest of the top Nazis, seated side by side in the dock, Göring, Hess, Ribbentrop, Speer, Frick, Keitel, Jodl, once so powerful, now humiliated. And this at Nuremberg, the site of so many glorious Nazi triumphs. 'It wasn't us,' they said. 'It was Himmler's SS.' Ernst Kaltenbrunner, the most senior remaining member of Himmler's SS in the dock, the man who took over from Heydrich once he'd been assassinated in Prague, got the blame. One after another these top Nazis pleaded 'not guilty'. Only twelve were sentenced to death. The reasoning: that these trials were not only to convict the guilty. They were there to show the German people what they had allowed to happen to their country. Day after day, week after week, the evidence of the horrors perpetrated by the Nazi regime was laid before them, each day more shocking than the last. It was the first ray of sanity.

Else, living in her small flat in Cologne with her child Renate and her *Grossmutter*, read the recently re-established *Kölner Nachrichten* local newspaper every day once she was back from her work at the savings bank. Was it true? How could it be? And yet, and yet. Deep down, deeply buried, were memories of neighbours – Jews, Socialists, Communists, people she'd known well enough, who ran the local shop, the local surgery, the local coal business – who'd disappeared overnight. She remembered some being shot in the street, she remembered reports in the press of people accused of 'defeatism' being sentenced to death by the local People's Court. And now these top Nazis were pleading 'not guilty' and blaming the SS for everything. Fried's SS. Else searched every column, sat through every newsreel at the local cinema, even those showing the horrors of the concentration camps, for news of him. Never mind what he might have done – might have been forced to do. As long as he was alive.

But then came the trial of the *SS-Einsatzgruppen*, named as extermination units, which confirmed that through them alone, as ordered by *Reichsführer-SS* Heinrich Himmler – Fried's chief and *Kamarad*, the man who'd made sure she was well cared for at the Steinhöring *Lebensborn* home, the man who was Renate's godfather – 2 million Jews had been liquidated in mass-shootings. And that was not to include those other 4 million Jews killed in ghettos or on transports or in local *Aktionen* or in the concentration camps.

The American prosecutor, Mr Thomas J. Dodd, produced Document 3421 PS, containing the testimony of Lieutenant George C. Demas, who certified that parchment found when the US Army liberated Buchenwald was 'tattooed human skin'. Also 'the shrunken heads of two young Poles who had been hanged for having relations with German girls. The heads were the size of a fist and the hair and the marks of the rope were still there.' Apparently it was something Camp Kommandant Karl Otto Koch and his wife Ilse enjoyed.

Later came the 'Doctors Trial'. It was shocking how many once-eminent 'scientists' were in the dock, including one woman: Herta Oberheuser, a doctor at Ravensbrück. Apparently the evidence ran to 1,000 printed pages. 'The defendants in this case are charged with murders, tortures and other atrocities committed in the name of science. The victims of these crimes number hundreds of thousands,' accused the American Chief Prosecutor, Brigadier-General Telford Taylor. 'These defendants did not kill in hot blood, some of them may be sadists who killed and tortured for sport, but they are not all perverts, they are not ignorant men. Most of them are trained physicians.' They had treated their fellow men as less than beasts, he said. 'This case offers a signal opportunity to lay before the German people the true cause of their defeat. The insane and malignant doctrines account alike for the crimes of these defendants and for the terrible fate of Germany. A nation which deliberately infects itself with poison will inevitably sicken and die. These defendants and others turned Germany into an infernal combination of a lunatic asylum and a charnel house...' Another ray of sanity, then. Another small ray stating how it was. So it could not be denied.

Then came the trial of the big industrialists and others who had funded the Führer and the Nazi Party from early on, which took place in the same US Military Court and in the same Palace of Justice rooms as the main trials a year earlier.

The Krupp Trial, as it came to be known, was headed 'The United States of America vs Alfried Krupp et al.'. The 'et al.' referred to the eleven Krupp directors, all charged with war crimes and crimes against humanity. It came after the trials of the two other big industrialists who'd funded the Nazi Party. First, Friedrich Flick and five directors of the Flick Gemeinschaft, charged with the use of concentration camp and slave labour, as well as plundering, and of belonging to 'The Circle of Friends of Himmler', donating into his 'Special Account S'. Then Carl Krauch of the chemicals giant IG Farben, along with several of his directors, was charged with the same, making special mention of their production of Zyklon B which was used to exterminate Jews in the concentration camp gas chambers. Himmler's SS was designated a criminal organisation.

At the end of the trial Krupp was sentenced to twelve years in prison and he had to forfeit all his property and businesses. In the event he only served three.

Finally it was Case No. 8 at the American Military Tribunal No. 1: 'the RuSHA case', which included the *Lebensborn* organisation. There were fourteen defendants, including Max Sollmann, Dr Gregor Ebner and Inge Viermetz from *Lebensborn*, as well as members of the Race and Settlement Main Office, the Office for the Repatriation of Ethnic Germans and the Office of the Reich Commissioner for Strengthening Germanism. All part of Heinrich Himmler's SS. 'These crimes included murders, brutalities, cruelties, tortures, atrocities, deportation, enslavement, plunder of property, persecutions and other inhumane acts . . .' spoke the British Attorney-General, Hartley Shawcross, for the prosecution. 'It was a systematic programme of genocide, aimed at the destruction of foreign nations and ethnic groups, in part by murderous extermination and in part by elimination and suppression of national characteristics.'

The Indictment stated that 'The object of the programme was to strengthen the German nation and the so-called Aryan race at the expense of other nations and groups by imposing Nazi and German characteristics upon individuals selected therefrom (such imposition hereinafter called Germanisation) and by extermination of "undesirable" racial elements.' It went on to list nine methods used:

Kidnapping those considered racially valuable
Compelling Eastern workers to have abortions
Taking away children born of Eastern workers, for extermination or Germanisation
Executing or imprisoning Eastern workers who had sexual intercourse with Germans, and imprisoning the Germans
Hampering reproduction of enemy nationals
Evacuating enemy populations from their native lands and resettling ethnic Germans
Compelling foreign nationals to become German citizens and join German armed forces
Plundering public and private property
Participating in the persecution and extermination of the Jews

There followed a concise description of the fundamental purpose of *Lebensborn*: 'to safeguard the "supposed" superiority of Nordic blood and to exterminate all sources that might dilute or taint it' and 'to assure Nazi dominance over Germany and German dominance over Europe in perpetuity'. The judgments were handed down in March 1948. They were surprisingly lenient, the main perpetrator and instigator, Heinrich Himmler, already being dead.

The trial of *SS-Obergruppenführer* Oswald Pohl was one of the the worst. Pohl had been the Chief of Himmler's SS Administration Office and thus party to all SS actions, from extermination in the camps, to breeding the pure Aryans in the *Lebensborn* homes, to stealing blond, blue-eyed children from occupied lands like Poland. By May 1945 Pohl had fled Munich and was on the run. He got as far as Bremen, where he was captured and brought back for trial at Nuremberg, and sentenced to death by hanging. The *Lebensborn* administrators Max Sollmann and Gregor Ebner were each sentenced to two years and eight months. Sollmann had tried to argue that the *Lebensborn* Decree No. 67/1 referred to its charitable work for unmarried mothers and the like. But he finally had to admit that the unmarried mothers had to be racially pure and that stealing and Germanising Polish children had been part of it. And that about 12,000 so-called Aryan babies had been born in *Lebensborn* homes in Germany and the occupied countries. All the defendants pleaded not guilty.

So much for the Aryan race and the Thousand-Year German Reich. In all, 45 million people were dead. Poland alone lost over 6 million; 1,356,900 Poles were sent into slave labour, including 380,000 boys and 225,000 girls. The USSR lost over 20 million. The rest of the Allies lost 3,682,000 among them. And then the Jews: over 6 million Jews exterminated.

Thirty years later, when I was talking to Else, fit and well in her eighties, sitting in her pleasant flat in Cologne, she still spoke of her love for Fried – the love of her life, she said, button eyes sparkling. She no longer denied the Nazi atrocities, but she'd managed to extricate her memories of Fried from it all. And she'd managed to make a life for herself and her child too, working in the bank and later, in her retirement, educating herself by reading and going to lectures. She was quite a person, was Else. Lively. Very likeable. Admirable even. But back in 1948 it was a different matter: then she was still holding on to her illusions. Still hoping Fried was alive. Still happy that she'd found nothing in the papers or anywhere else to say he'd been captured by the Russians. And when Renate and *Grossmutter* were safely asleep she often took that bundle of letters tied with red-satin ribbon out from under the floorboards and read them, again and again. And kissed the photograph of handsome Fried in his SS general's uniform.

As for Renate, aged seven in 1948, she missed the freedom of her life at Straubing. And she hated her *Grossmutter* – a mean, strict, humourless woman. They lived, the three of them, in that small flat, each with their own resentments and concerns, getting by as best they could. Once Renate was older she began to understand what it must have been like for ordinary Germans like *Grossmutter* – all that disillusionment and guilt and hardship, going through two world wars and their aftermath – but she couldn't forgive her. And she couldn't understand why *Mutti* put up with it, never saying a word except very occasionally to stand up for Renate, who early on showed signs of rebellion and high spirits. *Grossmutter* hated high spirits.

Around the age of ten Renate started fantasising. Their flat in Cologne looked out on the busy street below, with screeching trams coming and going. She could see the tram stop from the window, and every day it seemed a former soldier released from a Russian prisoner-of-war camp would get off, kitbag or sack flung over his shoulder, and start walking home – someone's father, someone's husband, someone's son. They looked terrible, those men, haggard, skeletal, half-dead. But they were home, and often as not there'd be a wife and children there to greet them, calling out, '*Pappi! Pappi! Vati! Vati!*' strangers now, but their *Pappi*s nevertheless. And alive.

Renate, watching, longed for her own *Pappi*. And saw him, many a time, as she told me thirty years later, shaking her head at the memory of that child who'd once been her. '*Pappi!*' she'd call out from the window, waving. And apparently sometimes a soldier would look up and wave back. She started putting a piece of cake aside for him whenever *Mutti* did some baking. And if she saw a prisoner of war walking down the street alone she ran out on to the landing and peered down the stairwell, waiting for the tread of his boots coming up the stairs. Else was perplexed. What should she do? Should she stop her? Should she be cross with her? 'Tell her he's dead,' said *Grossmutter*.

But Else couldn't. She wanted too much for Fried to be alive.

School was hard for Renate. Children with missing fathers were given free meals, but not if they didn't have a known father because they couldn't be registered. Renate lied of course, saying her *Pappi* was still a prisoner of war in Russia, but they knew it wasn't true.

'What's his name?' her classmates would challenge. And when she didn't answer: 'She doesn't even know who her father is!'

'Friedrich,' she said finally, revealing her *Mutti*'s secret.

'Friedrich who?'

The worst by far was visiting the relations on Sunday, every Sunday. They who'd once been so proud of their connection to the high-up SS officer now treated them like dirt. That's how Renate described it later. Like dirt. Suddenly her mother was the unmarried woman with the illegitimate child, no longer the proud bearer of a racially pure child for Hitler. Now every time Renate came into the room conversation hushed and significant looks were exchanged, purse-lipped. And what did *Mutti* say? Nothing. 'Oh yes, she was quite happy to be a doormat. She thought she deserved it!' said Renate, still smarting from it years later.

Poor Else. Caught between her critical, bitter *Mutti*, her disapproving relations and her angry child, she hardly knew where to turn. And where was Fried? It took a long time before she knew the truth, that he was dead, and even then she told herself: he's not dead to me. He'll always be alive to me. I'll always love him. She never married.

Luckily she liked her job at the bank and she was good at it. The truth is, Else had a natural intelligence and a lively curiosity. She'd left school at fourteen like most children from poorer backgrounds in the Germany of those days, but she always liked to read, and she wrote a good letter too. One of the things she'd loved about Fried, she told me, quite forgetting to watch her words for the moment, was that he seemed to know so much about the world and what was going on in the Reich – the rights and wrongs of things. In fact she was surely cleverer than Friedrich, who had a narrow, literal mind, as it later turned out. Else's intelligence was obscured by her circumstances: her minimal schooling, the harshness of growing up during the First World War and its terrible aftermath. And now there was the shame of having an illegitmate child. Else bowed her head and suffered in silence.

Perhaps there were better times to come. Just as Fried promised.

Renate started to ask her mother questions when she was about fourteen. Awkward questions. It was 1955 and the pupils at her school were just beginning to learn about the war, though hardly the Holocaust. Up till then even the war had been more or less taboo in Germany, let alone the concentration camps. The subject was skirted around – it was just too terrible to admit. Time and again Renate heard a teacher explain that it wasn't the German people as a whole who'd committed those war crimes, it was the SS. Some teachers even implied that the Allies were lying, or at least exaggerating. No one wanted to ask their *Vati* what he'd done in the war. Many men were still prisoners of war in Russia. Or dead, in an unknown grave or ditch. Later it turned out that only a third ever returned from Russia, so terrible were the conditions in those camps. The Russians had lost some 27 million during the war – civilians as well as soldiers – so there was no forgiving and no forgetting.

By now Renate knew her *Vater* had been in the SS – that he'd been an SS general in fact. Her mother had a framed photograph hidden away in her bedroom, nowadays under her woollens in the wardrobe. It was of *Vater* in his SS general's uniform, looking straight at the camera, smiling, handsome, confident. Splendid. 'Do you think *Vati* is alive?' Renate would ask her mother again and again. 'Do you think he'll come home one day?' Else tried to avoid it by saying, 'I pray every day that he'll come home one day.' Not so *Grossmutter*.

'He's dead,' she said.

'But what did he do?' Renate pursued. 'If he was in the SS, what did he do?'

'Stop asking questions and don't talk to anyone about him,' said *Grossmutter*, 'or there'll be trouble.'

'He was a good man,' Else kept saying. 'Whatever he did must have been for a reason.'

Else had to believe it, not least because as she grew older Renate looked more and more like him. She had his eyes, she had his hair. She even walked like him. '*Ganz wie Fried!*' as she told me, eyes shining. The very image of Fried. For Else it was a sort of miracle. Everyone in the family who'd met Friedrich Jeckeln could see it. But if once this was a good thing, now it was bad. Renate's character was like his too, they said. Bold. There was nothing shy or retiring about Renate. She wasn't like Else at all.

During all these years Else held Fried close, secretly, for herself and no one else. She knew there was another Fried, a gentle, loving Fried, who suffered silently. You only had to read his letters. In between the lines, you could tell. Hadn't he admitted that he often drank, just to get by? He called her his balm, his good angel. He often told her that. He even introduced her to his friend and *Kamarad* Struppi. What fun they had, the three of them. Four times she went for a few days to Fried's hunting hut during her summer holidays – not for the whole week, but most of it. She had five photographs to prove it, tiny black and white ones with those serrated edges, a bit blurred, but unmistakable. And what a joy those times were, for both of them. You could see him relax and put all the cares of his working life away. They drove there in his car! Deep into the forest. How she loved waiting for him to pick her up at the railway station. The excitement of it. She didn't mind how long she had to wait. She understood he couldn't always get away from his heavy duties on time. She just sat on the wooden bench in the second-class waiting room, savouring every minute. She never thought such a thing could happen to her. Even the short meetings snatched here and there were a thrill. And then she got pregnant. Oh joy! And Fried was very happy about it. He told her. Years later she still seemed not to realise, or accept perhaps, that he was pleased for dubious reasons which had nothing to do with her own. He arranged everything for her lying-in at the Steinhöring *Lebensborn* home, she told me. She was treated so well there, she said, because they knew the father was high up in the SS. Unlike most of the other fathers, he'd accepted paternity. He didn't give his name, but he accepted paternity. And who paid for it all? The *Reichsführer-SS* himself!

At this point Else always checked herself. It wasn't good to talk about the *Reichsführer*. Not any more. She didn't say it out loud now. Just that she still loved Fried, whatever he'd done.

The war had changed everything. Fried said it was a necessary war, a fight for the survival of the German Reich which had been cruelly denied them by their defeat in the 1914–18 war. The stab in the back. Her own *Vater* had often said how unfair the Versailles Treaty was, so she knew what Fried meant. And off to war Fried went. Only she understood what a terrible time he'd had in Ukraine. And then in Russia. He was transferred to Latvia in the very month Renate was born! He wrote to her often from Riga – strange letters full of optimism one month, low the next.

There was only one person who was sympathetic to Else after the war. Astonishingly, it was one of Fried's sisters. In one of his last letters from Riga he'd mentioned this sister, telling Else to contact her if anything ever happened to him. She would help her, he said. She lived in Braunschweig, like most of the family. Fried included an address. So once they were back in Cologne, having a hard time, Else plucked up her courage and wrote the letter. The sister answered and agreed to meet halfway. None of the other members of Friedrich's family wanted to have anything to do with her, and she told no one.

They met a few times, always on neutral ground. Renate called her *Tante*, aunt. Else never forgot that first time *Tante* met Renate, who was about seven by then. '*Ganz wie Fried!*' just like Fried, she said, smiling, looking Renate up and down. And she said it as though this was a good thing, not bad. But it turned out she was already ill when they met. If the war had killed over 6 million Germans, soldiers and civilians alike, the post-war years did away with another estimated million – so exhausted and starving and disillusioned were Hitler's *Volk*. *Tante* died when Renate was ten, and that was the end of that.

Else had an album of Renate as a baby, the photos taken by Else on one of her rare visits to the Steinhöring *Lebensborn* home. She'd left the home once her lying-in was over, as all the mothers did, and gone back to her parents in Cologne, back to the bombing. But unlike the other *Lebensborn* mothers, she'd hadn't borne a child to hand her over to *Lebensborn*. She'd had her baby at Steinhöring so she herself could be well taken care of, as Fried said, and the baby too – just till the war was over. Renate was her child, and Fried's child. Four times she'd managed to visit Renate during the war, in spite of the distance and the danger of the train journeys, stopping and starting all the way, with the train sometimes left overnight in a siding till the bombing raid was over. After the war the *Lebensborn* children, those who hadn't already been adopted, were left scattered about the Reich in various children's homes with no idea who they were or where they came from, wanted by no one. But not Renate.

The photograph album was small and red with a red tassle. As far as Renate knew, her *Mutti* had left her in a normal children's home because of the war, for safety, and came to take her home as soon as she could. It wasn't till much later that Renate learned about what it meant to be born in one of Heinrich Himmler's *Lebensborn* homes. Even *Mutti* didn't seem to know, though that was hard to believe.

'Is that nurse Elfrida?' Renate pointed to a nurse, holding Renate in her arms.

'Yes, that's her. You really loved her...'

'Why aren't you in any of the photos?'

'Because I was taking the photographs *natürlich*.' Else laughed, but Renate smelled a rat. 'How could you afford a camera?'

Well, Friedrich had given it to her of course. A box camera. It took surprisingly good photographs – small, black and white. And there was baby Renate in nurse Elfrida's arms, which is how Renate knew about her in the first place. The nurse was in a crisp outfit, starched, white apron and cap, hair pinned neatly back. You couldn't see the giveaway SS badge, so there was no telling. But she belonged to the Brown Sisters, who were part of the SS – the same Sisters who played havoc in Nazi-occupied Poland – but how was Else to know? And of course you had to be a member of the Nazi Party to join, but for the time being Renate knew none of that. Not even Else really knew. Or did she?

Else just stopped herself telling Renate what Friedrich had told her: that these *Lebensborn* homes prided themselves on the best possible care for their children, with the best possible nourishment and plenty of fresh air, because one day, once Germany won the war, these children would inherit the Thousand-Year German Reich. And she never told Renate that Friedrich was married either, with children of his own. Luckily, Renate hadn't found the five or so loose photographs Else had hidden under the floorboards in her bedroom, of herself and Friedrich. Nor the bundle of letters he'd sent her from here and there, many from Riga. No, they were well hidden. Even *Grossmutter* didn't know where they were.

Renate was a rebellious teenager. She was bold, as the relations said, bright too, and good-looking with her thick hair and strong blue eyes. After school she went to college to train as a teacher, then took a job at a 'progressive' school which included the disabled in everyday school life, treating them the same as other pupils. Renate loved that. It seemed to make up for some deeply buried wrong. She taught all subjects, but especially Germanic studies, English, French and History, her favourite. The pupils loved her. She had a way of saying '*Ja!*' with vibrant enthusiasm and a shining smile whenever they did good work. Dimples, she had. A golden girl. But beneath Renate's bright manner there were dark doubts. They gnawed at her and wouldn't let her go. Every time she went to a library or into a bookshop she searched the shelves for new information about the war, but most of all about the SS. She demanded her mother tell her everything she knew. When Else hesitated, she shouted at her and made her cry. 'She lied, all the time!' Renate told me.

Whenever Else started to cry Renate walked out of the room in disgust. And yet she loved her *Mutti*. Admired her even. Because, when *Grossmutter* died, worn out and embittered, Else, feeling free for the first time in her life, started educating herself and travelling. Art history was a favourite. She read anything to do with other countries, faraway places, with lives unknown to her. Later she went on coach tours, seeing the places for herself. Southern Germany. France. Italy. Finally she went to Russia. Yes, Renate admired her for that.

But she never gave up asking her questions. 'Tell me about Vater! Show me the photographs. I know you've got some, so show me!' Else fended her off for as long as possible, but finally, one rainy afternoon, she retrieved her secret cache from under a floorboard in her bedroom and they sat side by side on the canapé looking at them – five tiny photographs, black and white, with those serrated edges. The letters were under the floorboard too, but Else said nothing about that.

Oh, they were delightful, those photographs, thought Else: so happy, so carefree, taken on a stolen weekend in 1938 or 1939 at Friedrich's hunting hut deep in the forest. They were too small for Renate to make out details, except a man in plus fours and woollen knee-socks and boots, wearing a hunting jacket, and, once, a feathered hat. And her *Mutti*, unmistakably her *Mutti*, in a summer frock, seated on a tree trunk, or, in one photo, standing beside a car. A car! His car, obviously. Renate scrutinised each photograph again and again. 'Where was that?' 'When?' 'Who knew?' She was . . . what was she? Fascinated. Disgusted. Angry. Troubled.

'Did you know?' she asked.

'What?' Else tried to change the subject.

'Did you know what he did?'

Renate, well informed about the history of the war and the Germans' war crimes by now, just wouldn't give up. She couldn't, as she told me many times. She just had to have the truth. Renate was a stickler for the truth. She couldn't stand the way her *Mutti* tried to avoid the truth. Refused to face it.

'What he did?' Else might say, looking confused.

'*Ach! Mutti!* What he did in the war!'

Else would start to close the photo album, close the subject.

'This was before the war.' Avoidance, endless avoidance.

'All right! What he did in the SS, then!'

Sometimes Else tried to defend herself.

'He told me the SS was keeping order in the Reich.'

'With concentration camps?' Renate said it used to make her wild, this refusal of her mother to face the truth. 'You know about the concentration camps, don't you, *Mutti*?'

'It was important to keep order. The Communists...' Else began to cry.

'And the Jews?' Renate said she knew she should stop. But she couldn't.

'I didn't know...' wept Else.

Oh dear, not that one again!

'The Holocaust. You know about the Holocaust, don't you? You've seen the pictures, haven't you? The piles of bodies. Who ran the extermination camps, *Mutti*? You know it was the SS! Admit it!'

Renate said she often ended up shouting. She wasn't proud of it, but she couldn't stop herself.

'*Genug* Renate! Enough! Stop!'

But of course she didn't.

'What was his name?'

Else would sigh, 'You know it.'

Renate would persist: 'No! his family name.'

'Jeckeln,' said Else one day, finally giving up. 'Jeckeln.'

She was sobbing now, face buried in her hands. Renate felt terrible. Ashamed of herself.

That's how it was.

It was time to move into a place of her own. She found a pleasant flat in Weissenburg Strasse, on the third floor, about half an hour by tram from her mother's. It had a largish sitting room overlooking a street shaded with plane trees, two bedrooms, a decent-sized bathroom and a kitchen at the back overlooking the inner courtyard. She furnished the flat to her taste: simple, modern 1960s style, with some Turkish rugs on the floor and plenty of bookshelves. She painted the walls white. The second bedroom doubled as a study. She gave a home-warming party for all her friends, including her current boyfriend Jürgen, a teacher at her school. Renate never lacked men interested in her, with her striking looks, and good fun too. Few saw her dark side, and none knew that she was becoming more and more obsessed with her *Vater* and what he might or might not have done. The most people saw of Renate's secret was her honesty. It was excessive. She couldn't bear any sort of avoidance of the truth, however small.

One day she found the book she was looking for. It was hidden away on a shelf in her local library under 'German History', and when Renate held it in her hands she literally trembled with fear. *Anatomie des SS-Staates*, Anatomy of the SS State. It was published in 1965 by Walter-Verlag and was based on research done at the Institut für Zeitgeschichte, the Institute for Contemporary History. On 20 December 1963, after five years of investigation, the trial of twenty-two former guards and administrators at Auschwitz concentration camp had opened in Frankfurt. It was the first large-scale case of its kind tried by Germans before a German judge and jury. The book was based on four depositions on the organisation and function of the SS given to the court before the trial began by members of the Institute. The first section was on the persecution of the Jews, then a section on the structure and origins of the SS, then one on the concentration camps, and a final section on SS activities in Russia. Renate went straight to the Index. And there, for all to see, were three entries under his name: Jeckeln, Friedrich, citing pages 62 and 235 and 586.

The entry on page 62 came under the heading: The Final Solution. Part One was 'The decision and how it was put into effect in the occupied zone of Soviet Russia'. Apparently Hitler, encouraged by Joseph Goebbels and Martin Bormann, had already issued Himmler, as *Reichsführer-SS*, with instructions about the 'progressive destruction' of the Jews after the French campaign in 1940. Then, not later than March 1941, he issued a secret decree, never put in writing, that all the Jews should be eliminated. What he openly declared was that all political commissars in Soviet Russia, Communists, were to be executed. No exceptions. It was Himmler's *Einsatzgruppen* who would carry it out. They'd already had plenty of practice in Poland.

By May 1941 the *Einsatzgruppen* were ready to go into action in Russia. Himmler's right-hand man Reinhard Heydrich was in overall charge. In a written memo, which had only recently come to light, he 'summarised' the 'basic instructions' to the four *Höhere SS- und Polizeiführers*, HSSPF for short. Jeckeln was one of the four, first as HSSPF Russland-Sud, and then from late 1941 onwards as HSSPF Ostland und Russland-Nord.

The Institut für Zeitgeschichte deposition added that there could be no doubt that apart from the *written* memorandum to the four HSSPF to shoot all Jews in the service of the state and Party, the *verbal* orders were to shoot all Jews, regardless. The killing had started on

4 July 1941. It was in Lithuania, carried out by *Einsatzgruppe A* and local Lithuanians in Kowno – 416 Jews shot, including 47 women. From August onwards they were shooting Jewish children 'almost daily', Hitler and Himmler believing that they constituted a danger in the future if left alive. For example, in Moletai and Utena on 29 August, 1,469 Jewish children, 582 Jewish men and 1,731 Jewish women were killed – the women being a special danger as far as *Reichsführer-SS* Himmler was concerned as the bearers of future Jewish children. Getting into their stride, there was a build-up of executions by all the *Einsatzgruppen* in November 1941, the month Renate was born.

Renate didn't remember how she got home, and she told no one. Nevertheless, she took the book with her and read the rest once she felt stronger.

On page 235 she found a letter written by her father from the Baltic States on 9 February 1942, pointing out some organisational problems: 'I, the HSSPF and the commanders of the *SS-Oberabschnitte* on duty in the field have a staff of approximately company strength, including drivers of radio vehicles etc. But we have no disciplinary powers . . . The same applies to the question of promotions. The only method of obtaining decorations for members of the HSSPF staffs is to make application to the *Wehrmacht*, which from time to time deigns to make available one or two War Service Crosses Second Class.' Evidently the German Army and the SS were not on good terms.

In the Appendix she found Jeckeln's personal details: born 2/2/95; SS No. 4367; Party No. 163348; *Sturmbannführer* 15/3/30; *Führer Oa Mitte*, 1937; *HSSPF Russland-Sud* 1941; *HSSPF Ostland und Russland-Nord* 1941.

'You knew about *Kristallnacht*. You can't say you didn't know about that!'

Renate was on one of her weekly visits to her mother. They were sitting in Else's kitchen having the midday meal. Else had made Renate's favourite potato salad, she still remembered that. They were having a perfectly pleasant talk about Renate's school work – her History classes, and how they seemed never to get past Bismarck. And now this again, thought Else!

'*Lass doch!*' Leave it. That's what a lot of the parents of Renate's pupils said too: '*Lass doch!* Leave it alone! You don't understand! You weren't there.'

'*Kristallnacht, Mutti*. It happened here in Cologne as well.'

'Yes. Not as bad, but...'

Renate told me about this conversation, not Else. But knowing Renate's extreme honesty, I guess it proceeded pretty much as she described. Else said it was terrible. She saw it on her way to work.

'What?'

'Smashed shop windows. Broken glass. People looting.'

Renate felt they were getting somewhere, but then Else added:

'There are bad people everywhere, Renate. It's not that simple...'

Ach! There she goes again, avoiding.

'What did *Vater* say?'

'*Vater*?' Else repeated it as though she'd never heard the word.

'*Vater*.'

'He said it was terrible. He said he couldn't understand it.'

Renate nearly left there and then, she said. She didn't tell her mother that she'd just read that Jeckeln had been one of the main organisers of *Kristallnacht* in Braunschweig, his home town, where he lived with his wife and children.

'I want to read his letters,' she said next time.

Else didn't answer. How did Renate know?

'No!' she said. 'They're private.'

'I have a right!'

'No!'

That went on for some days, weeks perhaps. But in the end Renate won. Else went to her bedroom, closed the door, took the letters out from under the floorboard. Handed them over without a word.

Renate was astonished, she told me. Absolutely astonished. She'd expected a dozen or so. There were eighty-three, all bound up with a red ribbon. The first was dated 20 July 1937, the last 26 February 1945.

Renate sat and read them all, line by line till it was getting dark. Else meanwhile had gone out shopping. She couldn't bear to stay.

'Little Renate this, little Renate that!' Renate told me later, riffling through the pages, because at first sight they looked like love letters. 'All this "my brave soldiers". Protecting them from their hard duties! And why didn't he write for a month, till' – she riffled through again, beside herself – 'till 24 January 1942. Too busy?

'Here the war is full of difficulties,' she read out. 'He calls it "difficulties". He even felt sorry for himself! He often needed schnapps to get by, he writes here.' Renate pointed to the passage, disgusted, distressed. 'Then the usual stuff about the winter weather, snow, ice, temperature twenty-five degrees below zero.' Her finger ran down the page. 'The Jews were naked!' she was in tears now, but she read on: 'I myself have managed to bear it pretty well so far...' And all this work schedule information he keeps writing about, so self-important, without admitting anything that's really happening!

'But he couldn't!' Else, back home now, had protested before she could stop herself. Renate didn't understand, she said. She'd never been in a war.

Renate said she just carried on then, unstoppable, no thought for her *Mutti*: 'My belief remains unshakeable, though I have doubted myself sometimes.' What was that meant to mean?! She turned another page. 'Actually my only real worries are about my children. I'd like to be able to do things for them, but it can't happen, because I'm still not allowed home leave.'

When she was telling me all this, years later, she stopped here and gave an imitation of her reaction:

'Children?' she asked. 'Children?'

Else said nothing apparently. Looked out of the window.

'He was married, *Mutti*? With children?'

Else shook her head, close to tears.

'How many, *Mutti*!'

'Five,' said Else.

She didn't mention he'd probably had others outside marriage. Renate asked if she could take the letters home to read them again, in less of a rush. Else hesitated. Then agreed. She was exhausted. She felt she couldn't say no, given the circumstances. 'But bring them back when you come next time!'

Renate sat on the floor of her living room, surrounded by the letters, reading out bits to herself. 'Look at this, look at that!' He wrote once a month on average, long letters full of how excellent he was feeling, the good food provided by the field kitchen, the Bolsheviks running out of steam, his 'brave troops', his 'heavy task', how often he thought about Else, his good angel, and 'little Renate'. How he would love to visit, but unfortunately he couldn't. He knew Else would understand. How pleased he was to hear she'd managed a visit to 'little Renate' and so on. 'The war against the Reds will surely be decided this year, and then transform itself into a colonial one,' he wrote in March, whatever that was supposed to mean. In April he wrote that they'd celebrated the Führer's birthday with 150 of the men. In May that the *Reichsführer-SS* had visited for a few hours and promised to look after little Renate if anything happened to him. What on earth did he mean? Heinrich Himmler, *Reichsführer-SS*, himself? The letters were headed *Gefechtsstand* 'bunker' now. He'd been in Germany for a few days but again hadn't had the time to see Else. 'The war requires sacrifices of everyone!' he wrote in July. 'But what matter personal sacrifices when the German *Volk* is at stake. Nothing but victory to complete extermination counts. England will be next.' He was worried about the Cologne bombings. He thanked her for her letter(s) and the sweet photographs of the *Spatz*, the sparrow. He scolded Else: stop worrying, and be happy. He was hoping for some home leave. He had a Messerschmitt 108 at his disposal. And always what the weather was like. And always ending 'With heartfelt greetings. *Heil Hitler!* Your Fried.'

Renate was caught between fury and distress. How could he write like that? So sweetly, so heroically, when he'd been doing what he was doing in Riga? All that about his 'brave men'. All that soppy talk about 'little Renate'. And why? That was the big question for Renate. Why? Even as late as February 1945 he was telling Else how fine things were. Lying, always lying. She was left with nothing, Renate told me, except: *wie*? How? Why?!

He must have got his home leave in autumn 1942, because there were no letters for almost four months. Then Renate's heart sank. No, surely four months was too long for home leave. According to the records, there was more killing in Riga that autumn. More Jews shipped in from elsewhere to Salaspils concentration camp. Had he told her something of what was going on? Had her mother destroyed the letters?

'I came back yesterday,' he wrote from Riga on 16 November 1942. He had to return to his work. He thanked her for both her letters. The rest of his holidays had gone well. His flight was delayed. He'd had a short stay in Berlin before returning to Riga, and spent a nice evening there with two of his children, Klaus and Ilse. Klaus had just joined the Luftwaffe. 'So now he's a soldier too... Ilse is a sweet girl. Heavy work duties awaited me in Riga.' Renate knew that Salaspils concentration camp wasn't shut down till October 1943. He told Else to think happily of their last meeting, admitting that he had a nerviness these days which probably affected their time together, grabbed here and there, so he wasn't as carefree as before. He knew 'little Renate' still wasn't with her yet, but she would be be soon. He'd talked with Pohl about their situation, and all was in hand. Else could contact him any time, but head the letter '*persönlich*', personal. Renate read that bit again. Who was Pohl? After some further research she found out. Oswald Pohl was the chief adminstrator of the *Lebensborn* 'charity', based in Munich.

There were fewer letters in 1943. The Battle of Stalingrad, ending in February 1943, had changed everything. Ask any soldier at the Eastern Front.

There were six letters in 1944, more like quick notes, assuring her he was well. 'My dear girl,' he wrote in April. 'You haven't heard from me for a long time, but don't be cross, I'm no longer used to writing... Thank you very much for your letters. Unfortunately your visit to Riga didn't work out.' Renate felt like tearing up the letter, she said. Else wasn't ever going to Riga. Lying was evidently second nature to Jeckeln. He was back in a filthy Soviet bunker, he wrote, going back to Riga every now and again 'where lots of work awaits'. He'd been in Munich too, but had unfortunately been unable to see 'little Renate'. Even though Steinhöring was only a few kilometres away. He desperately needed some rest! Poor man, Renate thought bitterly. And he hadn't heard a word for months from his two eldest sons, who were both in the marines. 'Even if I don't write, I think of you. *Heil Hitler!*'

There was just one letter in 1945 – his last.

Renate was desperate to find answers – any answer. How much time did her *Vater* spend in Riga? What work was he doing there in 1943? And what was he doing in 1944? She searched for more books, more articles. She began talking about it to close friends, especially about the Holocaust which was finally being openly discussed in Germany. But there were no answers. And life went on.

Then she found *Hitler and the Final Solution* by Gerald Fleming, published in London by Hamish Hamilton in 1985. And there he was again: Jeckeln, Friedrich. Her *Vater*. His evidence at his trial by the Russians had been kept in the Historical Archives in Riga. On page 44 she read that her *Vater* had gone to the SS Headquarters in Prinz-Albrecht Strasse on 10 and 11 November 1941, just days before she was born in Steinhöring to see Heinrich Himmler and received 'precise liquidation instructions' from him. The solution now was 'evacuation' to the East. In a footnote there was a quote from his trial in Riga on 14 December 1945: 'Himmler said I should go over it with Lohse, and even if he was against it, the Riga ghetto was to be liquidated. He said "Tell Lohse it is my order, which is also the Führer's wish."' Lohse was the civilian *Reichskommissar Ostland*.

On page 75 and 76 came a report by the *Komandant* of *Eisatzgruppe A* of 5 January 1942, presented at the post-war Nuremberg Trials: 'The Higher SS and Police Chief in Riga, SS Obergruppenführer Jeckeln, began a shooting action on Sunday 30 November 1941, eliminating an estimated 4,000 Jews from the Riga ghetto and from an evacuation convoy that originated in Germany.' Fleming adds that the correct number was actually 14,000 Riga Jews and 1,000 Jews from Berlin. In his testimony on 14 December 1945 Jeckeln stated that he had taken part in the shootings three times. 'All the Jews went by foot from the ghetto in Riga to the liquidation site. Near the pits they had to deposit their clothes, which were washed, sorted and shipped back to the Reich. Jews – men, women, and children – passed through the police cordons on their way to the pits, where they were shot. When asked if he'd notified Himmler, he answered in his usual precise way: 'Yes, indeed. I notified Himmler by phone that the ghetto in Riga had been liquidated. And when I was in Lötzen in December 1941, I reported in person too.' There were additional convoys in January 1942, destination Salaspils concentration camp. 'Himmler said he had not yet determined how he would have them exterminated, whether to have them shot on board their convoys, or at Salaspils, or whether to chase them into the swamp somewhere... It was my opinion that shooting would be the simpler and quicker death. He listed that Jews had been transported from France, Belgium, Holland, Czechoslovakia, as well as Germany. 'To give a precise count of the Jews in Salaspils camp would be difficult. In any case, they were all exterminated.' Then, surprisingly, he told the court he wished to make an additional statement, which the court allowed. It was about Göring, who had denied all culpability about the Holocaust. But it was a lie, said Jeckeln. From February 1942 Jews could only be shipped East with Göring's approval. He stressed the word 'only'. He went on to accept his own culpability.

'I have already said that I discussed the extermination of the Jews in Salaspils with Himmler in Lötzen. That alone makes me an accessory to this crime.'

Renate couldn't read any more, she told me. Not then. But later she went back to it, like a moth to a flame.

By page 99 her *Vater* was listing the numbers. 'I can give you approximate figures. The first convoys arrived in November 1941. Then in the first half of 1942 convoys arrived at regular intervals... Overall in eight months, no less than 55 and no more than 87 convoys arrived at the camp. Given that each convoy carried 1,000, that makes a total of 55,000 to 87,000 Jews exterminated in the Salaspils camp.' On page 101 of the Fleming book Jeckeln is quoted as saying he inspected five of the pits, which were dug by 300 Russian prisoners of war on 28 November 1941. They measured 12 square yards and 10 feet deep, plus a ramp 'so the victims could descend into the pit.' A footnote on page 70 turned to the gassings. 'Were there gassings used in Ostland?' asked the Russian prosecutor. 'Yes,' said Jeckeln. 'Three to five gassing vans were used in Salaspils and Riga in the second half of 1942.' Apparently a certain doctor Lange was in charge, and offered Jeckeln a demonstration, which he refused. 'He told me how the people inside began to scream loudly and bang on the walls with their fists after they had been inside for five minutes, then lost consciousness, then finally their lives.' On page 193 Fleming estimated that 4,975,499 Jews lost their lives in the Final Solution.

Renate was into her thirties before she realised that she loved women more than men. Lesbian wasn't an easy word in the 1970s. Perhaps bisexual was better. If Else noticed that her daughter no longer had boyfriends and wasn't getting married, she said nothing. Nor did Renate. They just let it go. But then Renate fell in love, and there was no hiding it after that.

Edi Seebauer was an actress, talented, humorous, good-looking – thick dark hair and large brown eyes, said Renate, smiling and laughing. She'd arrived in Cologne to join a local theatre group in late 1978, where she met Anna, Renate's current girlfriend. Anna invited Edi for supper to Weissenburg Strasse. Renate wasn't back from school yet. The two women were chatting in the kitchen over a glass of wine when she walked in. 'She was *entzückend*!', enchanting, Edi told me. She had dimples when she smiled. They talked about their lives, filling in past information.

'Where are you from?' Edi asked.

'Here in Cologne,' said Renate, hesitating.

'But where were you born?'

Renate mumbled something about Bavaria.

'But where? I'm from Bavaria,' said Edi.

'Oh, a small village. You wouldn't have heard of it,' said Renate, offhand.

Edi persisted now because she could sense something hidden, something interesting. That was Edi. Always curious.

'Steinhöring,' Renate reluctantly said, as if giving up a secret.

'Steinhöring!' Edi couldn't believe it. 'But that's where my parents live!' She beamed at Renate. 'Fate!' she said.

She knew at once that Renate would be the love of her life, she told me later, once I was helping Renate find out more about her *Vater*.

Emboldened by Edi's love and support, they set out to find some answers about Jeckeln, once and for all. They went to see Helmuth Krausnick, one of the authors of *Anatomie des SS-Staates*, but he knew nothing more than the few paragraphs already written. They wrote to the archives, with little more success. They read Fleming's book *Hitler and the Final Solution* together. Then they went to the SS *Lebensborn* home at Steinhöring where Renate was born, now a home for disabled children, which almost made them laugh – the sheer irony of it. 'Look!' said Edi. Woven into the wrought-iron work of the gates were those SS runes, and the V runes of *Lebensborn*. And, hidden in a circle of high shrubbery, they found the monumental stone statue of the *Lebensborn* mother and child.

'Typical Nazi bad taste,' said Edi.

'Typical Fascist style,' said Renate, stroking the stone. 'But beautiful in a way.'

Edi disagreed, disgusted. 'They couldn't bear to pull it down, so they planted trees all round it.'

'Read this!' said Renate, once again surrounded by her *Vater*'s letters. She was reading his penultimate letter to Else, written on 4 November 1944 from somewhere on the northern flank of the Eastern Front. Apparently most of Else's letters had gone missing in the field post, but he thanked her for the one which had reached him. He was pleased to hear what life was like for Else and her mother now they were out of Cologne, 'which must be real hell', and living at Straubing. And very happy that this gave Else a chance of having little Renate living with her at last.

'The war is a real trial now,' Edi read out. 'But that after all is why we're here.'

'Typical heroics,' said Renate. Apparently the Russians had reached the outskirts of Riga on 12 October 1944 and his lovely ten-room villa in the Kaiserwald was completely destroyed. He'd been the last soldier to leave Riga that night, at midnight. Then all the bridges were blown up. He'd gone north, back to his troops at the Front. His house in Braunschweig had been bombed and lay in ruins. On 27 September his grandson Manfred was born. 'I am in excellent health, and my morale high, and full of energy. The enemy is on the attack, but it doesn't disturb us too much. One day the sun will shine again.'

'There wasn't much fighting going on that far north,' said Renate, who'd read it up.

Fried's letter went on as though he were just chatting to an old friend. 'My family have moved to West Prussia, and they're fine. My mother was seventy on 2 November.' Then it was back to reality. 'The war is hard, and every man has to do his duty to the highest degree.'

'Ugh!' said Renate and Edi.

'In the end we'll get a fair peace, which will protect our future...

I can't say more in writing... I think often in my loneliness of our happy times. Heartfelt greetings to you, little Renate and *Grossmutter* and for you a loving kiss. *Heil Hitler!* Your Fried.'

Finally, in 1984, Renate and Edi decided to go to Riga. They knew from Krausnick that Himmler had appointed Jeckeln as HSSPF of the whole of the Northern Russian region in late 1941, and that there had been a concentration camp there called Salaspils. Nothing else. They had to go with an organised group – it was the only way in those pre-Perestroika days – but they managed to slip away to try and find out more.

In the event they didn't find out much and it was an unhappy visit. What remained of Salaspils was just a wide windy space, a concrete wasteland, with an ugly neglected memorial in the middle and deep forest beyond, no buildings except a small museum with a few blurred photographs of the camp as it was during the war. Renate looked at them long and hard. Surely that was her *Vater* in the middle of the square? Perhaps not. Later they visited the old Jewish ghetto as once was, but when they asked people in the street about it no one seemed prepared to talk. There were plenty of anti-Semites left in Riga apparently. The only person who would was the Jewish lady who ran the museum. She agreed to meet them later, in a café. She was cautious about what she told them. Life as a Jew in Riga was still difficult. She told them German snipers had started shooting the Jews from the rooftops as they were marched in columns out of the ghetto to the pits in the Rumbula Forest. Renate wept. Edi sat silently by. The woman felt sorry for this troubled daughter of the monster Jeckeln. No, she couldn't tell her all of it, she thought. It would destroy her.

Eventually Renate made a decision. It was a huge step and the start of everything else. She'd heard about a therapy group at the University of Wuppertal for the children of Nazi war criminals. It was unbelievable, really, but the times were changing. The group included Martin Bormann, the eldest son of Martin Bormann, as well as Dirk, the son of the Gestapo Chief of Braunschweig, and Gudrun, the daughter of a euthanasia doctor. Like Renate, they were all trying to come to terms with what their fathers had done. Edi encouraged Renate to join. She herself was training to be a therapist by then, and she thought Renate needed a different kind of help to face her dark past.

News of this shocking group soon got out. One day in 1991 the telephone rang at Weissenburg Strasse. There was a woman on the line who said she was from BBC television in London. She spoke German. Would Renate consider meeting and talking about a possible documentary?

Edi remembered how long and hard she and Renate discussed it before agreeing to meet the woman – all the pros and cons of it. It depended on what this woman was like. Could she be trusted? Could she make a good film? But the deciding factor was the BBC. They knew that the BBC, with its international reputation and its research expertise and clout, would be able to find out what they hadn't managed to find for themselves. And there was this thing, typical of Renate: she wanted the truth. And she wanted it out in the open. She told Else what she was going to do. Once Renate made up her mind about something, she did it. The woman from the BBC was me, of course.

The first thing we, the BBC team, filmed was Renate and Edi bicycling through the rich farmland near Steinhöring, on their way to visit the *Lebensborn* home where Renate was born. They saw the birth register, the SS and V runes in the gates, the statue of the mother and child. Then came the main interview with Renate, at home in Cologne. She wasn't a bit nervous. She wanted to get on with it. She described how shattered she'd been when she came across the Krausnick and Fleming books, and finally knew who and what her father had really been. She read out from some of her *Vater*'s letters.

Her *Mutti* Else agreed to let her do it. She even agreed to be filmed with Renate, looking through the photo album. Then Renate asked her to do a short interview. And Else agreed to that too. Renate was surprised and didn't know why she did it, though Edi kept telling her Else had agreed for Renate's sake and nothing else. Else went to the hairdresser to get her hair done, then she put on her best blouse and sat, eyes bright, quite composed, facing the camera. '*Ganz wie Fried!*' she kept saying, describing how year by year as Renate grew she looked more and more like him. The very image of Fried. She smiled, pleased to say it, in public. And no, she didn't know exactly what Fried had done in the war. But she knew he was also a good man. And she'd loved him. She still did. And that's enough, she announced, standing up. The interview was over.

Then came Riga. Renate and Edi knew nothing of the detailed research which had been done by the BBC team, nor of my resarch trip to Riga, where I'd found a small archive of what had gone on there during the war, hidden in an abandoned church deep in the forest. The archivist was friendly and helpful. Yes, they had some photos of Jeckeln in Riga, even some newsreel film off-cuts. The short bits of film were spellbinding and shocking: out of his field caravan Jeckeln steps, a handsome, powerfully built man in SS uniform, smiling at the camera before settling down to work on his files at a table in the open air, smoking his cigar. And here he was again, talking with *SS-Kamaraden*, laughing, smoking his cigar. And here he was inspecting his troops. And he was, indeed, the very image of Renate, even the smile. Even the gestures.

Then: here was Jeckeln at his trial in 1945, gaunt, almost unrecognisable, but standing upright, like a soldier, listing in precise detail how many Jews he'd killed, thousands of them, by shooting them into pits five miles outside Riga, in Rumbula Forest. The Riga Jews – men, old and young, women, children, mostly naked – shot by the soldiers under Jeckeln's command, and local Latvians. Then came all the other Jews, transported in from all the other places. 'I have to take full responsibility for what happened in Ostland, with the SS, the SD, and the Gestapo. This greatly increases my guilt,' go the transcripts of his trial. 'My fate is in the hands of the High Court, so I ask only to pay attention to mitigating circumstances. I will accept my sentence in full repentance which I will consider as worthy punishment.'

All ten defendants were found guilty and sentenced to death. The pubic hanging took place on 3 February 1946, in the main square of Riga. Archive film shows each man seated in the back of separate lorries, on chairs, feet and arms bound with rope, heads shaved. Then they were strung up in a line on wooden gallows, and left there. Four thousand came to watch and cheer. It was shocking. There was no point showing Renate.

But we did go to Riga together. It was easier to visit now, after 1989, and we had a good local 'fixer' called Sylvia Limane. We filmed Renate in a café meeting Jeckeln's old Latvian driver, still living there, healthy and hearty. We settled them in a café, the two sitting opposite one another, each drinking a glass of tea. Yes, he knew her father well, he said. A fine man. 'You look just like him,' he said. 'No mistaking you are his daughter.' Renate sank down into her seat, head bowed, in tears. The driver said he didn't know what happened to Jeckeln once the Russians came. Who knows if he was telling the truth.

Next we went to the old Jewish community centre. It was once the thriving hub of the Riga Jewish community, numbering over 2,000. Now it held twelve. One of them was Izak Kleimanis – Isaac Kleinmann as was – but it was better to avoid a Jewish name in Riga, even in 1991. Isaac was a teenager during the war, and on the run. He survived because two sisters, Jehovah's Witnesses, took him in and hid him for the full two years of Jeckeln's reign of terror and beyond. He and Renate sat in the airy upper room of the community centre and talked. Edi sat nearby. 'It is not your fault,' said Isaac, a wonderful, impressive and compassionate man. 'The sins of the father are not visited on the children.' Renate wept. He told her what it had been like for the Jews once Jeckeln arrived in 1941 – all the hounding and shooting and exterminating – and the pure terror people had of this seemingly sanguine man who appeared quite unperturbed by his work. Renate wept again. Edi handed her a handkerchief and put her arm round her shoulder. 'It's not your fault,' repeated Isaac. 'You are very brave to come here.'

The next day we went to the pits in the Rumbula Forest. They were half-overgrown, hidden in the woods, but still there, still recognisable – long rectangular mounds, filled with the silent dead. Some had small photographs in metal frames stuck into the earth. There were poems. Some prayers. But mostly it was just mounds.

More of Renate's bravery was required for our last interview. Sylvia Limane had found one of the translators at Jeckeln's trial in 1946. We filmed in the old courtroom, a hollow derelict place, full of dark atmosphere. The proscenium stage where the Russian military tribunal had sat was still there, festooned with some faded red drapery. It was easily recognisable from the off-cuts of film I'd viewed in the archive in the woods. We could work out exactly where Jeckeln stood, haggard but upright, answering his accusers. There were a few Jewish witnesses who'd managed, like Isaac Kleinmann, to survive. And some others too, Communists and Socialists mostly. In the documentary we could cut straight from the former courtroom to the archive film of the uniformed members of the Russian military court, seated at a long table, lined up, taking notes, asking further questions, then pronouncing their verdict: the death sentence by public hanging.

'He admitted everything,' said K, the translator, a clever, sharp man, still angry.

Renate was so tense she didn't understand what he was saying.

'This was good?'

'No. He just wanted it on record. How many Jews he'd managed to exterminate. He remained a racial ideologist to the end. How many Jews from the Riga ghetto, how many who'd arrived in transports from Hungary and elsewhere. How they'd shot them, into the pits. A record.'

Renate was devastated. Should we stop filming now? No, she had a key question she wanted to ask K. And she wanted it on record.

'Was there . . .' she searched for the right words, trying not to plead. 'Was there any little good . . . anything . . . cultured in him?'

'Young lady,' said K. 'You must know, a man can be cultured and still do terrible things. But no, your *Vater* was not a cultured man. Nor a good man. I am sorry.'

Renate wept and had to sit down. We stopped filming. K took his leave.

Renate kept in close touch once we were back in London, in the BBC cutting room with the editor Alan Lygo, wanting to know how the film was progressing, step by step.

'I think you have some film of him, yes?'

'Yes.'

'Will you use it.'

'No.'

'I want to see it.'

'You will be horrified.'

'I want to see it. And I want my mother to see it. Then we'll decide.'

It's hard to imagine the scene: mother and daughter sitting side by side watching the VHS tape we prepared. I have no doubt Else did it for Renate. Or did she want to see her Fried, whatever he'd done? Within days the answer came back. Use it. The only caveat: don't transmit the documentary in Germany. Anywhere else, fine, but not Germany. For Else's sake.

I can't pretend I wasn't pleased. The filmmaker in me knew what a difference it would make to the documetary, titled *A Child for Hitler*. We cut straight from a headshot of Jeckeln to a close-up of Renate. Two peas in a pod. In appearance, but absolutely nothing else. But no, we didn't film Renate and her *Mutti* watching it.

Renate and Edi came over to stay with us in London for the transmission. We watched it together in our sitting room, along with our teenage children. Renate wept, head in hands. Edi too. Us too. The next day we went sightseeing round London. Hyde Park. Buckingham Palace. Piccadilly. To Renate's amazement, and mine for that matter, many people came up to her in the street. 'We saw you on the BBC last night,' they said. 'Well done, well done! You're a brave woman!'

As it happens, Renate was only halfway through her journey. The dark past was gradually receding. The future beckoned. But that's for later.

CHAPTER SIX

JOE TELLS HIS STORY

New York in the 1950s was one hell of a place, teeming with life and post-war optimism, teeming with immigrants, mostly from war-torn Europe, mostly Jews.

The Albek family arrived on 21 March 1949 on one of those great ocean liners, the SS *Ernie Pyle*. The previous year President Harry Truman had signed a law making it possible for Jewish Holocaust survivors to come to America, echoing the foundation of Israel as a nation which happened that same year. It had not been easy for Truman. Congress was against. So were the majority of American people. But in his 1948 State of the Union address he held firm, making no compromises on his liberal programme for health insurance, housing, education and a minimum wage, and calling for immediate legislation on immigration 'so that this nation may do its share in caring for homeless and suffering refugees of all faiths. I believe the admission of these people will add to the strength and energy of the nation.'

But before being admitted, immigrants had to have the necessary documents. The Albeks were helped by relatives already settled in America, especially their uncle Simon Goldfeld, to whom they'd written in 1939 hoping to get out of Poland. He hadn't managed it then, but now he did his best, providing the extra information to prove they were eligible, and helping out in general once they arrived. Unfortunately David Orlanski, Yadzia's fiancé, was not eligible because he'd been an officer in the A.K. Polish Home Army, considered a foreign army by America even though they'd fought the Germans. Poland was Communist now, which apparently changed everything. His friend Sevek Dutzenman was likewise ineligible because he'd served in the Russian Army. So both men decided to go to Australia instead. Yadzia, torn, finally decided to go to Australia with her fiancé. The sisters' parting on Hamburg docks, with the great ocean liner rising high above them, was one of the most painful Lonia ever experienced, following all those other terrible partings. They'd managed against the odds to survive the Warsaw ghetto, Poniatowa concentration camp, the Nazis, the Russians, the sewers of Warsaw, the trek over the mountains of Czechoslovakia in the deep snow with Lonia pregnant, the Displaced Persons camp in Germany. And now this! It was another case of small lives caught up in big historical events. The war was over. America was heady with victory and had a thriving post-war economy. But the next war was already on the horizon: the Cold War, between democratic, capitalist America and Communist Russia. By 1948 Truman was overseeing the Berlin Airlift, saving as much of Germany from Communism as he could.

Joseph was three by the time they arrived in America. He didn't remember that parting on the Hamburg dockside and he hardly remembered the sea journey, but he vaguely recalled the famous Statue of Liberty looming out of the mist, beacon of freedom held high. Or did he just think he remembered it, so often did his parents Mendel and Lonia talk about it, eyes shining, but with darkness and sorrow always close behind.

Whether he remembered it or not, there was uncle Simon Goldfeld waiting for them, in suit and tie and Homburg hat, waving a newspaper, 'Over here! Over here!', once they got through the queues and questions and document-checking on Ellis Island. 'Was your journey fine? Were you seasick? How's the young man?', patting Joe on the head. Lonia was crying, Mendel was shaking his hand again and again, Joe was looking up from among their legs, confused by all the emotion. 'Come, come!' said Uncle Simon, leading the way to the ferry, helping Mendel, Lonia and Joe with their cases and their bundles. And then there they were crossing New York Harbor, leaning over the rail of the ferry, gazing in wonderment at the Manhattan skyline – their new life, their golden future. Twenty-five minutes is all it took. And now here they were, squashed together in a bus in the teeming traffic, cars bigger than anything they'd ever seen, Chryslers, Fords, Buicks, Packards, yellow cabs, motorbikes and trucks either side honking their horns, the pavements crammed with people, the stores crammed with food. And the billboards, and the flashing neon signs, and noise and the dirt. And those skyscrapers. 'See! Look!' said Uncle Simon in a mixture of Polish and American and Yiddish, pointing this way and that out of the grimy bus window.

Lonia couldn't take it in, she told me years later, sitting in her Boston apartment, looking back at it all. Really she couldn't. Nine years of hell, and now this.

They were making for a district called Brooklyn, over the great Brooklyn Suspension Bridge, all eight lanes of it, the massive steel girders rising high above. There was a two-bedroom apartment available in a building at 1780 West 7th Street apparently, which was a small miracle given the housing shortage. It belonged to Mr Lemberger, the husband of another Goldfeld aunt. One of Lonia's cousins, Phyllis Schneider, also lived there, along with her husband Jack, a big, burly, cheerful guy. Phyllis was only eighteen, a good twelve years younger than Lonia, but they instantly became the closest of friends, with Phyllis showing Lonia the ropes, walking her around the district holding Joe by the hand – the grocery stores and bakeries, the haberdashers, the newsagents, the dress shops, the tailors, the toy shop, the Italian ice-cream parlour, the picture house on the corner, the subway and bus stations, the local park with its swings and slides, and introducing her to their neighbours, most of whom were immigrants like Lonia, some recent, some not. Their building was right next to the subway, so you could hear it screeching all day and all night long. But the rooms, ranged in a line down a long dark corridor like a railroad, which is what they were called, were spacious, with high ceilings in the old style and large windows letting in the spring sun. And polished wooden floors. And soon enough it felt like home. Because it felt safe.

Actually, they weren't Mendel and Lonia any more. They were Milton and Lily. And Joseph, once upon a time, long ago, Heinele, was Joey. And they weren't Albek any more either. They were Albeck – a world of a difference in one letter of the alphabet. The Albecks were Americans now.

Phyllis taught Lily English. She didn't need to teach Milton – he'd always had a gift for languages, speaking three already, and soon he was talking like an American, albeit with an accent, but he lost even that with time. Lily was different. She never lost her accent. She never became fully American either. Perhaps it was psychological: deep down she couldn't give up who she really was. It showed in many small ways, including the way she shopped, going to the grocery store every morning to buy whatever was 'fresh'.

No tins for Lily.

As for clothes, when she bought an outfit for a special occasion it was always elegant, in a quiet way. Not for Lily the flashy 1950s frocks with their low necklines and wide skirts worn by some of the immigrants heady with their new money and new freedoms, parading their chunky jewellery and winter furs. When Lily was Lonia Goldfeld, in Warsaw before the war, she wore the most expensive clothes, made by her dressmaker – beautifully cut, beautifully sewn, never showy. So now she did the same, only on a smaller scale. It went with an inbred superiority – a certain manner and tone, which was resented by some of the other immigrants who'd been less well-off back in Poland. Back in the old days. '*Who does she think she is!*' they'd say, watching her going about the district in her way. And then what did she do? She went and ordered a telephone!

The worst were the immigrants who'd arrived in America earlier, before the Holocaust. These included some of the more distant Goldfeld relations from back in the 1920s, escaping the mounting anti-Semitism in Russia or Poland or Germany, take your pick. They didn't understand what people like Lily and Milton had gone through. You couldn't really blame them. Who could possibly understand? In fact, many of them resented these new arrivals with their broken English and heavy accents and their strange dress and manners, some holding on to the old religious ways, crowding them out, giving them a bad name. They didn't want to associate with them. So Lily and Milton stuck to their close family and a small group of friends, most of them survivors of the Holocaust like themselves. As for Joey, it was uncle Simon Goldfeld and his wife Greta who stepped in. They lived close by in Brooklyn, in another of those large old apartment buildings, just a few streets from the Albecks. They came often for family meals round the mahogany table, nicely laid up by Lily with a white tablecloth and flowers. Equally Lily might drop Joey off at their apartment, though he was soon old enough to get there by himself. The Goldfelds hadn't had any children of their own, and now they had this: a beautiful and clever boy – a grandson more or less. The three of them might stay in the apartment, playing board games or cards and eating cookies. Or they might go out to Prospect Amusement Park with its carousels and swings and ice cream and candy floss, 'You choose Joey!' Or they might even cross the great Brooklyn Bridge to Manhattan. Either way, Joey was happy as could be in their company.

Except that darkness never lay far beneath the surface.

It might happen during one of those family meals. They'd all be sitting round the table, enjoying Lily's chicken soup and *kneidlach* matzah balls, when Lily would stop, ladle midway, eyes filled with tears, suddenly overcome with the loss of all those people – her mother, her father, her brothers, Mendel's father and sisters, aunts, cousins, school friends, neighbours – who should have been sitting there round the table with them but weren't. She just couldn't bear it. Milton felt the same, and didn't even dare to remember his last parting from his own father at the *Umschlagplatz* in April 1943. But he was better at putting it to one side. Better at embracing Uncle Sam. Better at life in general, perhaps. Lily was half-dead somewhere deep inside. It rarely showed, because she was a whirlwind of activity and helping others out. But it was always there, dark under the golden surface.

Actually it could happen any time, that sudden abyss, that feeling of empty chairs round the family table. And Joey, growing up fast into an all-American boy, calling his parents Mom and Pop and speaking only English, never Polish, took in that dark past without even knowing he was doing it. 'Silently, invisibly,' as the poet William Blake put it.

One practical thing: Milton had to get a job and earn some money to keep the family going. But what to do? Finally he found work in one of the handbag factories in Manhattan through someone who'd worked for the Goldfeld factory in Warsaw, back in the old days. He was put on the counter which attached the golden metal clasps to the leather bags. Only trouble was: he'd never worked in a handbag factory and he had no idea how to attach the clasp. So he was fired. So he went to the next handbag factory. So he got fired again. By the eighth factory he'd got the hang of it. It was piecework, and he was paid ten cents a bag. And he did that for the rest of his working life. Years later, Joe wrote a poem about it: about the humiliation of this handsome, clever man, his father, having to work in a lowly job in a handbag factory for his entire working life, crossing that Brooklyn Bridge early every morning and back again every night, tired out. He titled the poem 'Polish Jew', and the first lines went:

> Humiliation
> is what my father felt
> Rage, his and mine, commingled.

But in truth it was Joe's own humiliation and rage he was writing about more than his father's – having to watch the man he loved and admired lowered in this way, day by day, year by year. Milton himself thought it was just a job, and work was an honourable thing. He'd come from a happy background in small-town Poland, gone through unimaginable hell during the war, and now here he was, safe and secure in his new life, with his wife and his son and a home and a job. In America. No, Milton was fine enough about it. But Joe wasn't.

America in the late 1940s was Democrat Harry Truman's America. He'd inherited the presidency when Franklin Roosevelt died in April 1945, but he gained it in his own right in the 1948 election, against all expectations. Everyone thought the Republican Thomas Dewey was bound to win. Everyone but Truman himself. Truman took to the road that hot July, electioneering for the best part of two months to every corner of the land, reaching out to large and small-town America – the ordinary, decent people of America who were ordinary and decent in the same way he was. He did most of his travelling in *Ferdinand Magellan*, the presidential train, with its galley and pantry, servants' quarters and panelled dining/conference room at the front, then four state rooms including the Presidential Suite with its own bathroom in the middle, and, further back, the offices and sleepers for the presidential staff and security and the press, plus a communications carriage with telephones which could be hooked up trackside, and a dynamo carriage to power the air conditioning and electricity. Lastly there was an Observation Lounge, and, right at the rear of the train, a platform from which Truman gave impromptu speeches along the way, speaking off the cuff and from the heart, with no notes.

Truman was a neat, dapper man from a modest background, conventional to look at but far from conventional in his beliefs and his language. A liberal Democrat by conviction, he talked to the people of America in a way they liked and understood, full of energy and plain speaking and humour, in his shirtsleeves, perspiring in the summer heat. 'The Democratic Party represents the people,' he'd say, no two speeches the same. 'It puts human rights and human welfare first.' He happily attacked the opposition: 'These Republican gluttons of privilege are cold men. They are cunning men. They want a return of the Wall Street economic dictatorship.' His listeners vividly remembered the 1929 Wall Street Crash and the terrible after-effects. 'I'm not asking you to vote for me. Vote for yourselves!' he'd say. 'Most Republicans are fine people. But there's a big distinction between the individual Republican voter and the policies of the Republican Party. They have a hard time hearing what the ordinary people of the country are saying. They have no trouble at all hearing what Wall Street is saying.'

The crowds grew and grew. They clapped and cheered. They knew he meant every word he said, and this at a time of great danger. Because Truman had recently given the go-ahead for the Berlin Airlift to counter the Communist threat in Europe, in the sure knowledge that it might provoke a further war. He'd discussed it fully with his advisors, as was his way, then made his decision. After which he never wavered. 'I believe that if we ourselves try to live as we should, and if we continue to work for peace in this world, eventually we will get peace, because that is the only way we can survive with the modern inventions under which we live. We have got to harness these inventions for the welfare of man, instead of his destruction. That is what I am interested in. That is what I am working for. That is much more important than whether or not I am President of the United States.'

And it worked – both the Berlin Airlift and the election, which he won hands down. Taking everyone by surprise, except himself.

Joey was a bright kid – both his parents knew that and were proud of it. But Lily was the ambitious one. She made sure that

Joey skipped kindergarten and was put straight into first grade in 1951, aged five. He had no real memories of school during those early years, he said, all his memories were of home life. Of Pop putting him to bed at night, tossing him in the air and on to the bed with Joey shouting 'Again! Again!' Of Mom in the kitchen baking his favourite cookies. Of Mom and Phyllis laughing together about some story they'd heard, or, once, of Mom consoling Phyllis who was crying because her Jack had been called up to serve in the Korean War. And of his outings with Uncle Simon and Aunt Greta. And of playing with his friend Ricky Lacerra, an Italian immigrant who lived a block away. And of that wonderful day when their first television set arrived, after which Joe got up every Saturday morning at six to watch his favourite programme, *The Modern Farmer*, with its enticing scenes of country life, followed by *Howdy Doody* with Buffalo Bob Smith and Clarabell and Chief Thunderthud.

But then, in 1953, came the move to Manhattan. Why did they have to move? Why oh why did Joey have to leave his neighbourhood and the friends he loved, not to mention his Uncle Simon and Aunt Greta? And Phyllis? Simple: Lily was pregnant, and they needed a bigger apartment. And Milton was earning enough at the handbag factory now to afford it. Which meant he wouldn't have to commute from Brooklyn any more. So the Albeck family moved to a larger railroad apartment on 209 West 107th Street in the Upper West Side – a mixed sort of neighbourhood, mostly Irish and Jewish with some Japanese-Americans and a few Black people. The Puerto Ricans were further south. Harlem was further north. But uptown was Riverside, so the district looked both ways, poor and rich, rich and poor.

The apartment building itself was typical: five-storeyed, with steps leading from the sidewalk to a small area by the entrance where people might sit out during the hot summers if they weren't sitting on the rusty iron fire steps round the back. Inside there were landings on each floor, with an apartment left and right. The Albecks' apartment was on the first floor, to the left. There was no elevator. Thank God Lily didn't have to traipse all the way up five flights with her grocery shopping like some of the other moms. The apartment had the usual long railroad hallway with rooms leading off. The first room was large, with windows facing the street. That was the living room. All the other rooms had windows to the side facing the Church of the Ascension next door. Then there was a bathroom, and a room for the baby. And a separate room where they put the television. Joe had a room to himself. The kitchen was the last room at the far end of the hallway, with a pantry facing the back of the building on 108th Street. All in all, a great improvement on the Brooklyn apartment thought Lily. But not Joey.

Joey was enrolled in his new school, PS 165, on 109th Street between Broadway and Amsterdam Avenue. It teemed with traffic and dirt and noise – apartment blocks and garages and all-night stores and fenced-in basketball courts, and all the rest of it. And he was devastated. As far as the seven-year-old was concerned, Manhattan was as far from Brooklyn as the moon.

Years later Joe conceded that what really bothered him was the arrival of his baby brother, Robert. The usurper. The cuckoo in the nest. All that talcum powder and smelly nappies and gurgling and oohing and aahing and 'Sssh don't wake the baby!' All that putting baby to bed, when it used to be him. All that love. Because Robert was born at a time when Lily and Milton were happy and settled – at least as much as they would ever be – not in a Displaced Persons camp, which is where they were, frightened and traumatised, when Joe was born. No, they were in a new apartment, light and airy. In New York! They never knew how Joe was feeling – his waves of jealousy and anger – for the simple reason that he never told them.

Joey was always a good boy, and clever. So he did well at his new school, and showed not a trace of his inner feelings at home. Except for once. One day his feelings were so overwhelming, he thought: *I'll show them!* He was nine years old. That evening, lying in bed, he could hear his parents talking in the kitchen – not the words, only their murmured voices. They sounded just fine. *I'll show them! Then they'll be sorry!* He crept out of his bedroom and down the hallway to the bathroom, opened the medicine cabinet and took out a small brown glass bottle. 'Iodine', the label read. 'Poison!' It had a red rubber stopper. He opened it. Swallowed the lot in one gulp. Wiped a brown drop of iodine off the bottle, neatly, so as not to stain the sink, because he was still a good boy. Lay down on the cold tiles of the bathroom floor and waited. How would death come? Would he faint? Would he have stomach ache? Would he just fall asleep? He waited and waited. Nothing happened. He could still hear his parents talking. Why hadn't they come to rescue him? Finally he got up and went into the kitchen and told them what he'd done. They were utterly perplexed. Why had their beautiful son done this? They took him to the hospital, where the doctors pumped him out. Then they all went back home again.

The 1950s were a long way from recognising that the terror and trauma experienced by survivors of the Holocaust would never really go away, just be buried under the appearance of normal, everyday life, be it in New York, Melbourne or London. Even further away was the recognition that in avoiding conversations about the subject with their children, in order to protect them, they passed it on to them without even knowing. Milton and Lily were perplexed by Joey's suicide attempt because he was always such a good, happy, clever boy. Their golden boy. Whatever got into him? Perhaps he was just jealous of the new baby. It never crossed their minds that it came from their own dark pasts. Or if it did, they never said.

Whatever the reason, Joey's suicide attempt was something of a turning point for him, and he never did it again. And from now on he was Joe, not Joey. He picked up his life in Manhattan with renewed enthusiasm and, perhaps inevitably, a renewed determination to be good. And American. He was doing it for his parents' sake, though he didn't know it. All his life he felt he had to be good for their sake. Make it up to them, though he hardly knew what for. They all kept silent, each for the other.

In 1955 the Albecks got American citizenship. So that was that. No more dark past. Just the golden future.

Yes, the 1950s were the good times in America. Dwight D. Eisenhower, known by everyone as Ike, the national hero of the Second World War, led the Republicans to victory in 1952 and again in 1956. He won because the people liked him and trusted him, a decent man, a religious man, acting for the good of the country not just the good of his own party. He ended the Korean War and strongly supported NATO. He presided over a decade of capitalist prosperity and economic expansion. His new Interstate Highways opened up the countryside to people fed up with the noise and grime of the cities. They moved in their millions to newly built spic-and-span suburbs with their rows of neat houses and front and back yards and stay-at-home moms baking cakes in their pretty 1950s aprons or doing the housework with the latest domestic appliances, as advertised on the new television set. Vacuum cleaners, fridges, a car with tailfins parked in the driveway for Pop to drive to work every morning and return at six every evening. At weekends there was baseball and a Saturday-night hop in the local church hall. There was church on Sundays. There was Hollywood and rock'n'roll, with Elvis shaking his hips, and the ice-cream parlour or the milk bar down the road where the teenagers could meet and horse about.

For Lily it was heaven. Heaven after hell. She was more than happy to be the stay-at-home mom. Milton had a good job now, the boys were doing fine, the country was at peace. Never mind the dark underbelly, the McCarthy era, witch-hunting suspected Commies, who were hiding everywhere apparently, in the schools and universities, in Hollywood, in the street where you lived. Lily wasn't bothered really. Just look at the state of Poland now, under the Communists. No, the US of A was just fine for Lily and Milton. Safe.

Joey soon made new friends in his neighbourhood, a motley crew of Irish, Italian, Jewish – tough boys, most of them, second-generation immigrants. In the hot summers they played stickball in the street, hitting a 'spaldeen' rubber ball between the cars parked by the sidewalk, then racing round the makeshift bases. Joey was smaller than the others but he was a fast runner, and, what's more, he was small enough to retrieve the spaldeens when they landed in the grilles of the basements, which was often. So that's what they did, day after day, during those long hot summer vacations. In the winters they fought it out with snowballs instead, singly or in teams, scooping the snow off the street and the roofs of parked cars, because by the mid-1950s almost everyone in America had a car, taking a handful of snow, packing it hard, then whacking it at someone, shouting: 'Got you! You're out!' Real street fights were rare, but if Joey was ever caught up in one he ran fast. As a last resort he could fight it out, because he was tougher than he looked.

It was the same at school. He made new friends. He was good at sport. He did very well academically. By the time he was in third grade, aged nine, he was walking to the public library on 100th Street every Friday after school and taking out the six books allowed and returning them the following Friday to take out another six. One of his favourites was J. B. Bury's *History of Ancient Greece*, all 900 pages of it. At the end of his fourth-grade year in 1955 his teacher Mrs Marton recommended him for the IGC, the class for Intellectually Gifted Children. Their classroom was the school library and the pupils were allowed to study there in their free time too. Joey found himself a nice perch on an empty shelf in the store cupboard and lay there, stretched out, reading to his heart's content. By the time he graduated at the end of sixth grade he'd read pretty much everything the library had to offer. He was made class president and was voted best athlete. His favourite athlete was Gil Hodges. His favourite sport: football. His favourite book: *The Swiss Family Robinson*. His favourite song: 'The Yellow Rose of Texas' – this all written in his graduation autograph book signed by his classmates before they moved on to their senior schools. 'Take a local, take an express, don't get off till you reach success!' wrote Sally Süskind. 'I expect to see you on a list of Phi Beta Kappa,' wrote Mrs Rosenthal, one of the teachers. As it duly turned out.

'A scout is trustworthy, loyal, helpful, friendly, courteous, kind, obedient, cheerful, thrifty, brave, clean and reverent,' intoned Joe along with all his other Junior High School friends joining Boy Scout Troop 560. They went on weekend camping trips and hikes and a whole week's camping during the summer vacation, getting away from the noise and dirt and the general mayhem of Manhattan. Then, in 1959, when he was thirteen, it was on to a more serious matter: his Bar Mitzvah at the local synagogue. Being a good boy, Joe was word-perfect reading his section of the Torah in Hebrew, though he was less perfect at the celebratory meal afterwards when he was meant to give a speech about the meaning of Judaism in his life. He refused. He was sitting next to his best buddy Teddy, another child of Holocaust survivors, and he flatly refused. His parents and guests

were astonished, especially since his father had grown up Orthodox and was still a practising Jew. Whatever got into him? Perhaps he felt it was hypocritical, seeing as he wasn't a true believer. Or perhaps it was the first signs of independence. But Joe wouldn't budge.

'I'm going to apply for reparation from Germany for my properties,' Lily announced one day to Milton. They were having breakfast at the Formica table in the kitchen, and she said it in Polish. Joe was instantly alert.

Milton said, 'That's a bad idea. Pointless. You'll just get distressed.'

'Well, I'm going to do it anyway,' she announced, quite the old Lonia of Warsaw days who knew she was right.

'Think about it, Lonia, before you do anything,' said Milton before he got up and went off to work.

Joe remembered the scene vividly over thirty years later, because although he couldn't understand the words he understood the essential meaning, the significance. It was something about the past again, but this time it had a confidence about it, a determination, which was quite different to the usual sadness and oppression.

The point is: Lily had been seeing a psychiatrist to help with her nightmares. It didn't help. Her psychiatrist had no idea about the lasting effect of the Holocaust on survivors. He didn't believe in all that stuff. Pills were what he believed in, which was how it was back then in the good ol' USA, 1950s-style. It was years before anyone gave serious thought to the possibility of post-traumatic symptoms. Lily's psychiatrist reckoned she was simply suffering from the loss of all the wealth and position and servants she'd had back in Poland. Before the war. And that she hated being poor, and her lowered status. Lily was left high and dry, just like all those other Holocaust survivors struggling with their new lives.

So she left the psychiatrist and put her efforts into getting that reparation instead. Against Milton's vehement opposition, she ploughed ahead. Finally she was awarded a small sum. 'Blood money', she called it. It didn't make the nightmares go away.

By 1960 Joe had moved up to Stuyvesant High School. You had to pass a city-wide entrance exam to get in, and of course he passed with flying colours. Unusually for an academic school, Stuyvesant insisted that their pupils, all male, did mechanical drawing and woodwork too. Joe loved it. Most of the teachers were excellent, and he responded in kind. Though not in French. '*Vous parlez le Français comme une vache Espagnole*,' you speak French like a Spanish cow, Mrs McGillicuddy told him, though being Irish her own pronunciation wasn't that great either. Dr Kelly was Joe's home room teacher. He was close to retirement and everyone could see why. 'Albeck, Baumbach, Berger, Bernstein, Brown,' he shouted every morning at roll call. 'Get out! You're no damn good!'

In 1960 the Albecks moved back to Brooklyn, to a row house not far from the subway station, which was just as well seeing as Joe went on attending Stuyvesant High School in Manhattan which meant an hour's commute each way. He continued to excel there, including at sports. Baseball was his best game and he played shortstop. His batting average was high and he could still run like the wind. Not long after Joe joined the Baseball League his father, always sporty himself, volunteered to be an umpire for the weekend games. So there they were, father and son, all kitted out, cheered on by the locals and, on big match days, by the band and the girl cheerleaders in their short skirts and high boots and their pom-poms. All-American, they were, Albeck father and son.

But money was still short, so Joe started to take odd jobs to see him through school and, later, college. His parents told him he didn't need to do it, they could manage. But Joe wanted to do it. Do his bit. The most lucrative job was as a hat and coat check-person in the evenings and weekends at various Jewish venues in Brooklyn – Bar Mitzvahs, weddings, birthdays – when the tips were often better than the pay. It was strange: Joe just couldn't get over the feeling that he had to contribute to the household budget, make it up to his parents for all the unnamed suffering they'd gone through in the dark past.

'Who was Henek, Mom?'

They were sitting in the kitchen over a cup of coffee, Joe and Lily. Lily was taken aback by the question, out of the blue as it seemed to come, though Joe had in fact been thinking about it for some time. Henek was a name that floated into the conversation from time to time, always loaded with darkness. And now Joe reached the age, perhaps sixteen or so, when he wanted to penetrate some of that darkness.

'Henek?' Lily spoke the name as though it were a sacred name, from a far-distant land.

Joe waited. It was another of those scenes he could remember like yesterday thirty years later, telling me about it.

'He was a little cousin,' said Lily. She pronounced 'was' as 'vas' and 'little' as 'liddle'.

Joe waited on.

'A liddle orphan.'

There was that awful, laden silence again.

'Henek...' Lily already had tears in her eyes. 'He came to live with us when his parents were killed. In Warsaw. The Nazis, you know?'

'What happened to him?'

'He was only eight...'

Lily wasn't safe in her Brooklyn kitchen now. She was back in the ghetto.

'He lived with us and I looked after him. Henek. But things got worse, you know? Very bad. So we decided: safest place for him was Jewish orphanage. So many shootings, so many deportations. Best place for Henek was with Janusz Korczak. You know about Janusz Korczak?'

'No.'

'A saint. A holy saint, God rest his soul...'

More silence.

'He ran an orphanage in Warsaw, already before the war. Before the ghetto. He could have stayed on the other side of the wall, you know, but he came in to the ghetto to run the Jewish orphanage. He came.' Lily shook her head at the memory. 'You would not believe it Joe. He looked after those kids, those orphans, fed them, taught them school, even put on shows, liddle plays, you know...'

'Incredible,' said Joe.

Silence. Lily was lost again.

'So what happened to him?'

'Henek?

'Both...'

'They were killed,' she said, matter-of-fact. 'All.'

'How many?'

'Two hundred maybe. We watched them walk along the street, you know? To the *Umschlagplatz*. You know the *Umschlagplatz*, don't you Joe?'

'Yes.'

'Janusz Korczak walked ahead. No hat. Leather belt. Boots. Holding a liddle one by the hand. Some nurses too. And the children... Henek. I loved that boy...' Lily shook her head. 'The children holding hands, singing. They thought they were going on a vacation. They had clean clothes. How did Korczak manage that? A knapsack. A toy. Each child had a toy or a book.'

She started to cry, wringing her handkerchief.

Joe didn't know what to do.

'Then it was us, you know?'

'Yes, I know,' said Joe. He was speechless. Trying to hold off the darkness.

In September 1962 Joe joined fifty other Stuyvesant graduates to start Freshman Week at Columbia University. He exchanged his room at home for a students' dorm, and he didn't tell a soul about the darkness, not even Steve O'Neill, his room-mate, who came from Indiana. They shared that tiny room with bunk beds and a small desk each for the first two years of college, but in all that time Joe never told Steve about his parents and the Holocaust – not even after one of Lily and Milton's regular visits, laden with enough food to last for weeks. Lily had quite an obsession with food, for obvious reasons. No, Joe never told, and Steve never asked. Steve wouldn't have a clue anyway, thought Joe. But the truth is, Joe was hiding it – from himself as well as from others. It made him introverted, and communication with other students difficult. Years later he came to understand it. But for the time being he was looking to the future, not the past. That's all.

Serious and clever as he was, he started out studying Chemistry. It was something to do with the idea that you needed to know about things – how the world worked, what made it tick. What lay beneath the surface. He enjoyed the lectures and the experiments, which were demonstrated in the large auditorium. And he enjoyed the other students, who were a lively bunch, up to all sorts of pranks while the professor's back was turned writing something or other on the blackboard with his chalk. Years later Joe still laughed, telling me about Everett Bovard, the ace joker, taking a white apron out of a bag and pinning it round the neck of the student in front, then using a comb and some scissors and calmly proceeding to cut the guy's hair, like they were in a barber's shop. When the professor turned round he watched them for a while, then continued with the lecture. Good sport. Once done, the recipient got up and left the auditorium. At which point another student took his place. And so on, till the end of the lecture.

Yes, it was good fun. But, really, Chemistry wasn't for Joe. Soon enough he'd transferred to the pre-Med courses, taking Oriental Studies on the side and learning about the religions and history of India and China and Japan. Preparing to be a medical student came naturally to him. He would make the world a better place. Heal the sick and wounded.

For all four years at Columbia Joe had an in-college job – fifteen hours a week helping with administration in the Radiation Lab in the Pupin Physics building. It paid well and had the added advantage of keeping him up to date with the latest technology, especially the new Xerox machines which made copying texts so much easier. He joined the soccer team, co-captained the debating team and joined the Columbia College Citizenship Council, which concerned itself with doing good works in the poor communities of the district – Morningside Heights, Harlem and East Harlem. Sometimes he'd bump into former Junior High School classmates, Puerto Ricans and Black Americans. A guy might be working in a local store stacking shelves, a girl might be pregnant or pushing a baby carriage, already a mother at eighteen. He noted that his white classmates were all in college somewhere or other, but not the Puerto Rican or Black people. So much for the American Dream, thought Joe. He joined the committee of the Council, which sent volunteers into city schools. If there was one thing which might make a difference it was education, he reckoned. Though Joe soon noticed that what the pupils lacked in education they made up for in vibrant vitality, sparking with energy and loud humour and street know-how. It was your regular *West Side Story*. Full of confidence, they were, in their own way. But still, they needed education, and Joe was there to offer it.

Another reason for joining that committee was girls. Columbia was all-male, as were most Ivy League colleges in the early 1960s. America might be two years into the Kennedy administration with its liberal agenda, but the conservative Eisenhower 1950s still ruled. Ed Murrow and Walter Cronkite still dominated news reporting, *The Lone Ranger* and *I Love Lucy* were still the most popular TV shows, Hollywood still preferred their movie stars innocent and wholesome, like girl-next-door Doris Day and hunky Rock Hudson. Women were still supposed to be mothers and housewives. Elvis Presley was the only rebel in town. No wonder all the girls fainted when he came on stage with his quiff and his curled lip and his shaking hips and

'Jailhouse Rock'. But luckily the all-girls Barnard College was just across the street from Columbia. And they were keen to volunteer for the Citizen Council. Heady stuff for shy Joe, to be working alongside a nice, clever girl who was attractive to boot. Columbia boys were not allowed beyond the Barnard dormitory entrance doors in those old-fashioned days, but Barnard girls, for some odd reason, were allowed into Columbia dorms, at least during daylight hours, with the proviso 'a book in the door, and a foot on the floor'. Unsurprisingly, the book most often used was a book of matches.

Joe still found it hard to communicate easily with anyone, being weighed down with his parents' darkness, but he found it even harder with girls. Which was puzzling for the girls, because he was very good-looking. Nice too. And clever. It didn't make sense. But dating was the thing then, always accompanied by plenty of cigarettes – rooms, subways, restaurants, cinemas all filled with smoke. Joe first dated a nice Jewish girl from Brooklyn College. She lived in the Bronx, which was a three-hour trip by bus and subway, but Joe reckoned it was worth it – helped along by the fact that Pop had a car now, and being a loving father he sometimes let Joe borrow it. Next there was a girl from Barnard. She was a volunteer on the Citizens Council, clever and lively with beautiful red hair, and perhaps Joe was properly in love for the first time. They were soon 'going steady', seen as 'a couple' by the other students. It lasted a whole two years, right up to graduation. And then, out of the blue, Joe broke it off. Years later he still wondered why he did it. At the time he told himself they were too young to get married, which was certainly true. But later he realised it was more not to hurt his parents. Lily said the girl was 'too pushy', which wasn't true. Milton kept mum. Joe was torn in two, agonised by it, but held firm.

Where was Joe when President Kennedy was assassinated by a sniper, or was it two, or even three, waiting by a window on the sixth floor of a book depository warehouse, driving through Dallas, Texas in an open-topped car sitting beside his wife Jackie in her pink pill-box hat, waving with that charismatic smile of his at the thronging crowds, his security detail in the front seats keeping a sharp eye out for trouble and surrounded by outriders on their motorbikes? Where was Joe that 22 November 1963? In point of fact Joe was just going up the wide stairs at Columbia, off to another class. He could probably tell you the exact step he was on when he first heard.

Everyone in the Western world could probably tell you exactly where they were at that moment. The question 'Where were you when you heard Kennedy had been shot?' echoed through the years. When Joe looked down the stairwell to the hall below all he could see was a crowd of stunned faces, trying to take it in.

So Vice-President Lyndon B. Johnson did the same thing Harry Truman had done when President Roosevelt died: he got sworn in unelected as President of the United States of America, this time on *Air Force One*, the presidential plane, in Dallas, two hours and eight minutes after the assassination, with Jackie by his side. And, just like Truman, LBJ was elected in his own right later, in a landslide victory. He'd already got going on his agenda by then. His 'Let Us Continue' speech of 27 November laid it out: the Democrats would press on with the Bill of Civil Rights, which was the Bill nearest Kennedy's heart. Johnson went on to expand Medicare, support education and welfare, fight poverty with the War on Poverty campaign and continue Kennedy's Apollo space mission, as well as Kennedy's fight against Communism during the Cold War. Later there were race riots and demonstrations against the Vietnam War, but for the time being America under LBJ, helped by a strong economy, progressed and thrived.

As did Joe. Outwardly at least. In 1965 LBJ's War on Poverty Act had just passed Congress. One of Joe's History professors at Columbia, David Shenton, joined the campaign. Now he needed students to draft a proposal for a scheme to enable bright but underachieving high school pupils to come to Columbia for a summer school catch-up.

It was called Project Double Discovery and it was awarded a federal grant of $167, 000 – over a million in today's money. The pupils were selected by the New York City school system. Shenton turned to the Citizens Council for volunteers, and of course Joe was in there fast, up and running. In July 165 students, girls as well as boys, came to stay in the dorms at Columbia for the summer along with forty of their high school teachers, with one student counsellor living in the dorms for every four pupils. They in turn were overseen by a supervisor. Joe was one of the supervisors. The mornings were spent in class, afternoons and weekends on field trips in and around New York and its cultural institutions. It was exhilarating. And exhilarating for Joe to be working with other young idealistic volunteers, including girls. The project still runs today. Over the years 90 per cent of the selected pupils managed to move on to a college education. An outstanding success, and Joe had been there at the very start.

By then he'd moved out of the dorm and into a two-bed apartment on Amsterdam Avenue and 119th Street. So much better for his social life. So much better for giving parties. So much better for lightening up and looking to the golden future, less the dark past. He was helped in this by his college flatmate Mike. Mike had crazy ideas. One night he took it into his head to go and steal a sign he liked the look of. It said 'Do Not Climb Cliff'. It was posted high on the cliff on the Jersey side of the George Washington Bridge, for obvious reasons. The lower level of the bridge was still under construction. No matter. Off the two daredevils went, scaling the hazardous cliff in the more or less dark. Unfortunately, close up, the sign was six feet long and made of metal. Somehow they managed to dislodge it and scramble down to the lower walkway when headlights appeared in the distance. The police! They found some steps to the upper level, but the steps were made of meshed metal, so you could see the Hudson River far below. *Don't look down, Don't look down!* Joe kept telling himself. Who knows how they made it back to the apartment, but they did, proudly displaying the sign on a high shelf, cliff-like.

Now that the boys were on their own, having to fend for themselves, Lily redoubled her efforts at providing food for Joe and Mike. Every two weeks or so she and Milton would arrive laden, and nothing could stop her, she who had known real hunger and starvation back in the black old days in the Warsaw ghetto. Joe found a solution by passing most of it on to the girls who had the apartment above them, which had the added advantage of getting to know them, and sometimes sharing parties with them. As for Lily and Milton, it gave them a chance to check up on their elder boy and complain to him about their younger one. Robert had grown into the typical 1960s teenager, with not a care in the world, hippy-style. He appeared completely unaffected by his parents' dark Holocaust past. Not interested really. Joe was half-envious, half-amused, half-irritated. Lily and Milton shook their heads. Joe had been such a good boy. Now look at Robert! He seemed to inhabit another planet. He seemed to think school was for social life and nothing else. Where on earth did he come from?

Joe meanwhile moved on with his studies. He applied to several medical schools, and, when they asked why he wanted to become a doctor, could answer in complete honesty: because he wanted to make a difference. The place he favoured was Harvard, and lo and behold, when he arrived for his interview with Professor David Hubel, there on the desk lay a book: *Teach Yourself Japanese*! What a bit of luck. The interview proceeded with plenty of talk about the Japanese language and culture, which Joe knew all about from his Columbia extra studies. He was accepted there and then, along with six other Columbia students. Another piece of luck: two years later Professor Hubel organised a course in neuroscience. Could there be anything more suited to Joe than the study of the brain?

But before he started at Harvard Medical School in Boston he had a carefree summer to dispose of. For some of the time he worked as a volunteer again. For the last three weeks he decided to go to Europe on a student Euro Rail pass. On his own. London, Paris, Florence, Munich, Copenhagen. Not Warsaw, because by 1966 the Iron Curtain had come down hard on Poland and the rest of Eastern Europe. In London he went to see the Mother of all Parliaments, in Florence he gazed in wonder at Michelangelo's statue of David, in Paris he visited the Louvre and smiled back at Mona Lisa, in Copenhagen he joined a course studying Danish social institutions, visiting a housing project which consisted of one-third disabled people, one-third nursing staff and one-third subsidised families with children, who all looked out for one another. What an eye-opener! What a contrast to America, thought Joe.

The nearest he came to the dark past was on the overnight train from Florence to Germany. He'd fallen asleep and woke with a start at the German border with uniformed border police asking to see his passport, and suddenly he was overcome with a feeling of pure panic. His own brief experience of Germany, where he'd spent the first three years of his life, gave him no cause for it. It was his parents' panic, passed on to him silently, invisibly. And there it was at the German border, waiting for him. The border officials were polite, neatly dressed. They looked at his American passport and handed it back. '*Kein Problem.*' No problem. How strange it was. Even stranger was that when he visited Dachau, the first Nazi concentration camp, situated a few miles from Munich, just a day trip, he remained in control. No panic at all. It took years before he understood: abruptly woken at the German border he was still half-asleep, still in his unconscious mind. When he visited sanitised Dachau he was fully conscious, fully prepared. But it took years to understand that.

For the summer vacation from Harvard Medical School in 1968 Joe decided on an internship in Psychiatry at Mount Zion Hospital in San Francisco – West Coast, not East, and the other side of the world as far as Lily and Milton were concerned. It was something of a turning point for Joe, that summer of 1968. Firstly, it decided him in his future medical career: he would become a psychiatrist. Secondly, he broke up with his current girlfriend, who constantly complained, like all the others, that he was too cut off, often completely unreachable in fact. Thirdly, he met Isabelle, who would become his wife and remains so to this day, fifty-five years, three children and seven grandchildren on.

It happened like this: Joe was planning to drive across America, tourist-style, before starting his internship. He asked a friend in New York to put a 'looking for travel companions' notice in a couple of restaurants, given as Joe was in Boston, not New York. A few days later the phone rang in his Boston dorm. It was a girl's voice, and it was foreign. Apparently she and a girlfriend, also foreign, were ending their year as au pairs in New York and wanted to take a trip across America before they went back home. One was Swiss, the other French. Viviane and Isabelle. They were twenty-one, he was twenty-two, and bliss it was to be driving across the States together, three carefree spirits, out for a good time. How could Isabelle know what complexities lay beneath the surface of this handsome, charming, clever, apparently light-hearted medical student. South Dakota, Chicago, Wyoming, the Nevada Desert, on and on they drove, having a blast. When the odd mishap occurred Joe noted that Isabelle remained calm, humorous even. Nothing much rattled her. And he knew why too: through those long driving days there was plenty of conversation about their pasts and childhoods. Needless to say, Joe kept quiet about the darkest parts of his own story. But Isabelle described a happy, uncomplicated childhood in France, surrounded by a large family, the father an admiral recently retired from the French Navy, the mother, always known as *bonne Maman*, running the home. Very French. Very bourgeois. Very Catholic. And all that difficult history of French collaboration with the Germans during the war firmly deposited in the past. No trauma, just a blind eye.

'Not because I have anything against non-Jews,' Joe was quoted as saying two years earlier, in a newspaper given out by the Copenhagen project. He was talking about the fact that he wouldn't marry a non-Jew, 'because I would hurt my parents terribly by doing so. My parents had to flee from Poland, and were the only survivors of the Hitler regime out of a family of twelve, so I understand their attitude. I may, some day, break it if I happen to fall in love with a non-Jewish girl, but for the sake of my parents I do not hope so.'

But he did fall in love with a non-Jew. And after much hesitation and anxious deliberation, Joe asked Isabelle – lovely, humorous, steady Isabelle – to marry him. And Isabelle said yes. 'Fifteen minutes on the phone to Paris,' he wrote in his diary on 17 March 1970. 'And she said yes! Good to go on!' And it did indeed cause consternation with Lily and Milton. And with Isabelle's Catholic parents too.

'Dear Mr Biseau!' wrote Joe's dad, Milton, after long discussions with Joe, and Lily too of course:

> First I want to tell you that I know exactly how you feel, and I think I can also understand the motives behind your refusal to allow your daughter to marry out of her religion. Believe me that in the beginning I was also very much against it, and probably for the same reasons that you have. You see I have always tried to raise my son religious and to instill in him a sense of religion and to make him a good human being. I think that I have succeeded in this respect, and I am

very proud of that. My own family background, and also my wife's, is a strictly Orthodox one and our son was raised the same way. But you have to realize that the young generation now looks at our convictions and beliefs in a different way than we look at them, and that they express their love for God with love for humanity, and they can't agree to our conception of love for God, when at the same time we are filled with prejudices and sometimes even hate for people different from us, be it religion, or race or color. Personally I think they are right, because how can we be so hypocritical to say we love God with all our heart, soul, and all our possessions, and at the same time not to practice the one thing that He considers the most important, namely that all people are His children and that all people are the same in His eyes. And that is why my wife and I decided that if your daughter and my son are in love and they feel they can be happy together, not to interfere and to give them our blessing. We will consider your daughter as if she was our child, and if it is all right with you, give them all our support and help we possibly can. I hope and pray you will change your attitude and try to understand and look at the situation the way it really is. I hope that your wife feels better.

Very sincerely Milton Albeck.

But the real problem was Joe, still the good boy trying to make up for his parents' dark pasts, even now with Isabelle in his life. Outwardly he was fine, inwardly he was unable to trust anyone enough to tell them what was in his heart. So he was lonely. And depressed. When President Nixon gave the go-ahead on 3 May 1970 for the US Air Force to bomb Cambodia without the authorisation of Congress, Joe took to wearing a black armband to symbolise his mourning for the US Constitution. And he joined the Harvard Medical School strike committee to protest, along with others at over a hundred colleges across America. They'd protested about the Vietnam War and torn up their draft papers, now they were protesting again. Joe, based in a makeshift office in the Medical School's Anatomical Museum, worked day and night, hardly sleeping, till he was utterly exhausted and spent. Later he realised he was mourning for his parents' dark past as well as America under Nixon, but not yet. Finally his classmates stepped in, seeing what he himself could hardly see – that he was cracking up. They took him to the Emergency Room at the Massachusetts Mental Health Center, where he was put on antidepressants. He took them for some weeks, then he changed tack. He got on a flight to Paris.

Joe and Isabelle were married at Notre-Dame de Versailles on 17 June 1970 in a full Catholic wedding ceremony, High Mass and all. The presiding priest was Patrice Flichy, Isabelle's uncle. Isabelle's parents and her six siblings were in attendance, along with numerous family friends, and Swiss Viviane too. But no Milton and Lily. Instead, Joe had the rings Milton and Lily, that is Mendel and Lonia, had used at their own wedding in 1942, in the Warsaw ghetto. Simple gold rings, laden with dark meaning. Lonia had hidden them on 23 April 1943, or perhaps given them to Yadzia to hide, before she and Mendel were transported along with the remaining workers at the Többens factory to Poniatowa concentration camp. She retrieved them in May 1945 at the end of the war, once she and Mendel emerged from the sewers of Warsaw, having miraculously survived. And now here they were, those same rings, golden in the light from the stained-glass windows, under the high dome of the Catholic Baroque church and in front of an altar decorated with great displays of summer blooms. '*Oui*,' said Joe in his recently acquired French. 'Yes, I take Isabelle to be my lawfully wedded wife, to love and to hold till death us do part.'

It should have been happily ever after, but it wasn't.

After a short honeymoon in Fontainebleau Joe went back to New York to look for an apartment. He found one on the corner of 12th Street and Broadway in Manhattan. It was on the eighth floor, with a large bedroom, a nice living area and an alcove kitchenette. There was very little furniture, but Lily and Milton helped with that. And they presented Isabelle with a diamond engagement ring when she arrived, to show that they meant to be good and loving parents-in-law and, God willing, good grandparents in the fullness of time. Isabelle, for her part, kissed them on both cheeks, French-style, full of her natural affection and optimism. A second wedding ceremony was to be held in the apartment two weeks later, officiated by the Jewish chaplain from Columbia. Lily and Milton were appeased. They could see how much Joe and Isabelle were in love, and who were they to disagree;

they who'd married under the most inauspicious circumstances in the Warsaw ghetto all those years ago, and look at them now.

Isabelle soon found a job in the accounting department of Saks Fifth Avenue. Joe was working all hours as an intern at Bellevue Psychiatric Hospital. And then, apparently out of the blue, he fell back into depression and exhaustion. He took some time off, tried to sleep, had hot baths to relax. It didn't work. Poor Isabelle had occasionally glimpsed Joe's depressive side, but not this! She tried to understand it, but she couldn't. Hardly surprising. Not even Joe really understood it. He turned, as he had often in the past, to poetry, to writing it down. He titled the poem 'It's So Hard':

It's so hard to let it in –
To feel your love inside my skin
To take in your warmth
And let our life begin

It's so hard to let it in
To feel you know my fear
And forgive me all my pain

Thankful that you are near
I still sing the same refrain:
It's so hard to let it in
It's so hard

With time the depression eased, but it never really left him. What was going on?

Then came two great events: the first, their daughter Simone Juliet was born on 17 May 1971. She was named after Simon Goldfeld, the uncle who'd helped Lily and Milton, then still Lonia and Mendel, to come to America back in 1949. The second: Joe was listed to be drafted, probably to Vietnam. As a doctor he knew he had little chance of escape. He decided the best way to avoid Vietnam was to volunteer, then he could decide for himself which service to join. He chose the Army Medical Corps, which turned out to be a good idea. He and Isabelle moved into officers' housing on the army base at Fort Eustis, Virginia, which had about 16,000 troops, and Joe started work at the base hospital. In his entire two years in the army he never had to handle a firearm. A year earlier he'd been protesting against the war in Vietnam and Cambodia, now he was tending to troops who'd been or were going there, and he would possibly even have to confront protestors in Washington. He held the formal rank of captain. He was twenty-four.

Before he left, Yadzia and her husband David came to visit from Australia. It was the first time the two sisters had met since that terrible parting in 1949 at Hamburg docks. The swings of history. They wept, they talked and talked, they laughed, they held each other tight, quite unable to match the dark past to the golden present. No, the past was too dark. For brief hours they entered the present: went shopping in the big, bright department stores on Madison, took the Staten Island ferry out to the Statue of Liberty, went for walks around Manhattan with Joe and Isabelle, pushing Simone in her pram, ate ice cream on Coney Island, queued up outside the Rialto movie theatre on Times Square to see *Love Story* with Ali MacGraw and Ryan O'Neal. But always the dark past lurked – the Warsaw ghetto, the transports, Poniatowa, the sewers, the desperate escape across the mountains in the deep snow. The parting at Hamburg docks.

Still, life went on. 'Hello folks,' wrote Joe cheerfully to Lily and Milton from Kéramézec during the first of their annual summer visits to Isabelle's family home. 'Fondest greetings from beautiful Brittany. We arrived safely and speedily via a US Air Force plane landing at Frankfurt, Germany. Then a quick over-night couchette to Paris followed by a pleasant day at one of my brothers-in-law there. Then we took a train to Brest that night and arrived Saturday at 7 a.m. (we left Virginia Wednesday). The family house here in Brittany befits a former admiral: a large, stone, three-story-plus-attic building, with high ceilings and large rooms with central heating. It's about 20 kilometers from the coast. The grounds are about 30 acres of beautifully planted gardens, and fields. There is also a much-used tennis court.' Nothing like pre-war Warsaw, then. Even less like post-war Warsaw, reduced to rubble. Isabelle's father had retired from the navy by the 1970s. He'd been commander of a battle cruiser in July 1940, evading the British Navy after Churchill ordered the seizure and sinking of the French fleet at Mers-el-Kébir in Algeria. By November 1942, when the Nazis tried to seize the French ships in Toulon harbour, it was Isabelle's father who received and transmitted the order from the British to scuttle all seventy-seven warships sheltering there. Another swing of history.

The early 1970s, and the 'times they were a-changing' in America. President Nixon declared his war on drugs, given the thousands of young men returning from Vietnam with a heroin habit. PTSD, post-traumatic stress syndrome, wasn't yet named, though there was plenty of it about. The army base had twenty-five doctors and just one social worker. The social worker began behavioural therapy sessions, the latest thing, treating the sick mind rather than the sick body. Joe went to have a look, and with it his future working life was decided. When he left the army he took a post at McLean Hospital in Boston, originally known as the Asylum for the Insane. He stayed there for the next forty-five years.

Two more children were born, David and Margot. His parents moved to Florida. His father got ill with pancreatic cancer. He died on 24 September 1974, with Lonia/Lily at his bedside. It was unbearable for her, losing him – the person she'd shared everything with, good and bad, had loved and respected through all these years, the only person who knew every detail of their dark past, the one who'd kept them all going with his innate decency and optimism. In the same year Yadzia died too, worn out by her own dark past. And now Lonia was alone.

Joe had been there at the hospital just days before Milton died. 'I recall my last view of my father,' he wrote, years later, because he couldn't face it before:

> A thin, thin man in the anonymous degradation
> Of a hospital gown, standing straight,
> Holding up a kiddish cup, praying powerfully

For the memory of his own father,
Before collapsing suddenly, at prayer's end,
In a heap of weakness on to the bed,
To receive what proved to be
My final, silent kiss on a forehead
Over eyes I had not the courage to meet,
Though they still sparkled and shone.

I recall too, that my father had last seen his father
Standing in line at the *Umschlagplatz*
In Warsaw, in April 1943.
My father escaped that line,
And returned that same night to that infernal place,
Calling his father's name again, and again.
But there was no answer. There was no farewell.
That scene was my father's recurrent dream,
Which he spared me until just before his own end,
But which I did not fully understand until this moment
Until this Kaddish, in this consecrated time and space.

Father, where are you?
He asked... I ask... Job asked...
Our question cried to the heavens, which remain silent.
The silence must be our comfort,
As it is theirs... Farewell, Father... Farewell.

Still, during the 1970s, by his own admission, Joe hardly gave the Holocaust a thought. The odd Remembrance event, the occasional visit to the Synagogue at Rosh Hashanah, and now, following the Arab–Israeli war, Yom Kippur. That was about it.

But Lily did – all the time. Came the day in 1978 when Joe paid her a visit, to make a suggestion. He and Isabella had moved the family to Miami by then, feeling that Lily was spending too much time alone after Milton's death. Joe, ever the good son, said he wanted Lily to be a full-time grandmother to his three children. Isabella, the good wife, could see that Joe had a deep need to protect his mother. He took a post at the Jackson Memorial Hospital, heading the St Luke's methadone clinic, dealing with multiple psychiatric problems. Now he'd been invited to an international conference on addiction in

Warsaw, he told Lily. Wouldn't this be the perfect opportunity for her to go back and visit the old home with him, put to rest some of the old fears? No, said Lily. She didn't think she could or would be able to do that. Joe persisted. Lily gave way. Perhaps she did it for him.

Being back in Warsaw was almost unbearable for Lonia/Lily. It was so changed, Communist Poland. So poor. So grey. And yet and yet, there it was, the past, buried in the rubble of what had once been. They found the old apartment block on Grajewska Street, divided into many flats now, dilapidated, scarred by shrapnel, unfriendly. No, the new inhabitants didn't know who had lived there before, and they didn't want to know either. And there was 22 Nalewki Sreet, miraculously still standing. Lonia stood on the other side of the street, looking up at the windows one by one, hearing the old voices, the talk, the laughter – her mother, her father, Julek, Sevek, Frania. All gone. And, Lord preserve us, there was the *Umschlagplatz*. And Dr Korczak accompanying the children, including Henek, two by two, to their deaths.

They visited Stephania Przesnyska, their old maid, who had hidden Lonia and Mendel when they were on the run after their escape from Poniatowa. And they visited Eduard, the ethnic German who had rescued them from Poniatowa on his motorbike – for a price, it's true, but risking his life nevertheless. He was living in the poorest circumstances, and almost blind now. Lonia had sent both of them some US dollars from time to time and had tried to get them added as 'righteous Gentiles' at Yad Vashem, the Holocaust Remembrance Center in Jerusalem, which would entitle them to a pension. But it didn't work. They'd been paid for their help, so it didn't count. Paid with Nicha's gold coins. Finally, they went to the Jewish cemetery, wild and neglected now. Beautiful in a way. They were looking for Lonia's mother, Nicha Goldfeld's grave – Nicha who had died before the war and whose forethought to hide away those gold coins, just in case, had saved Lonia and Mendel's lives. Lonia wandered this way and that, quite lost. Was it near this tree? Was it down that lost lane? Finally they found it, a slab of black marble buried under dense weeds. Lonia wept and wept.

They weren't far from Auschwitz, Oświęcim now in Polish, and Joe was keen to go. They went with a guide. But they'd hardly passed the horror of the entrance gates with the words *Arbeit Macht Frei* still emblazoned high above when Lily/Lonia said she couldn't go on. She was done for. Joe went on alone, past the piles of discarded shoes and spectacles and the mounds of hair, and the gas chambers and the barracks, row upon row of them, and met her again on the way out. Out and away, for ever more.

In March 1980 Joe and Isabelle decided to move back to Boston. Was it hard to tell Lily? Joe never said. But knowing them, they did it mostly for the children. And knowing Lily, she probably encouraged them to do it. The decision was made easier by the fact that Robert, Joe's brother, now lived in Florida. And he was soon getting married, so there'd still be family, hopefully grandchildren, to keep Lily company and busy in her old age. Perhaps the move was also to help Joe. He got a job at McLean again, and they settled back into East Coast life, more European than Florida, more to their taste. But it didn't help Joe. He still had his periods of depression and hypomania which hung about him, darkening his life. And it caused trouble in his marriage too. He and Isabelle quarrelled more often now, mostly about the children. He was too soft on them, she said. She was too hard on them, he said, disciplining them in the old-fashioned French style. Both knew the children stood for something else, something deeply wrong with Joe, which he could only partially face. They went to couples therapy. They tried to work it out. Isabelle was enrolled in a PhD course in Psychology. She gave it up after two years to concentrate on family life, she said, and to help Joe with his depression. Joe wrote more and more poetry.

The thing that made the difference, eventually, was Joe joining a One Generation After group. There were more and more such groups now, therapy groups for the children of Holocaust survivors, all experiencing emotional problems of one sort or another, all puzzled by it, as Joe was, because surely they were the loved ones, the treasured ones, the golden ones, making up for their parents' dark pasts. And yet and yet…

It was the legacy of silence which they shared. Their parents held their silence about that dark, terrifying past, wishing to protect their children from it. But it turned out, again and again, that the children knew. Silently, the horror had been passed on to them. And the children, again and again, displayed signs of distress and confusion. Sorrow, anger, nightmares, desperate attempts to be good, oh so good, to make up for their parents' dark pasts. Just like Joe.

Came the day when Joe found a book actually titled *Legacy of*

Silence, written by an Israeli psychologist called Dan Bar-On. It turned out Bar-On was currently a visiting professor at MIT, the Massachusetts Institute of Technology in Boston. Joe asked him to come and talk to his group of One Generation After. Was it chance, was it fate? One way or another, it was another turning point in Joe's life.

CHAPTER SEVEN

DAN: CHILD OF ISRAEL

Shemà
You who live secure
In your warm houses,
Who return at evening to find
Hot food and friendly faces:

Consider whether this is a man,
Who labors in the mud
Who knows no peace
Who fights for a crust of bread
Who dies at a yes or a no.
Consider whether this is a woman,
Without hair or name
With no more strength to remember
Eyes empty and womb cold
As a frog in winter

Consider that this has been:
I commend these words to you.
Engrave them on your hearts
When you are in your house, when you walk on your way,
When you go to bed, when you rise.
Repeat them to your children.
Or may your house crumble,
Disease render you powerless,
Your offspring avert their faces from you.

10 January 1946
Primo Levi, *Collected Poems*
(translated by Ruth Feldman and Brian Swann)

So quoted Dan Bar-On at the beginning of his book *Legacy of Silence* in 1989. He was fifty-one years old, living in Tel Aviv with his second wife Tammy and embarking on the most audacious, shall we call it 'mission' of his life. A mission which would elicit plenty of hate mail, and even the loss of some friendships.

But to understand this quite reckless decision of Dan's we have, as ever, to go back to the beginning. Which was in Haifa, in Palestine, on 3 October 1938. That, at least, was Dan's beginning, a joyful one for his parents who were building a new life for themselves there. Haifa was beautiful, they thought, situated on the northern tip of Palestine, with a large port and harbour, its whitewashed buildings spread out in the flat plain between the wide bay of the blue Mediterranean and the foot of ancient Mount Carmel which rose green and rocky high above. A lovely place to bring a child into the world.

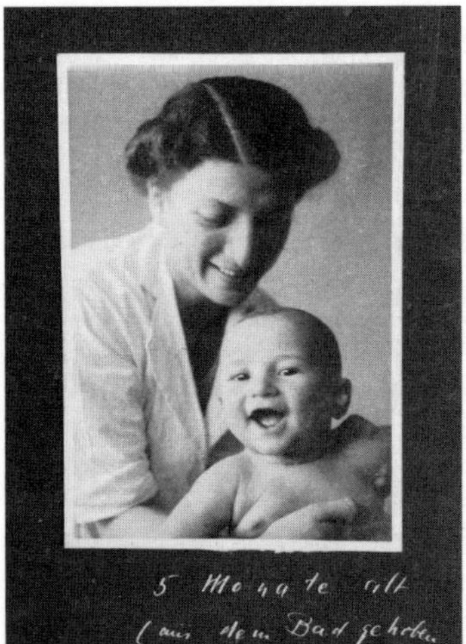

Photographs of Haifa in the late nineteenth century taken from Mount Carmel, black and white and blurred, show little more than a small town with scattered Arab houses, square and white, and a small harbour. At the eastern gateway Arabs squat with camels, bringing their sacks of grain to trade. Beyond the western gateway is a 'European' street of about sixty houses which run straight to the foot of Mount Carmel. Here everything is tended, writes a traveller in 1886: a pavement, houses built of local limestone, gardens with roses and cactus hedges. There are English, and German, and Swiss and some Scandinavians. Businesspeople, mostly. No Jews as yet.

There is a school, an excellent hotel, a steam-powered mill, a small factory making olive oil soap and a windmill. The first Palestinian railway travels the short distance from Haifa to Beisan and then on to Lake Tiberias.

In the 'native' town the narrow streets show men in Arab dress, tunics and long robes with the check keffiyeh headdress or the taboush flat woollen hat, herding goats or leading donkeys laden with produce in wicker baskets – vegetables and fruit from the surrounding fields, bundles of wood from the lower slopes of Mount Carmel, making for the marketplace. The men in trousers and Western dress are Christians, both European and Arab Christians, though the Arabs might just wear a jacket over their usual tunics. There are few women to be seen, and if at all they are robed and veiled. It looks quiet and peaceful. But it didn't last. Because the big events of history soon overtook those small lives, changing everything.

It was the League of Nations, no doubt with the best intentions, who intruded, back in 1922, three years after the end of the First World War. The Ottoman Empire, allied to defeated Germany, was being broken up and redistributed among the victorious Allies. Palestine came under British administration, the so-called Mandate for Palestine. And in fact, over the next several years Palestine prospered and developed under the efficient British. If progress was what you wanted. And if you didn't mind being controlled by another power. But the Palestinian population did mind, leading to sporadic fighting between the British troops stationed there and the rebel Arab population.

The British quickly had their eye on the village of Haifa, so beautifully and usefully situated on the Mediterranean, and already furnished with a small harbour. Over time Haifa became a larger town, the small harbour became a large port, and later a major industrial one transporting crude oil from the Middle East to every corner of the Western world. With it came a new railway replacing the old one, the so-called Palestine Railway, plus a new road to facilitate local communications, but mainly for trade and security. There were new administrative and civic buildings. And an oil refinery next to the port, close to the British Army barracks. And a new electrical power station. And a new population, first Arabs from the surrounding villages seeking work, then Jews fleeing the anti-Semitism in Europe, much encouraged by the Balfour Declaration of 1917 which had promised a 'national home for the Jewish People'.

The Declaration was no more than a letter from Arthur Balfour, British Foreign Secretary, to Lord Rothschild, leader of the Jewish community there. 'Dear Lord Rothschild,' Balfour wrote from the Foreign Office on 2 November 1917,

> I have much pleasure in conveying to you, on behalf of His Majesty's Government, the following declaration of sympathy with Jewish Zionist aspirations which has been submitted to, and approved by, the Cabinet. His Majesty's Government view with favour the establishment in Palestine of a national home for the Jewish people, and will use their best endeavours to facilitate the achievement of this object, it being clearly understood that nothing shall be done which may prejudice the civil and religious rights of existing non-Jewish communities in Palestine, or the rights and political status enjoyed by Jews in any other country. I should be grateful if you would bring this declaration to the knowledge of the Zionist Federation.
>
> Yours sincerely, Arthur James Balfour

So far so good. Except that Chaim Weizmann, a leader of the Zionist movement which had long been arguing that Palestine was the traditional homeland of the Jews, and David Ben-Gurion, who became the first Prime Minister of Israel, the former born in Russia the latter in Poland, had other ideas. Weizmann was always for a separate 'national home' within Palestine. Ben-Gurion wanted the whole. 'I don't regard a state in part of Palestine as the final aim of Zionism, but as a means towards that aim,' he wrote to his wife in 1938, the year Dan was born. 'After the establishment of the state, we will cancel the partition of the country and we will expand throughout the Land of Israel.'

Of course not all Jews were Zionists, not even the majority, but that is what the Zionists planned early on and increasingly as the situation in Europe, but especially in Germany, grew worse and worse. Not to mention the situation within Palestine itself, where there were daily skirmishes with the Arab population who had no intention of sharing their land on an equal, even less on a subjugated, basis with the Jews. In 1918 the population of Palestine was approximately 512,000 Muslims, 61,000 Christians, mostly Arab, and 66,000 Jews;

35,000 more Jews had arrived by 1923 and 82,000 more by 1930. In 1922 the population of Haifa, as recorded by the British, had grown to some 24,000, roughly divided between Muslims and Arab Christians and the newly arrived Jewish population. By 1931 this had doubled to 50,000, with the Jewish population now almost 16,000. By 1938, thanks to Nazi Germany, the Jewish number had risen to 52,000 – half the population.

Originally it was just a few hundred Zionists who made the great journey across the ocean from Europe and Russia to Palestine, fleeing the pogroms, seeking a new, freer, safer life. Theodor Herzl, founding the Zionist movement in 1896, called it a reclaiming: 'The Idea which I have developed... is a very old one: it is the restoration of the Jewish State.' The term 'national home' was used for the first time at the first Zionist Congress in Basel a year later. There followed a small but steady flow of Jewish immigrants to Palestine, though many soon left again, seeking their new life elsewhere, often in America, because life in Palestine was simply too harsh. But the hopes persisted. By January 1915 Herbert Samuel, a Liberal MP in the British government and a Zionist, submitted the first of three memos to the Prime Minister, Herbert Asquith, anticipating the victorious outcome of the First World War. 'The course of events opens a prospect of change, at the end of the war, in the status of Palestine,' he wrote. 'I am assured that the solution of the problem of Palestine which would be the most welcome to the leaders and supporters of the Zionist movement throughout the world would be the annexation of the country to the British Empire.'

Samuel was British to the core. His great-grandfather Menachem had emigrated from Poland to England way back in the 1770s. 'It is hoped that under British rule, facilities would be given to Jewish organizations to purchase land, to found colonies, to establish educational and religious institutions, and to spend usefully the funds that would be freely contributed for promoting the economic development of the country. It is hoped also that Jewish immigration, carefully regulated, would be given preference so that in course of time the Jewish people, grown into a majority and settled on the land, may be conceded such degree of self-government as the conditions of that day may justify.'

And so the idea spread, slowly at first, appealing to a younger, more politically active generation who rejected the rampant anti-Semitism which affected every aspect of their lives. David Ben-Gurion was typical enough. Born into a relatively well-off and educated family in the small town of Płońsk some forty-five miles from Warsaw, he had decided by 1906, aged twenty, to make a new life for himself in Palestine, which he was happy to call their national homeland. Ben-Gurion was a Zionist from the start, and given his energetic, restless and ambitious personality, he was soon one of the leaders. To make the point, he changed his name from David Yosef Grün to Ben-Gurion, the name of one of the leaders of the Jewish community in Jerusalem in the first century AD.

It was clear to Ben-Gurion early on that the Jews would have to fight to conquer their land. 'One doesn't receive a country, one conquers it,' as he put it. 'We will conquer Palestine by developing it.' He travelled back and forth from Palestine to the Western world, meeting people of influence, lecturing and writing articles and books, and looking for what he called 'pioneers' – young, idealistic, physically strong Jews keen to build a national home working the harsh land. They would need a 'group for self-defense' against the rebellious Arabs, he said, but at the beginning, at least, he was convinced it would be good for the Arab population of Palestine too, helping to transform that barren land. If only they could be persuaded. But they couldn't. By 1916, when Ben-Gurion returned to Palestine again after another of his travels, the Arab population was close to a million, a far cry from what he once described as 'a land without a nation' which 'awaited people'.

Then came the Balfour Declaration in November 1917. What's in a capital letter? Is a National Home the same as a national home? Is a Declaration the same as a declaration?

The letter began life as a general declaration of good intent and well-wishing to Zionists across the world and only later acquired the status of a Declaration. But Declaration or declaration, either way it wanted it clearly understood 'that nothing be done to prejudice the civil and religious rights of the existing non-Jewish communities in Palestine' at the same time as viewing 'with favour the establishment in Palestine of a national home for the Jewish people'. Even with that caveat, it was by no means considered a good idea by everyone. 'It was suggested that a question raising such important issues as to the future of Palestine ought, in the first instance, be discussed with our Allies, and more particularly the United States,' the War Cabinet minutes of 3 September 1917 record when the draft declaration was being discussed, not least because 'there was a very strong and enthusiastic organization (Zionist) there who were zealous in this matter'.

On the day news of the Balfour Declaration reached America there was rejoicing among the Jewish population there. They booked the Great Hall of the Cooper Building in New York for a celebration. It was the grandest of buildings, pillared and balconied, five storeys high, where Abraham Lincoln had once spoken, anticipating his Gettysburg Address. Now Ben-Gurion was one of the speakers. An appeal fund was launched. He needed money, and where better to find it than America, the capital of capitalism. Within weeks they had $40,000. Whether it was on that day, hearing that speech, or whether on some earlier occasion, Paula Munweiss, a Jew but no Zionist, fell for Ben-Gurion, and they were married within the week. It tells us plenty about Ben-Gurion. How on earth did he persuade a sophisticated New Yorker to leave the safety and comfort of America and go with him to Palestine, a harsh land with no electricity even! But he did, and by the end of the war there they were, young, energetic, idealistic, back in Palestine, embarked on the fight to establish a national home.

There were numerous reports and discussions in the lead-up to the Peace Conference convened at Versailles in January 1919, held to establish terms and draw new borders following the First World War as well as to found the League of Nations to make sure such a war could never again happen in Europe. The future of Palestine was only one of many concerns, not even one of the foremost. Sir Mark Sykes, attached to the Foreign Office as advisor on Near Eastern policy, suggested in a memo: 'My general impression is that there is a great deal of electricity in the air and that perhaps both parties think that the moment would be propitious to start a riot in order to draw the attention of the world to their varying claims... My opinion is that early measures should be taken to relieve the tension which is growing and if allowed to develop may result in a serious crisis.'

Brigadier-General Sir Gilbert Clayton, our man in Egypt, commented: 'Anti-Zionist propaganda has increased very considerably in Palestine lately and feeling is now running very high among Muslims and Christians who fear that political and economic advantages may be given to Jews in a peace settlement.' Field Marshal Viscount Allenby, until recently the Chief Administrator of Palestine, was worried about the appointment of the Right Hon. Herbert Samuel as High Commissioner of the new administration when the British Mandate came in: 'I think that appointment of a Jew as first Governor will be highly dangerous,' he wrote to the Foreign Office. To which the Foreign Office replied: 'Complete religious liberty will be maintained in Palestine. The places sacred to the great religions will remain in control of the adherents to those religions. A civilian administration for the country will at once be established. The higher ranks will consist of British officials of ability and experience. The other ranks will be open to the local population irrespective of creed. Order will be firmly enforced. The economic development of the country will be actively promoted.'

Samuel was duly appointed. The Arabs of Palestine were not reassured. The British continued to administer Palestine for the next twenty-six years.

The 1920s were years of mounting terrorist activity on both sides: bombs, shootings, Jews brutally evicting Arabs from their homes and lands, Arabs rioting and attacking Jews in the dark of night. On 4 April 1920 there was a riot in Jerusalem, Arabs breaking into Jewish homes, looting and raping. Five Jews and four Arabs were killed, and many were wounded, including seven British soldiers caught in between. On 3 May 1921 an Arab riot broke out in Jaffa, where there was a hostel for immigrant Jews. The Arabs, wild and way beyond the control of the British security forces, attacked and killed Jews in their homes and on the streets.

Ben-Gurion was on a visit to his family in Płońsk in Poland when he heard the news. He immediately left for Palestine.

The previous fifteen years since he first arrived in Palestine had been ones of unremitting dedication to the cause, a series of highs and lows, made worse by the fact that he himself was given to excessive bouts of optimism, quickly followed by days of despair. But he was a natural leader, and he led with Zionist purpose. Originally his cause was Socialist. Pioneering. He worked side by side with Arabs in the village of Sejera in Lower Galilee, ploughing the rough land with teams of oxen, though farm work was never his strength or interest. His interest was political, always. Early on he saw the need for a proper security force to protect the Jews. And a governing body. He was a man who thought long-term.

Then came the war. Ben-Gurion decided to go to America and gather support for the Zionist cause. He was dazzled by America –

the sheer energy of the place, the optimism, the wealth, the noise, the skyscrapers. His purpose was to find pioneers for his planned military force – that's what he called it officially. In private he called it a 'a group for self-defence in Palestine'. He went everywhere, lecturing, writing articles, meeting influential people, especially Jews.

In the last year of the war he joined the Jewish Legion, under the British. His work was more administrative than fighting in the trenches, but it gave him the time to think and plan ahead. Clearly, the tough Jewish Legion fighters, some 5,000 of them, were the perfect recruits for his new security force in Palestine once the war was over. Which is how the *Haganah* was formed, run by Ben-Gurion himself. And not only the *Haganah*. Also the *Histadrut*, an early government for the emerging national home, concerning itself with housing, employment and health as well as security. In fact one of his main problems regarding security in those early years was containing the brutal actions of the Irgun and Stern gangs, self-appointed underground guerilla groups wreaking havoc on Palestinian villages, evicting the inhabitants by force, chasing them from their lands, shooting them on the spot if necessary in order to replace them with Jewish settlers. This was not the way to gain Western support for a future Jewish state, said Ben-Gurion.

By 1920, when the recently formed League of Nations was still discussing the future of Palestine, Dan's grandfather, Levy, had returned home to Hamburg after serving in the Medical Corps in the First World War. Like other Germans, he was profoundly humiliated by their defeat. He was a German so patriotic that he wore his military uniform on his wedding day. Yet when he wanted to follow an academic career after finishing his medical studies he was advised by his professor to change his name from Levy to something, how to put it, more German, less Jewish. He chose his father's first name: Bruno.

Many years later Levy's son, now Bruno, Dan's father, described how and why he made the decision to leave Germany. He too was a doctor, married, with a first baby, Dan's brother, Michael. He and his wife both came from assimilated, well-educated, well-off German Jewish families – bankers, lawyers, doctors. Dan's mother was an accomplished pianist. In January 1933, just before the Nazi *Machtergreifung*, Dr Bruno and his young wife set off on their usual winter holiday, leaving the baby in the care of the children's nurse. They thought the Nazis could never last, given they hadn't actually won the election and were only in power because of a highly dubious coalition with the centre and right-wing parties who were more afraid of the Communists and the Socialists than the Nazis, and the abysmal failure of the Socialists and the Communists to join forces against their common foe. But then: 'One morning, when we turned on the wireless in one of the alpine huts we heard the announcement of the Reichstag fire,' wrote Dan's father in his memoir written in Haifa forty years later. 'But we were so completely involved in the enchantment of skiing that we did not grasp the importance of the event. The next day we arrived in Munich and found the whole town covered with Nazi flags and swastikas. Back in Hamburg we went to a Furtwängler concert, showing off our deep tan and still-exalted mood. Our enthusiasm (today I would say euphoria) left us quickly when we met our relatives and Jewish friends: they were gloomy about political events.'

It took till April, when Joseph Goebbels ordered the boycott of Jewish shops and businesses, legal practices and physicians, for Dan's father to become fully alert to what was happening. 'Many of my patients turned up and said, "Doctor, I am not permitted to come to treatment today; but here I am." Where I was working in Hamburg there were mostly Socialists who hated Hitler,' he wrote in his memoir. 'My mother came to "comfort" me. I still remember our conversation vividly. I said, "You should know, *Mutter*, they start with a boycott and end with a pogrom. I shall definitely leave Germany."' She answered, 'How can you say this? Everything will blow over in a few months.' Dan's father didn't think so. It had taken the Nazis no more than three months to impose the boycott.

And not only the boycott. First came the Law for the Protection of State and *Volk*, which restricted press freedom and the freedom of assembly. Then came 50,000 extra 'policemen', mostly from the *Sturmabteilung*, which had been the Nazis' paramilitary force since the early years. Then, on 27 February, came the Reichstag fire which the Nazis claimed was the work of a Communist but was in fact the work of Hermann Göring and his cronies. In 'reprisal' they arrested 10,000 Communists, and passed another Law for the Protection of State and *Volk*, giving them emergency powers to 'restore order'. By March the first work camps, Dachau and Oranienburg, were up and running, for political opponents of the regime to be taken into 'protective custody'. Soon there would be proper concentration camps, hundreds of them, to be run by Himmler's SS, but they took time to build and organise, so 'wild' camps here and there were hastily set up for the duration. On 23 March came the Enabling Act, which allowed laws to be passed without the consent of the Reichstag, effectively making the Reichstag obsolete and Germany into a dictatorship and a police state. By April it was the Jewish boycott. Three months is all it took.

'The next few months I spent looking into where we would go when we left Germany,' wrote Dr Bruno in Haifa all those years later. 'I first travelled to Holland, where one of my mother's cousins worked as a doctor. He was willing to take me as his assistant till I could get my license there. I could not make up my mind immediately and promised to return some weeks later after having talked things over with my wife. When I came back to Scheveningen, where the cousin lived, the whole town, from the railway station to his home, was covered with Dutch Nazi flags. This decided the issue finally.'

He went through the same process again, this time considering Denmark, with a similar result. Then he considered going to one of the French colonies, perhaps Algeria, perhaps Morocco. Some of their friends chose China, others Brazil, some chose England. Finally, he chose Palestine.

'We had never been Zionists or shown any interest in Palestine before,' he continued in his memoir. 'However, our neighbour, Dr Wiess, had been a Zionist all his life. For months he had brought us *Die Jüdische Rundschau*, the weekly magazine of the German Zionists, without saying a word. His silence proved to be stronger than any eloquent propaganda. 'We left Hamburg on October 30, 1933. When we came to the Austrian border the German customs official checked our passports, saw our immigration visa to Palestine and looked at our little boy, sleeping on the bench; then he wished us all the best for our future. He seemed to be one of the "good" Germans.'

Good or not, during those early years of the Nazi terror regime no one was minded to stop Jews leaving Germany – as long as they left all their assets behind. Dan's mother was deeply unhappy and resisted leaving to the last. Hamburg was her home, her family, her friends, her everything. The only reason she finally agreed to go to Palestine was because it was administered by the British and was therefore considered safe, which, as Dan later commented, was highly ironic. The Brunos left just before *Kristallnacht* – just in time. Most of Dan's relations who didn't leave in time, whether from Germany or Holland, ended up in Bergen-Belsen or Auschwitz, including the cousin who'd offered to give his father a job as his assistant in Scheveningen.

So that is how it happened that Dan was born in Haifa in 1938.

The Bruno household in Haifa was completely German. Outside might be Arab life, poor and noisy and dusty in the burning sun, but inside it was German, shaded and cool and clean, with German furniture shipped over from Hamburg, including Dan's mother's piano, German china and cutlery and linen, German paintings, German books on the shelves, German records on the gramophone, German food when possible. But not the German language. Dan's parents made a decision early on not to speak that language, perhaps because they wanted their sons to grow up Israeli, perhaps because it was too painful. Instead they spoke either Hebrew or English, but mostly English since their Hebrew was not good. In 1935 Dan's mother had managed to persuade her parents to leave Germany and settle close to them in Haifa. Later came her brother and his family. Whatever she said, they all spoke German with Dan. He also spoke German with the new arrivals in the European colony of Haifa, those who managed to escape Nazi Germany, and at school where there were many German boys alongside the Christian Arabs and the well-off Muslims. Beyond that, he spoke English with the British troops who were stationed at the barracks near the port who constantly patrolled the streets, rifles at the ready to quell any outbreak of hostilities between the Palestinian Arabs and the Jews. Or any outbreak against themselves, which might come from either side. So that is how Dan, born three years after the maternal grandparents arrived in Haifa, grew up speaking three languages: German, Hebrew and English. But still no German at home. So his life was split in two, and it confused him. Was German good or was it bad? He just couldn't work it out. On the one hand there were all those stories of happy times back in the *Heimat*, all that nostalgia, all that longing for a lost paradise. On the other hand it was pure hate and horror. What was a child to make of it?

The problem for Dan's father was a different one: he couldn't find work. There were too many Jewish doctors in Haifa now – more doctors than patients, he joked. So he took a job as an auto mechanic in the garage beneath their apartment. But Dr Bruno was no mechanic. Useless in fact, as Dan later recalled, and probably only kept on as an act of charity. But he did it for five years because someone had to earn the money to keep the family going, harsh as their life now was, or how could they eat? Luckily Dr Bruno was later able to switch to working on a local kibbutz. It was still hard manual work, but better than garage work. The kibbutz movement had developed rapidly during the 1930s as more and more Jews fled Nazi Germany, then Holland, France and Poland. And the kibbutzniks needed all the labour they could get for their newly planted fruit trees and vegetables, their orange groves, their vines, their olives and their building projects. Building a new, future Israel. Golden.

But the gold was slow to shine. There had been Arab revolts and bombings throughout the 1930s as more and more Jewish immigrants arrived. In 1933 some 35,000 Jews settled in Palestine. In 1934 it was more than 45,000. In 1935 more than 65,000. The official and violent Arab Revolt lasted from 1936–9, but it was a constant underlying danger to the Jewish population, and the British occupiers who were seen as being pro the Jewish settlers. In retaliation to the Arab attacks the *Haganah* attacked the Palestinian population in the villages and towns, unofficially assisted by the brutal Irgun and Stern gang guerilla actions. By 1939, with tensions running higher and higher, the British convened an Arab-Jewish Conference. It broke down almost immediately. After which the British government took matters into their own hands and produced a White Paper: 75,000 more Jews could be admitted to Palestine, but no more after that without Arab approval. And the High Commissioner of Palestine would henceforth step in to prohibit the sale of land by Arabs to Jews in certain areas. Because that too was happening. It inflamed the Zionists, who now made the British occupying forces as well as the Arabs the focus of their attacks, making the Mandate virtually unmanageable.

Then came the Second World War. Dan's father joined the British forces as an army doctor, to fight the Germans. He was happy to do it. From his point of view he was fighting the Nazis, who had nothing to do with the German Fatherland he once knew. And he was more than happy to finally be a doctor again, as part of the war effort. In 1941 he was posted to a field hospital by the Egyptian border. He was effectively gone for the next four years.

Life in Haifa became even harsher without him but at least Dan's mother had his army pay now. And her piano, which she played daily, often close to tears. She tried and tried to accustom herself to life in Palestine, but she just couldn't do it. She was European to the core, wedded to German culture and civilisation, Beethoven, Mozart, Goethe, Dürer. Arab life and culture were completely alien to her. The Jewish Young Pioneers didn't please her either. 'They remind me of the Hitler Youth, marching around in their uniforms, singing. The regime here isn't that much different!' she said. It was a preposterous comment, she knew, emotional and irrational, but she couldn't help it. So a depressing feeling of loss hung about her which she never managed to dispel – unlike Dan's father, who had decided early on to embrace the new life in Palestine energetically, patriotically even, especially after joining the kibbutz. Both the boys followed their father, not their mother. They were young. They opted for life and optimism. Dan, especially, found his mother's constant criticisms of life in Palestine irritating and dispiriting. It wasn't till he was much older that he came to understand her distress and to recognise her courage in trying to deal with it. Growing up, he found it intolerable.

In 1945, at the close of the Second World War and after almost four years of managing on her own, albeit with the help of her parents, Dan's mother was finally allowed to visit her husband for a few weeks. Dr Bruno was stationed at a vast field hospital complex by the Suez Canal. Should she take the boys? Dan was seven, his brother thirteen. Encouraged by her husband and begged by her boys, she decided to risk it.

They travelled with the Palestine Railway, which had been so usefully extended by the British back in the 1920s. The stations might have been anywhere in rural England, small and provincial, built of stone, with proper windows and pitched roofs. The platforms had glass-encased timetables on the walls and there was a large round station clock. The steam engines were made in Glasgow, painted dark green, the sleeping cars were plush as an English drawing room, though there weren't many of them left by 1945, and most of the locals travelled on the hard benches in third class surrounded by bundles tied up with string, and live chickens, flapping and clucking in their wicker cages, and live goats. Arab porters, in their flowing robes and red tarboosh headdresses, stood about the platform waiting to take the travelling trunks and hat boxes of the first-class passengers to the carriages.

The journey to the Suez Canal took the best part of twenty-four hours with stops and starts. The guard blew the whistle, the train steamed slowly out of Haifa station, gaining speed along the single-gauge track, bare-footed beaming Arab children stopping their work in the fields to wave and shout greetings as the train sped by. The two Bruno boys, leaning out, waved back, as Dan still remembered with joy fifty years later. They were glued to that train window, he said, hypnotised by the precipitous drops from the railway bank down to the blue Mediterranean far below and the high bridges spanning great gorges, and the long, dark tunnels boring through steep mountainsides – fine feats of British engineering, all.

It was thrilling but it was dangerous, as Dan's mother knew, though Dan was too young to understand. The railway had been regularly sabotaged during the Arab Revolt, as the Palestinians again rose up against British rule and the Zionist forces, fighting to keep control of their land against both. The war brought a temporary pause in their guerilla activities, but then it was the Italians and the German Luftwaffe strafing the Palestine Railway – an important supply route for the North Africa campaign. And in 1941 and 1942 the Germans had bombed the port of Haifa. Now, post-war, the Irgun and Stern gangs, along with the official *Haganah* forces, were blowing up administrative buildings and transport lines, still determined to be rid of the British and their Mandate which had always favoured a two-state solution. The British placed army patrols at strategic points along the railway line, but still trains were derailed and stations blown up. Arab rebels or Jewish fighters. A losing battle either way.

Dr Bruno was working long days at the field hospital tending the war-wounded when the family arrived. But the reunion was a happy one, even though Dan hardly remembered his father, and seeing him in this busy place full of wounded and convalescents was bewildering. Then his mother caught typhus, which was rampant in the camps. So now she was one of the invalids, and when the time came for the three of them to return to Haifa she was unable to travel. Their father put the boys on the train on their own, telling Michael to look after Dan and never let him out of his sight. The tunnels and the gorges and plunges down to the blue Mediterranean were more frightening now, and it was almost a relief to steam back into homely little Haifa station, where they were met by a family friend who delivered them safely into the care of their grandparents.

Dan spent much of his time with his beloved grandparents, even after first his mother and then his father returned home. How lucky he was to have grandparents, he later realised: most of his school friends had none, left behind in Nazi Germany, now dead. But here he was, taking daily walks around Haifa with his grandfather, along the brown, dusty pathways lined with high cactus hedges, through green fields of vegetables and fruit trees and recently planted vines, up to the lower slopes of Mount Carmel where the monastery still celebrated the Feast of St Elias every 20 July, into the silent woods and back down to the town of Haifa and the noise and bustle of the Arab market. *Guten Tag! Guten Tag! Hello, Hello! Salaam! Salaam!*

But things were on the move. Politics, war, victory and defeat – all the big stuff of history was coming once again to mess up small civilian lives. By 1947 the population of Haifa had shifted dramatically. Now the Arab population stood at 71,000, half Muslim, half Christian, and the Jewish population was over 74,000. It wasn't hard to see that the earlier clashes and disputes between the old and the new population was ready to burst into flame again. In 1920 there had been fifty-five Jewish settlements in Palestine, by 1939 there were 218, many of them fortified. And now the British, busily divesting themselves of their colonies after the war, decided to end their Mandate and leave Palestine to the Palestinians. But who were the Palestinians?

Ben-Gurion knew who they were. And what to do. In 1946 the first Zionist Congress since the war and the Holocaust was convened in Basel; 2,500 delegates attended to vote on the future of the Jewish population in Palestine. Should they support the British Mandate or should they plan for a two-state system, or settle for a federal arrangement? Ben-Gurion knew the British were keen to divest themselves of the whole sorry business of Palestine, but he was determined it shouldn't be yet. Because he wasn't ready yet. More precisely, the *Haganah* wasn't ready yet. It needed more men, more training and more weapons to defend the future state of Israel. 'If England does not want to or cannot maintain the Mandate,' wrote Ben-Gurion to Chaim Weizmann in the run-up to the Congress, 'it must agree to the establishment of a Jewish state, even if not in all of Palestine.' He knew that the timing was good because the world, following the horrors of the Holocaust, favoured the Jews. But he wanted rid of Weizmann, currently the president of the Congress, who saw no further than a two-state solution. Weizmann duly bowed out with grace, leaving Ben-Gurion in control.

For the time being Britain continued with the Mandate. But there were more and more ships arriving from Europe filled with illegal Jewish immigrants. It had to stop. On 18 July 1947 another ship, the *Exodus*, bearing 4,500 Jews, was intercepted by a British destroyer and escorted into the port of Haifa. The British authorities despatched it back to France, whence it came. In Britain it made the Gaumont weekly newsreel in the local cinemas. Why were their boys fighting in that distant land?, the British public were increasingly asking their government. By October 1947 the UN Special Committee voted for the partition of Palestine into two states. 'It is truly the beginning of the Redemption,' wrote Ben-Gurion to his wife, 'and even more than the beginning.' To a colleague he wrote: 'We need to prepare for war.'

Dan, aged eight in 1947, noticed that life in Haifa was changing. It wasn't just the constant threat of Arab attacks. It was all the new people arriving. Each time another ship docked in the port he raced down to the quayside with his friends to watch as hundreds of ragged refugees made their unsteady way down the gangplank clutching their bundles tied with string and their battered cases and their dark, wide-eyed children – illegal immigrants according to the British, but how was Dan to know. Then there was his everyday life at school, increasingly filled with these new boys and girls who were Jewish and yet not Jewish, at least not the sort Dan knew, rougher, talking a different language, less polite, many hardly educated. And on the other hand there were his Arab school friends, the children of well-off parents from the professional class, whether Christian or Muslim – traders, shopkeepers, civil servants, lawyers, doctors – who had started disappearing, so that now, many mornings when his teacher read out the class register, there'd be another of his Arab friends missing, the family having gone overnight to their holiday home in Beirut or Nablus and Amman, or to their extended families living in America or Europe, leaving their houses abandoned, fleeing the coming storm which threatened from the moment the British announced their intention to withdraw from Palestine in September 1947 and the United Nations announced its Partition Plan the following November. Shops and workshops started to close, offices of the political and economic leadership emptied, policemen shed their uniforms and melted into the crowd. By May 1948 there was only one member of the Arab Higher Committee, Dr Husayn Khalidi, left in his post.

It was a scandal, how the wealthy Arabs and absent landowners sold their land and properties to the fast-growing Jewish population, showing no care for their workers, the Fellahin living in the villages, labouring in the fields and the factories and the oil refineries, who were left to fend for themselves – which was impossible given they had no money, no weapons, no support, no leadership. Already in 1935 the Grand Mufti of Jerusalem had been forced to issue a fatwa order against those well-off Arabs who sold their lands to Jews. But the story later told about the poor Palestinians – that they left their villages willingly, encouraged by the Arab leadership – is not borne out by historical documents. In the thousands of monitored reports, including those of the BBC and Arab radio stations, there is no mention of it. On the contrary, there were repeated calls from Arab wireless stations for the Arab population of Palestine to stay put. But how to stay put if there was no one of their own to protect them? The wealthy Arab population had left, the Zionist Jewish population were on the march, taking over Palestine as fast as they could to build what they saw as their rightful homeland. Where was the impoverished Arab to go?

'Establish a Jewish state at once, even if it is not the whole land... the rest will come in the course of time,' Ben-Gurion wrote to his wife Paula in 1947, in one of his 'up' moments, filled with a euphoric optimism, echoing the hopes and aspirations of other Zionists, but not the doubts of the Jewish majority.

In Haifa the days of reckoning were 21 to 22 April 1948. Down from Mount Carmel the *Haganah* came, with tanks and mortars and machine guns, advancing through the Arab quarters after attacking the outlying villages, dragging people from their homes and clearing everything which stood in their way. The Arab militia, such as it was, didn't stand a chance. Thousands fled into the British-controlled port area, laden with bundles of hastily gathered possessions, and scrambled on to waiting British boats, protected by British troops who shipped them to the relative safety of Acre to the north. And thence to vast refugee camps in neighbouring Arab countries, or to safer areas of Palestine like Gaza and the West Bank. By the end of April 70,000 Arabs had fled Haifa. In all, over 700,000 Palestinians fled from Eastern Palestine, which now became the State of Israel.

'The Land of Israel was the birthplace of the Jewish people,' stated Ben-Gurion on 14 May 1948, inaugurating the State of Israel. 'Here their spiritual, religious and political identity was shaped.' He didn't mention the United Nations Resolution on Palestine of 29 November 1947, which called for the creation of separate Jewish and Arab states in Palestine. In the event 500,00 Arabs remained in the Jewish section, almost half the population, but only 10,000 Jews remained in the Arab section of 735,000 inhabitants.

By May 1948 it was war. It was called the Arab–Israeli War, or Israel's War of Independence, fought by the newly organised and well-equipped Israel Defense Forces, the IDF, against a disparate and not well-coordinated group of forces from the neighbouring Arab countries and Palestine, jointly known as the Arab League. On 11 July the IDF occupied the Arab town of Lydda. Lydda and Ramleh were the two towns situated on either side of the main Jerusalem–Tel Aviv Road, about ten miles from Tel Aviv, both causing the IDF plenty of trouble. On 12 July Lieutenant-Colonel Yitzhak Rabin, as part of Operation Dani, issued the order that 'the inhabitants of Lydda must be expelled quickly without attention to age'. Two hundred and fifty Arabs and four Israeli soldiers had been killed in the fighting the previous day. A similar order was issued for the inhabitants of Ramleh. In all, some 60,000 Arabs were expelled and marched eastwards towards Ramallah, laden with their bundles and their children and some animals, where a tented refugee camp was set up which later became a lasting concrete one. The war was over and won by the IDF within weeks. A United Nations Special Investigating Team concluded: 'Lands have been taken quite unlawfully from the Arab population which was compelled to leave their villages.' But nothing was done.

The Arab states had not been much help. Egypt, Jordan, Lebanon, Iraq, Syria – all had sent troops to Palestine, fighting to establish a 'United State of Palestine', but they were under-equipped, under-trained, under-funded, and not everyone was convinced they were putting in their best efforts. President Truman, watching from the sidelines and seeing plenty of trouble ahead, suggested a delayed partition. All to no avail. By 1949 Armistice Agreements were being signed by Israel with one after another of their Arab neighbours. The Arabs who remained in the half of Palestine which was now Israel became Arab citizens of Israel. The Gaza Strip was occupied by Egypt. The West Bank, including Jerusalem, by Jordan. Most of the vast refugee camps which were set up in the neighbouring Arab states remain to this day. Fighting in Palestine continued between militias on both sides, only now it was guerrilla warfare.

In Haifa David Hacohen, a member of the Haifa branch of the Mapai, Ben-Gurion's Socialist-inspired political party, argued that, in spite of the outcome of the war, eventually 'we must not forget, we will also have to live with them [Palestinian Arabs]. We talk with them [of] peace and we must abide by our declarations . . . There is Arab terrorism . . . but most of the Arabs want to live quietly.' After the Lydda and Ramleh expulsions the Mapai, who had largely held their silence during the war, spoke out. 'During the past weeks and months, positions (that is, attitudes or policies) have come into being which cause dissent among all of us in this House,' said Yosef Sprinzak, the Mapai secretary-general, addressing the Histadrut. 'This applies to the robbery, the looting, and the behaviour in general of the Jewish occupation forces.' He conceded that 'It is possible there are security reasons. But there must be a limit.' It was the same old conflict between the hawks and the doves, the Zionists and the others.

As far as Dan was concerned, the war meant moving house and moving to a new school, because the district around Mount Carmel had become a security risk. He didn't mind the new house, which was effectively set up in much the same way as the previous one, German-style. But he did mind moving school. By 1950 Haifa, as part of the State of Israel, was inundated with Jews fleeing Eastern Europe. Dan's new school was full of these recent arrivals, and they were completely alien to him: different languages, different cultures, different attitudes. Worse, he was now in the minority, no longer one of the majority holding the power and the say-so. He hated it and couldn't wait to leave. In addition, his brother Michael, the academic one, six years older, a maths genius and their father's favourite, had graduated from their previous school with honours and was now at university, set to become a distinguished economist, fulfilling all his expectations. Which Dan did not. Perhaps Dr Bruno was harsher on his second son than he needed to be because he himself was having trouble adjusting to life in Haifa as it now was. He was back to being a doctor, but it was at a local kibbutz which was filling up with the new arrivals from Eastern Europe with their rough-and-ready ways and manners. Completely gone was that old-fashioned German respect for the doctor. Just get on and do your job, Bruno, like the rest of us, the kibbutzniks said.

When Dan was sixteen and he and his father sat down to discuss his future. What profession was Dan aiming for? Dr Bruno asked his son. As Dan told it to me years later, it was a hopeless conversation, filled with misunderstanding. He thought he might become a farmer, said Dan. A farmer? What do you mean, a farmer? On a kibbutz, explained Dan. Hardly what you might call a profession, said Dr Bruno. Well, that's what he intended to be, said Dan. What's more, he added, becoming belligerent, he was leaving school. He'd already looked into it and there was an excellent agricultural college he could attend, starting the following term. Dr Bruno shook his head. But then came the surprise: Dan's mother stood up for him. Likewise the grandparents. Dr Bruno gave way.

Dan didn't really understand it himself at the time, he said, but years later he knew what his decision was about: he wanted to go his *own* way. Every time he talked about it, he stressed the word *own*. And *own* meant Israeli, not left-over German. Not the past. Not all that longing for a lost world, but the here and now. The future. Israel. He was tough, with big strong hands, he loved nature, he wanted to work on the land. By the autumn he was at his agricultural college.

Three years later he was living on Revivim kibbutz, far from Haifa, far from home, in the Negev Desert close to the border with Egypt. It wasn't that he didn't love his family, but he needed to make his *own* life, in his own way. He changed his name from Bruno to Bar-On.

From Levy, to Bruno, to Bar-On. Fifty years is all it took.

Revivim kibbutz was founded in 1943, mostly by European Jews fleeing the Holocaust. At first it was little more than a tented community in the middle of miles and miles of flat, empty desert. But by 1945 a well had been sunk and simple structures built out of the local stone, everything communal, expressing the basic concept of the kibbutz movement: communal housing, a communal centre with a dining hall and a communal kitchen, a school and a communal dormitory for the children, because from the start the movement believed in sharing everything, including the children. The work was agricultural. A rough road led to the fields. Fruit trees and vines and olives were planted. By the time Dan arrived from agricultural college in 1958 Revivim was a beautiful oasis, green and fertile in the middle of the brown, dry desert. For the next ten years he worked the land as a member of the team tending the fruit trees. Soon he was the team's leader because, early on, it became clear that Dan was a natural leader. He married young. Elia was the same age as he was, another recent arrival from another agricultural college. They had three children in quick succession. Dan and Elia shared the same belief in Israel, and were keen to spread the word. Together they went to New York and back for four years, recruiting volunteers for the kibbutz. Then it was back to the fruit trees. Happy years, he said, smiling and nodding his head in that way of his, raising his eyebrows.

The army was always part of life in Israel. Dan had already belonged to the *Nahal*, the youth group. Then came two years of military service. Thereafter he was in the Army Reserve, always at the ready, a pathfinder, going ahead of the armoured troops. It was enjoyable, exhilarating even – part of being a proper Israeli. But then came the Six Day War in 1967. He was posted to a unit far from Revivim, with people he didn't know and didn't have much in common with, professional army types who'd been in many fights and skirmishes with Arab militias and had little sympathy for the Palestinians – unlike Dan, who remembered his old Arab schoolmates well, those who'd stayed, and the terrible exodus of the poorer ones from Haifa in 1948, carrying their bundles, making for the safety of the port and scrambling into waiting British boats, bound for the refugee camps.

The Six Day War was between Israel and its Arab neighbours, Syria, Egypt and Jordan. The Israelis claimed it was started because of constant Arab guerrilla attacks across the border of Israel by the Muslim Brotherhood, including Yasser Arafat, founding member of the Fatah political party in 1959, and later the leader of the Palestine Liberation Organisation (PLO). The Arabs claimed they were fighting to retake their occupied territory.

Dan was fighting in the Gaza Strip, then still occupied by the Egyptians, as part of a planned pre-emptive strike by the Israeli Army and Air Force to take Egypt by surprise. Which it did, destroying virtually all the planes of the Egyptian Air Force in one fell swoop. It denied the bombing of the USS *Liberty*, a spy ship, killing thirty-four and wounding 171, calling it 'a tragic case of misidentification'; but it later transpired that it had been a deliberate attack in order to distract attention from the fact that Israel was massing forces in Galilee to seize the Golan Heights. Dan's unit meanwhile advanced to Suez. Did he kill anyone? Yes, he said years later, and how he hated it. Increasingly, he couldn't understand what he was doing there, and why this had to be. It went right against his nature and his whole liberal European upbringing. Not that his parents shared his views, seeing it as a war to protect Israel. But then, they weren't doing the fighting. At the end of hostilities, the Israelis had gained the West Bank from Jordan, the Golan Heights from Syria and the Gaza Strip and the whole Sinai Peninsula from Egypt. In all, the Arabs lost more than 20,000 troops, the Israelis 1,000. But one of those was Dan's best friend from Revivim kibbutz, from the fruit tree team, who was in the same army unit as Dan, killed on the very first day of the war. As Israel celebrated the victories with jubilation Dan felt nothing but alienation. When he got back to Revivim he left the fruit tree team and turned to other work. He'd lost the heart to do it without his friend.

Then came the Yom Kippur War. It was October 1973 and life had more or less returned to normal for Dan at Revivim. But now here he was, called up to fight again. This time it was the Arabs who made the first move, taking Israel by surprise. They chose Yom Kippur because it was the Jewish holy Day of Atonement when people were fasting and praying and attending synagogue. Perhaps the idea of atonement had something to do with it symbolically too, but more likely the Arabs, led by Egypt and Syria, knew the Israelis would be fully occupied on that day, their minds on other matters. The aim of the attack was to regain the territory lost to them in the Six Day War, especially the Golan Heights and the Sinai Peninsula. And for the first few days they made swift progress, crossing the Suez Canal and advancing far into the Sinai. But the IDF soon counter-attacked. Within three weeks the course of the war was completely altered, with Israel close to outright victory. On 22 October 1973 the United Nations Security Council, led by the United States and the Soviet Union, the one backing Israel the other the Arabs, called for a ceasefire. It didn't last. It wasn't till May 1974 that the Americans, led by Henry Kissinger shuttling to and fro from Cairo to Jerusalem to Damascus and back again, managed to broker a peace settlement.

Dan had taken part in brutal fighting in the Golan Heights then advanced across the desert to the Suez Canal, fighting the Egyptian Army. But enough was enough. The peace settlement, fragile as it was, signified an end for him – an end of fighting, an end of being that kind of Israeli. Was it some kind of a breakdown? He asked for a transfer to the Army Psychological Unit. And then he enrolled at the local university to take a degree in Social Psychology. He tried to explain it to Elia like this: he had to decide whether to work on the land or with the people who tended the land, and he decided on the people. Because he'd finally realised it was human beings he was interested in. He wanted to help them live better lives, happier lives. He might have added: instead of killing them. Elia didn't really understand. She worked with the olive tree team at Revivim and she loved it. Why was Dan so complicated? It was clear that they were growing apart.

Dan continued to live and work at Revivim but at the same time he decided to continue his studies and do a PhD in Social Psychology. It included working part-time at a clinic in the Western Negev for people traumatised by their experiences during the Holocaust. He started talking to the older generation at his kibbutz, those he knew were Holocaust survivors. Few in Israel had any real understanding or even interest in it. It was in the dark past, another time and another place. Israel was the future, the golden future. Just look around you, the fertile greening of the once-dry, barren land! So the Holocaust survivors kept their appalling memories to themselves. In particular, they didn't talk about it with their children. They lived in silence, Dan later noted, because they wanted to protect their children from that dark horror.

One of the first people Dan saw at the clinic was a Holocaust survivor who brought her two sons to see him. They were in their teens by then and they were giving her a lot of trouble. Dan talked to each of the boys in turn and couldn't see anything seriously wrong with either of them. Before they left he asked the woman if she'd like to come back another time and see him herself? She looked surprised, confused even, but hesitantly agreed. It turned out she'd been a child survivor of Auschwitz – one of those ragged scarecrows you see on the harrowing bits of archive film taken by the Soviet liberators on 27 January 1945, walking towards the camera hand in hand, two by two, in their striped camp rags, legs and arms like sticks, faces hollow, eyes unnaturally large, wells of fear and suffering, walking past the barbed-wire fencing of their camp and out to freedom. But what kind of freedom? In the case of this woman, her parents and all the rest of her family were dead, her home was gone, her past erased, her future utterly unknown. Once she started, she couldn't stop talking. She carried on seeing Dan for three years. He saw that the real trauma lay with the mother, and the two boys, unknowingly affected, were expressing their inherited distress, never spoken about but felt nevertheless.

It was a turning point for Dan, talking to these Holocaust survivors, whether at the clinic or in the kibbutz. He started to actively seek them out and persuade them to trust him with their stories, breaking their long-held silence. The Holocaust might have happened years ago, but the past was still the present for them, so vivid in its horror it plagued them during the long hours of night, making them scream out in terror. When they started talking to Dan, weeping, heads buried in hands, the years fell away and they were back in Auschwitz, Ravensbrück, Buchenwald, Bergen-Belsen – on the ramp, in the barracks, by the gas chambers. Dan learned to tread with extreme care, listen quietly, never ask difficult questions.

Whether it played a part in what happened next in Dan's own life is hard to say. But by the mid-1970s his marriage to Elia was effectively over. And then a young woman called Tammy arrived at Revivim fresh from New York, young, attractive, full of American optimism and energy. She was recently divorced with two small children, and she was minded to start a new life at the kibbutz. In fact they'd already met some years earlier, in New York, when Dan was on one of his trips recruiting Kibbutz volunteers, and Tammy had come to Revivim for the summer vacation as a member of the youth group. But she was just a teenager then, and Dan a 'married old man' as she put it years later, laughing her full laugh, head back, smoking her cigarette. But by 1977 Dan and Elia were getting divorced, and he started living with Tammy, who turned out to be his soulmate. The split from Elia was amicable enough because theirs had been a very young marriage and as time went on it had become clear to both of them that they didn't have much in common, leaving aside the love they shared for their children, who were almost grown up by now.

Dan and Tammy went on living at Revivim, for the time being at least. They married in 1980. In 1981, and encouraged by Tammy, Dan left his work at Revivim to take up a post as a Professor of Behavioural Sciences at the Ben-Gurion University of the Negev. His main subject of research was still the survivors of the Holocaust, but now he increasingly turned his attention to their children, remembering an Auschwitz survivor's comment: 'Most of us are dead. The few who remain are old. Our children must tell our stories now. It is, after all, their story too.'

Within a year he'd formed a group for the children of Holocaust survivors, but it was in America, not Israel, perhaps because it was easier there. He held the meetings three times a year, in Boston, and one of the first to join the group was Joe Albeck. Joe was in his forties by then, and since joining the organisation called One Generation After, he felt the need to finally understand his own sadness and anger, buried deep beneath his thin veneer of rationality. So one day, when he heard of an Israeli professor, Dan Bar-On, who worked with Holocaust survivors and was currently on a sabbatical at MIT, he contacted him and asked if he'd come and talk to his group. Dan turned up and talked about his work and research with the children of the survivors of the Holocaust, and how they were affected by their parents' terrible pasts, often without even knowing it. Would they like to tell him their stories, Dan asked the Boston group. Joe thought about it carefully, as was his way, and then he agreed.

The sessions began simply enough, with everyone telling their stories. That was always Dan's approach: let people speak, in their own time and in their own way.

'Within a few weeks of the Germans invading Poland,' Joe told an early meeting, 'the Jews were ordered into the Warsaw ghetto. My mother's home, which happened to be in that district, had to take in a large number of other people, which included my father. So they actually met in the ghetto, in late 1939.' He told them that his mother had only recently started to tell him bits about the past: about Yadzia, her sister, being blond and blue-eyed and plump 'like a Polish peasant girl', who was able to cross in and out of the ghetto in the early years, smuggling food and money, and that after the first year or so you had to routinely step over dead bodies lying on the pavements to go to where you were going. 'On the other hand,' said Joe, 'I have a photograph of a New Year's Eve party in 1941 in the ghetto, the young people got together and had a jam session – posing for photographs, you know – lots of efforts to continue life as usual. Despite the fact, as you say, there was a high attrition rate.' He shook his head and smiled his wry smile.

'My parents are both Polish Jews,' said Julie, another member of the group. 'When war broke out, they went with their families into Łódź ghetto. I believe Łódź was the first ghetto that was formed, and it was also one of the largest. And one of the last to be liquidated.' Julie was a therapist in her early forties, married with two children. It turned out that many of the children of Holocaust survivors worked in the caring professions in one way or another. Julie neatly fitted the description 'Jewish princess' – attractive, with dark wavy hair and large eyes, naturally empathetic, the beloved daughter of survivors of the Holocaust who'd met and married in Germany after the war, determined to make a new life for themselves and their children, who were their golden future. Many survivors of the Holocaust married each other after the war, feeling that no one else could begin to understand what they had gone through. Julie's mother had also, like Joe's, only recently started to tell her a few details of that past, because her parents wanted to protect her and her siblings from the horror, she explained. A murmur of recognition went around the room.

Charley's parents had also met and married after the war. He was a radiologist at one of the large Boston hospitals, highly articulate, with a liking for the telling detail. His parents were more open about the past, so he knew a bit more about daily life in the ghetto, and he told the group one of those unexpected stories which throw light into dark corners: 'Actually, there were factories in the ghetto,' he said. 'And my father first worked in a woodworking factory, then became the foreman of that factory. And then became foreman of their second factory in addition, so now he was foreman of two factories. They made panama hats, which were popular with the Nazis.' He shrugged at the absurdity. 'They didn't have the right kind of palm leaves to make them, but he figured out some way of making them out of straw. And that idea, he thought, might enhance his security in the ghetto, which it probably did.'

'There was an incident with my father's older brother,' said Julie. 'My father would have been sixteen, his brother nineteen. The brother went on a work-detail outside of the ghetto and at the end of the day he had to go back in, through the checkpoint. One evening there were a couple of SS guards who decided to have some fun with him.' She shook her head and shrugged. 'And so they took a bayonet and kept running it backwards and forwards round his neck. Not hurting him, just, you know... having fun.' She stopped for a moment. 'He was dead within twenty-four hours. The way I understand it is he died of shock.'

Once begun, the stories got worse and worse. Thank God my father had the foresight to get the family out to Palestine before it was too late, thought Dan. Thank God my mother had the courage to stay. Thank God they managed to bring her parents out, so I had grandparents.

'Finally it came to a point where they decided to evacuate the ghetto and move people to the concentration camps,' Charley told the group on another occasion. 'My father, being a fine woodworker, built a hiding place, and the way that worked was this: by the entry to their rooms there was a small hall up which there were three steps leading to the rooms. And what he did was, bring the steps forward and create a false area three steps high, so people would step up sooner, and just walk on that false area. And in that false area, just three steps high and just the width of a narrow hallway, he, his mother and his sister's husband hid. The sister had already been transported to a concentration camp and killed, and his father had died in the ghetto from a bleeding ulcer. And they hid there for weeks and weeks as more and more round-ups were accomplished. And lots of times, when the Germans were searching the houses, they would stamp on the floor with their boots to see if it sounded hollow. Or actually poke a sword between the boards. And my father, having anticipated that kind of stuff, built struts there, making the floor sound less hollow. Unfortunately, those struts also made it harder to be there, so it caused them to be in contorted positions and cramped. But they did it for hours on end while a search was on. Which was a hard thing for both men to accomplish, but an extremely difficult thing for his mother. After some weeks of doing that she ultimately felt so stressed that she couldn't handle it any more. And she begged my father to capitulate – simply walk down the stairs and out into the street and give themselves up, feeling that remaining in that kind of terror in that contorted position hour after hour wasn't worth it, and that dying might be a preferable end. And so they did that...'

So the stories went on, session after session, with weeping, anger, incomprehension. And Dan saw more and more how the parents' dark pasts lived on in their children, passing silently from generation to generation, though they hardly knew it themselves. And he saw that, under the sophisticated Boston veneer, the children were traumatised like their parents, albeit in a different way. And that talking about it after all that silence was like a dam releasing pent-up floodwater – once begun, unstoppable.

'One story my father did tell me,' said Joe. 'Apparently, when they were taking people away, taking them to the *Umschlagplatz* square to be selected and transported, some managed to get away in the chaos. But his father did not. And my father described to me, just before he died, for the first time, about going back to the *Umschlagplatz*, at night, and calling out his father's name.' Joe could hardly go on – too choked with pain for his own father, the man he loved. 'And of course he didn't find him. So I . . . I am able to imagine what it must be like not being able to protect your own family.' And over time he told the group about Poniatowa work camp. And his mother's escape. And his father's terror every time an escapee was returned to the camp. And the giant frying pan.

And everyone sitting in that room accepted without a doubt that this had really happened, although it was literally unbelievable, because they'd heard similar stories themselves. Listening to it all, Dan thought, not for the first time: perhaps I'm making up for the fact of my parents' escape from Nazi Germany. Perhaps I feel a kind of guilt. And I'm doing this work to make up for it?

'The story of my mother's liberation from Bergen-Belsen is more than a little bit sad,' said Charley one day, trying to hold back the tears. 'The bottom line, at the end of it, was that . . . the war ended. At that time, that day that the war ended, she was already under a pile of naked dead bodies, because she'd had typhus. Not typhoid fever, she had typhus. And she was deep under that pile. And when the British forces marched round the edge of these pits filled with dead bodies, she cried out to them in English. And they were stunned to hear a voice coming from a pile of dead bodies. So they frantically pulled out body from body, until finally they came across my mother's, simply by following the voice. They told her to keep talking, and she . . .' Charley stopped, gathering himself. 'She was ultimately . . . saved.'

The more they talked, the more Dan realised how affected these children of survivors of the Holocaust were in their own lives. The past hung over them, never spoken about, passed on silently, in all its horror.

'Auschwitz was liberated by the Russians on 27 January 1945,' said Julie. 'Of course, by that time most of the inmates had been moved towards Germany, including my father, on a death march.' Everyone in the group knew about the so-called death marches, when the remaining SS concentration camp guards, fleeing the Russians, forced the almost-dead inmates to walk back to Germany at gunpoint, shooting any who fell by the wayside. And everyone had seen the archive film, black and white, taken by the Russians when they first arrived at Auschwitz: rows and rows of barrack huts, thousands of them, surrounded by a deep ditch and a high wall and barbed wire, watchtowers at regular intervals all along. It was snowing in January 1945 and there was almost no one left in the camp by the time they arrived except for corpses strewn about in the snow – just a vast, deserted, windblown camp. And those corpses lying on the ground or by the gas chambers or in shallow trenches, skeletons, head to toe, mouths gaping. 'What the Russian soldiers found when they walked through the camp to the warehouses', Julie went on, 'were these mountains and mountains of hair, packed in sacks. And I must say, when I see film of those mountains of hair, I remember how my mother's hair was shaved. And then the mountains of shoes – my mother's shoes, my father's shoes. And the mountains of eyeglasses...'

There was archive of Warsaw too, completely flattened, in late 1944. 'Warsaw had been levelled,' said Joe of the place which had once been his parents' home and which they'd somehow managed to reach again after their escape from Poniatowa work camp. 'So for the last months of 1944 my parents lived in the sewers. My mother told me, not long ago, that they only survived down there because they were part of a gang of criminals. Tough guys who didn't mind killing any German who came down on patrol and who went out during the night, scavenging for food. She said she never knew such people even existed in her old Warsaw life. But now she was grateful to them. Finally, on 14 January 1945, the Russians came, and my father says he remembered someone opening the sewers and shouting down, 'Hey! The Russians are here!' And at first they didn't believe them and they wouldn't get out – they thought it was another kind of trick. But finally someone showed up with some bread.' He smiled his wry smile and shrugged. 'And that was the beginning of the next episode of what happened to them . . .'

After each session in Boston Dan returned to Tammy and their son, now living near the Ben-Gurion University of the Negev, and transcribed all his notes, page after page of dammed-up pain. He could see how sharing their experiences with other members of the group was helping these children of survivors. And he could understand why most of their parents had told them so little, because most of the survivor community in both America and perhaps especially in Israel were in some kind of denial of the past, it being so unbearable. And he noted how many of his group of children of survivors had ended up working as doctors, therapists, teachers – healing others, yet unable to heal themselves. So he wrote up his research and published, hardly knowing if it was the right thing to do – keeping his fingers crossed that he was helping more than hindering.

CHAPTER EIGHT

DAN ENTERS THE DARK

In 1984 Dan's life had reached a certain point, a certain understanding about his past, and being Dan – clever, brave, a bit reckless – he decided to step over the edge, into the darkness.

'I know exactly the event,' he said, many years later. 'It was at a conference in Oslo. A woman came up to me and spoke in Hebrew. With an Austrian accent. She said she was born in Vienna in 1943. So she couldn't be Jewish. Which Jew was born in Vienna in 1943? She converted at sixteen and came to live in a kibbutz in Israel, where she remained. We talked, and I was fascinated. It turned out she had a father who did terrible things in Russia during the war. He would never talk about it. She'd lived with that doubt all her life. After that chance meeting I said to myself: I want to try to figure this out!'

That same year a professor from the University of Wuppertal in West Germany came to visit Dan's department at Ben-Gurion University at Beer Sheva. The two cities, Wuppertal and Beer Sheva, had recently been 'twinned' and the two universities had followed suit. Over the next few days the professor and Dan sat in Dan's office for many hours, talking about their shared field of Behavioural Science. Dan told the professor about his work with Holocaust survivors and their children, and how the subject was only now being spoken about openly in Israel, after all these years. It certainly hadn't been the case when Dan first started his clinical work five years earlier, first at the kibbutz, then the clinical unit attached to Ben-Gurion University. Wasn't it telling, they agreed, that the children of Holocaust survivors were so profoundly affected, even though most survivors didn't talk to their children about it, trying to protect them. A legacy of silence.

'What do you think happened to the children of the Nazi perpetrators?' Dan asked one day, out of the blue. The German professor was shocked, quite lost for words. Dan had walked into a complete taboo. In Germany people were beginning to talk more openly about the Holocaust, but never about the Nazi perpetrators. If at all, it was quickly dismissed, washed away, washed clean, with the same blanket statement the American GIs had first heard, arriving at Renate's *Lebensborn* home at Steinhöring in Bavaria: 'It was Himmler's SS. Not us. We knew nothing about it.'

Call it fate, but it turned out the professor's wife, who'd come to Israel with him, was the child of a perpetrator. After some persuasion she agreed to talk to Dan, in confidence. The conversation was shocking and moving in equal parts. And after that conversation, Dan always said, he was ready to go to Germany. Or was he ready all along, just waiting for the moment? Did his parents, fleeing Hamburg for Palestine in 1933 and thus escaping the Holocaust, unknowingly cause their son to want to return to Germany one day, to try and understand how such things can happen? How people previously leading normal everyday lives can turn into monsters?

One way or another, that is what Dan did – to the horror and incomprehension of most of his family and friends in Israel. 'We have enough troubles of our own,' they said, embroiled as they still were in their fight with the Palestinians and the surrounding Arab nations.

'Why do you want to tell their story?'

'To try and understand,' he'd reply.

'Understand what? Why?'

In fact, Dan had almost visited Germany once before. He'd been on his way to a conference in Stockholm, travelling by train from Zurich. The train stopped in Hamburg and he nearly got off to spend a night there and take a look at his parents' old home. But he just couldn't do it. Not then. But now he started to brush up his German, and he wrote to the professor from Wuppertal to ask whether he was prepared to help him contact some children of perpetrators. And if so, what the best way forward might be.

Luckily the professor turned out to be a courageous man. They decided the simplest method was to put an advertisement in some local newspapers and see what happened. They chose Wuppertal and Munich. 'I put an advertisement in where I said who I am,' Dan told me many years later in Tel Aviv, 'and that I was interested in people whose families had memories of the Third Reich, and I said the respondents should be between these and these ages, so they couldn't be soldiers in the Second World War. I said no more than that. In Munich I didn't get a single response.' Dan smiled and raised his eyebrows in that typical Dan way.

'In Wuppertal about twenty-five people responded, and they had to contact the professor there in each case. Then we put in another advertisement, more explicit: people whose fathers belonged to the SS or the SA. Twelve people responded.' A few people rang in to complain that the professor should stop 'digging up the past'. One complained that the German professor was helping 'a dirty Jew'. Dan smiled and raised his eyebrows again.

In August 1985 he arrived in Germany for the first interviews. Tammy went with him that time, because, frankly, he felt he couldn't do it without her support. But she only stayed for ten days because she had to go back and look after the children. Their son Haran was only six. Her fifteen-year-old son Yariv from her first marriage had been diagnosed with lymphoma. Over the next two years Dan went to Germany four times. By the end of those four visits the taboo subject was just beginning to be spoken about in Germany – a couple of articles, a TV documentary. It must have been the zeitgeist.

Dan went everywhere by train, miles and miles of travel, soon enough getting over his initial fears about the symbolism of trains in Germany. There were forests and meadows and lakes, the Rhine and the Mosel with their rising vineyards and ancient castles, cities with avenues of Linden trees, medieval university towns, industrial suburbs, neat houses with neat gardens, charming villages with cherry trees. He saw most of his people in their own homes because there was a lot to be gleaned from the places where they lived, he thought, which might not feature in interviews held elsewhere, on neutral territory. Most of the interviews were in German, so as time went on Dan reacquainted himself with the language of his childhood, feeling strangely at ease with it. And those German homes, how familiar they felt. His Haifa *Heimat* all over again.

His first stop was in a small Bavarian village, very picturesque, very German, very unsettling. He left Tammy sitting on a bench under a tree and made his way to the house. A white-haired old man answered the door, smiling – the father of the man who'd contacted him. Dan didn't know what to do. It was the first Nazi he'd ever met and it horrified him. And this one, a perpetrator. Should he shake his proffered hand? Could he? *Guten Tag, guten Tag!* He nearly turned tail and left. The man had been a physician in Auschwitz and been acquitted at his trial after the war thanks to Jewish witnesses who testified that within that brutal regime, run by the notorious Dr Mengele, he'd been humane, doing his best to lessen their suffering. Just a camp doctor, as he later put it.

So Dan went into the house, sat down on the settee in the nice German living room with the picture window looking out over green fields, Alps in the distance, and accepted a cup of coffee from a china set unnervingly like the one his parents had at home. He could hardly speak. He kept thinking of his own father, another doctor. Later he met the man's son, the one who'd answered the advertisement, who ran a local restaurant. They'd never talked about the war at home, said the son. But he left home as soon as he could, aged sixteen. 'Thank God we *did* lose the war,' he added.

Those early interviews didn't go well for Dan. He found he was either too aggressive or too empathetic. He couldn't get the balance right. Many a time he thought he'd made a terrible mistake, should never have come. He wondered whether it was pride before a fall. His colleague, the German professor, had arranged for Dan to use an office in his department at Wuppertal University and an assistant to type out the interviews, and furnished him with a tape recorder. One of his early interviewees refused to be taped. That was enough to set Dan off into paranoia. Was this a set-up of some kind? Ridiculous, he told himself when he left. Pull yourself together! The man just didn't want to speak on record. So gradually Dan got the measure of it. By his second visit to Germany, on his own without Tammy now, he was calmer, more professional. He reminded himself he was there to try and understand how such things could happen, and how the children of these perpetrators were able to live with their legacy thereafter.

His first interview on this second visit was with the son of a man who'd been the chief of the local *Rassenpolitisches Amt*, Heinrich Himmler's pet project, the Office for Racial Policy. His father was an ideologue and a rabid anti-Semite, said the son. He'd started out normally enough as a professor of genetics, but ended up as director of the local health services, which in those days meant racial health. For him people were either pure Aryans or not. Euthanasia was his speciality. 'The mentally ill were killed either by injection or, in the early years, by gas, in travelling vans,' said his son. 'After the war my father shot himself in the clinic at the university. He thought he would be arrested and found guilty at his trial.' The son reached for his handkerchief and wept. Dan stayed silent, waiting. 'He said goodbye to me in a very warm way, not at all how he usually behaved. He was crying. I can still hardly talk about it.' He'd overheard his mother trying to dissuade his father from killing himself. 'He carried me on his shoulders during a long walk through the forest, even though I was a heavy child. He sang German folk songs, the ones he used to play to me on the harmonica to send me to sleep. 'Brunnen vor dem Tore', that kind of thing. I can't listen to them today. The trauma gets worse as I get older, not better.' He'd studied German Literature at university and was now working at the local radio station. He liked to write poetry. He became and remained a strong anti-capitalist, he said. He could see the appeal of the Baader-Meinhof group.

Dan was quite done in when he left, walking to the railway station. He knew he wasn't far from Heidelberg, where his paternal grandfather's house had been. His father often talked about it, the spacious comfort of it, the beauty of the furnishings, the garden. He decided to make a detour and visit it. Take a break.

The house was in one of Heidelberg's most beautiful old streets. It was pouring with rain by then, but Dan just stood there on the opposite pavement, looking at the house – large, elegant, with the date 1909 painted on the upper wall in old Germanic script, the date the Bruno family had moved into their newly built home. He hesitated, not sure what to do, then suddenly decided – walked across the street and rang the bell. A man, perhaps in his forties, answered the door. It was evening and he looked surprised to have a visitor at that hour. But when Dan explained who he was and that his grandfather had once owned this house, the man called out to his wife: 'Louise! We have a visitor. From Israel!' and invited Dan inside. And there, right there off the entrance hall, was the grand mahogany staircase which Dan had heard about so often from his father – dark, highly polished, specially carved for the house – his grandfather's pride and joy. It was uncanny, the whole experience: the past, the present, what was and what might have been. When Dan left, he felt completely drained.

On his third visit to Germany Dan went to meet Martin Bormann, He was the son of Martin Bormann, Hitler's private secretary and his most trusted and devoted follower, who accompanied him everywhere. Bormann ran the Obersalzberg at Berchtesgaden in the Bavarian Alps, which featured so often in Eva Braun's home movies – men in uniform clicking their heels and giving the Hitler salute, *Heil Hitler! Heil Hitler!* or, if not in the military, wearing their best suits and kissing the ladies' hands, especially if they were Austrian. The women were mostly in traditional dirndl dresses, fresh-faced with that natural look the Führer approved of, hair done up Heidi-style, everyone standing about on the terrace chatting or gazing at the sparkling view of the white-peaked Alps, '*Ach! Wie wunderschön!*', pointing this way and that, waiting for the Führer to appear.

The Obersalzberg was Hitler's private retreat, his enclave, surrounded by an impenetrable triple ring of SS security, from which, increasingly, the brave Führer of the Third Reich hardly ventured other than to attend an occasional inspection of his troops, again for the benefit of Joseph Goebbels's propaganda machine feeding the weekly newsreels in the cinemas, reassuring the German public that the war was going well and victory was imminent. Then it was back to the safety of Berchtesgaden as quickly as possible, flanked by a fleet of outriders, the route lined with his personal SS bodyguard, so paranoid was the Führer that he might be assassinated by one of his enemies – German ones, not the British or Russian or American ones.

'Hitler was my godfather,' Martin Bormann told Dan once they'd settled down in Bormann's living room, tape recorder running, Bormann's wife hovering discreetly in the background. He was a tall man, Dan noted, with wavy brown hair and brown eyes, a good-looking man, with a friendly, thoughtful, polite manner, German-style. Dan couldn't quite believe he was actually talking to him, Hitler's godson, and he had no idea why Bormann had decided to be interviewed.

'We lived on the Obersalzberg with the other families who were part of Hitler's close circle, more or less cut off from the rest of the world. In the early years we used to go down to Berchtesgaden to school, but later that stopped and we weren't allowed past the SS security ring. Not in, not out. It was a kind of ghetto, like being locked up: three security zones and a whole battalion of SS who lived in the barracks down the Alp. The farmers who used to live there had all been moved off. I was the eldest of ten siblings. You can see me in Eva Braun's home movies, on the terrace of the Obersalzberg with my mother who is wearing her usual dirndl outfit with her hair braided in the traditional German manner, and various other regular visitors like Albert Speer or Joseph Goebbels or Heinrich Himmler, who was my brother's godfather. And my father of course. There's a nice bit where we children are playing out in the snow and I turn to laugh at the camera. And in one bit of movie we Bormann children are seen opening Christmas presents with Hitler, a Christmas tree in the background. But mostly we hardly saw him.'

Years later, in Tel Aviv, Dan said it took him quite a while to settle to the task that day, even though he'd made careful preparations. But then, faced with the man, Martin Bormann, he wasn't sure. How to proceed? What questions to ask, in which order? What tone to take? He reminded himself that Bormann had agreed to talk to him, so...

In fact, it wasn't difficult at all. Bormann seemed perfectly at ease telling his extraordinary story. He had that way about him: measured, calm, strangely open. 'I remember Chamberlain coming,' he said. 'Hundreds of extra SS troops brought in to line the route. Then the black Mercedes arrived and this very English gentleman in a dark pinstriped suit, not a uniform, got out. Perhaps he even had an umbrella!' Bormann smiled. 'The Italian Ambassador was staying with us for the visit.'

Small lives touched by the big events of history again.

'I was fifteen when the war ended,' Bormann said. 'My father had sent me off to a Nazi Party boarding school at Völkerdingen on Lake Starnberg. I'd been playing hooky too often from school and he was very angry. He instructed them to make a decent person out of me. From then on, which was 1940, I hardly saw him any more.

We didn't see him a lot anyway. He was always off with Hitler at the Wolf's Lair or somewhere. In the end, he was in Hitler's bunker in Berlin of course.'

'Did he survive?' Dan knew the rumours: *Vater* Bormann might have escaped just before the Russians reached Berlin, helped by a secret underground network, perhaps via the Vatican, and made his way to South America. 'Oh no. I don't think so,' Bormann's son replied, firmly. 'He died in the *Führerbunker* with Hitler.' Who knows, who knows, thought Dan.

Bormann's wife brought in some coffee. They chatted about this and that for a while. Then they went back to the interview and the tape recorder.

'Völkerdingen was not easy for me. I was only ten. It was like a military academy, draconian rules, run by the SS. Beatings for punishment. Lots of sport. I wasn't sporty. And it wasn't an advantage to be Martin Bormann's son either. There was a lot of bullying. Like in the Hitler Youth, bullying was considered good for boys, to toughen them up. In the five years I was there my father hardly ever visited. Once he came when I complained about the bad food. It turned out the staff had been stealing it for themselves. My mother never came. I went home three times a year. But my father was very strict during vacations. I always had to work, in the vegetable garden or on the farm.' Dan hesitated: 'So he wasn't a good father?' Bormann looked surprised. 'No, no, he was a good father! And the school didn't do me any harm. And I didn't become a stranger to my siblings.'

Dan was confused, not sure what to ask next. He needn't have worried. Bormann carried on calmly, in his measured way.

'I was fifteen at the end of the war. We knew we were losing, even from 1944 onwards. Everything was in chaos. The SS began to disappear. I had my last letter from my father in March 1945. He told me to be optimistic. He was still claiming to believe in victory. I didn't believe it. Classes had stopped by then and we had to build fortifications and we were given weapons. I had a small portable wireless and we listened to the BBC at night, so we knew what was happening. The mood got worse and worse as each boy heard his home town had been overrun. Then the school was disbanded. We were each given food for a week and 100 Reichsmarks.'

'Where did you go?'

'On 23 April we were all transferred to Steinach. It was late at night. The road was bombed. The railway destroyed. We stayed till the 29th. On the 31st someone, sent by my father I think, came to drive me to the local Nazi Party HQ. It had a deep bunker. It was full of diehards. At two o'clock in the night we heard on the wireless that the Führer had died bravely, 'in the circle of his loyal *Kamaraden*'. The mood was one of despair. The end of the world. During the next two hours eight people shot themselves. I thought I had to do it too. But then I went outside and there was a boy out there already. We talked each other out of it. We wanted to live. We were both crying. It was terrible. We agreed to escape. He went left, I went right, out into the night. We ran away.'

Dan noticed Bormann's usual calm was gone. He spoke in short sentences. His voice was breaking, though he tried hard to control it. It was excitement, Dan realised in some surprise. Not distress. Excitement. After all those years.

'I made my way back to Berchtesgaden. When I came to the house it was empty. Mother gone. Brothers and sisters gone. Father gone. My father's secretary was in the study, destroying some documents. When he saw me he said, 'What are you doing here? Are you mad?' He gave me some false papers with a stamp so blurred you couldn't read anything. Then he told me to disappear. What we feared most was getting caught and shot.'

Bormann fell into silence, lost in thought. 'When did you see your mother again?'

'I never saw my mother again. She died in 1946, of cancer.'

Later he admitted that his father had told her to commit suicide and poison all the children as well, like Joseph Goebbels. But he stuck to his story that she'd died of cancer. And that his father had died with Hitler in the bunker in Berlin, in spite of all those rumours that he'd escaped to South America. That's how he was, Martin Bormann: very open. Until he wasn't. Or perhaps he was telling the truth.

He hid out until nightfall, he said, then made his way further into the Alps, to the border with Austria. He didn't know where to go or what to do. After days of hiding and scavenging he was starving. He knew he couldn't go on like that but he didn't dare give himself up. One early morning he was high in the Alps when he saw a farmer and his wife on the steep slope outside their Alpine hut, scything, making hay for their cows, the woman in boots and apron and headscarf, the man in boots, rolled-up shirtsleeves and braces. They were very old, bent over, swishing left and right in perfect rhythm with one another. Bormann hovered by the edge of the field, uncertain what to do. The old man called him over. '*Komm! Was ist, junger Mann?*' Come! What's up, young man? He spoke a local dialect, old-fashioned.

Young Bormann didn't know what to do. Were they loyal Nazis? Friend or foe?

'I didn't know the world, you see. I'd always been cut off from it,' he explained to Dan. 'I only knew Hitler and the Nazis. But I knew that not everyone was a Party member. I knew about Communists.'

The old couple took him into their alpine hut and fed him. He ate like a wolf. He gave them a false name, but of course they knew he was someone on the run. A wooden ladder led up to a small loft and they told him he could hide there. There was hay, and they gave him a blanket. And a prayer book. The loft was made of wide wooden planks and there were cracks through which he could see down into the room below. He made a gesture with his hands, showing how he'd bend down and look through the cracks. The single room had a wooden table, a wall-bench, two chairs, an old iron stove with a big black pot on it and a bed in one corner. There was no running water. That was brought in wooden pails from a trough outside.

In the evenings Bormann went down to eat with the old couple at the table: cheese and bread, soup, occasionally a hen too old to lay eggs, head chopped off with an axe by the farmer that morning and boiled for many hours, occasionally a sausage bought from the butcher in the village down the Alp where they went to shop once a week, rucksacks on back, walking alpine sticks in hand. As time passed and nothing happened, young Bormann began to go out into the field and help the old couple with the hay-making or the cows and the goats. Every evening as the light faded he went up to his loft again. The cockerel, strutting and crowing, woke him at daybreak.

Dan listened quietly. There was no remorse, he noted, again surprised, just a factual account of what happened.

'Had you come to doubt what your father told you?'

Bormann hesitated. 'Not yet.'

Dan waited. Bormann became agitated.

'I didn't know anything about the Holocaust then,' he explained. 'We didn't have a wireless up the Alp. No electricity.'

At the end of September the old couple took their cows back down to the village and into the cowshed attached to their farmhouse.

Bormann went with them and only went up to the Alpine hut if there was some danger. The villagers accepted him as a farm help, making up for the old couple's three sons, all 'missing' somewhere in Russia. If they had their suspicions they kept it to themselves. The world was full of people on the run.

'The only people who repeatedly upset us were the Americans,' said Bormann. 'They'd go up the Alp and shoot the wild goats! Or even a cow sometimes. In liberated Austria!' His indignation was shocking to Dan. The Nazis had killed the Jews and Communists and the Gypsies. Not goats.

Perhaps Bormann noticed, because he continued: 'It was the photographs of Bergen-Belsen in the *Salzburger Nachrichten* newspaper which caused my first doubts. Who would have thought such a thing possible? We had a work-detail from the Dachau camp at our school, but they looked fine. They were kept in barracks behind barbed wire by the SS. But they came to work singing.'

He went silent for a while. Dan waited again. Singing?

'We knew about concentration camps, but we thought they were like prisons. Work camps. Nothing else. We knew there were different triangles for the prisoners, that different colours meant different things: green for criminal, red for political.'

Yellow for Jew, thought Dan. 'What about the Jews?' he asked.

'They never came to the school. Were there Jews at Dachau? I know homosexuals weren't allowed. Nor Jehovahs. They were considered dangerous to the population. I don't know when the death camps were introduced. Not till the war turned against us.'

Dan pointed out that the first death camps were in 1942. Bormann said, yes, but they were all in the east. He reckoned National Socialism had been an exalted idea, misused by a handful of criminals and 'outsiders'. Dan wondered if Bormann admitted to himself that his own father was one of the criminals. The exalted idea, Bormann added without apparently realising he was contradicting himself, was an insane idea based on racial theories, the superiority of the Germanic race. 'But all this actually started long before National Socialism.' Yes, thought Dan, but it didn't end in extermination.

It was an unsettling experience for Dan, sitting there with this man, a good man, an intelligent man, who nevertheless seemed to excuse some of the Nazi past, either out of a sincere confusion or, more likely, to defend his father.

'So when did you change direction yourself?' Dan was keen to move on. 'Was it once you were down in the village, hearing the truth about what happened?'

'No, it was earlier. And for another reason.'

Dan smiled and raised his eyebrows. This man was full of surprises.

'It was when we were still up on the Alp. After the evening meal I would climb the ladder to the loft for the night. I could see down into the room through the cracks in the boards. And every night the old man and the old woman would kneel side by side in front of a crucifix of Christ on the Cross which hung on the wall and pray, heads bowed. They were devout Catholics, you see. They kneeled there and said the rosary – the Hail Marys and the Our Fathers – with their rosary beads, crossing themselves. I watched them every night, deeply moved. At first I didn't understand because I grew up without religion of course, forbidden by the Nazis. But I recognised: this is what Good is. And then I understood the difference, finally, between Good and Evil. I started going to church.'

Dan looked at this man, sitting there, leaning forward, hands on knees, telling him about his religious conversion. He really didn't know what to make of it.

Before Dan left they talked a bit more about Bormann's father and Nazism and how it could have happened.

'Only God knows all the reasons,' said Bormann. It was a bit like an Amen.

Martin Bormann, son of Martin Bormann, entered a seminary in 1946 and became a priest. Perhaps it was a safe place to be as well as a profound experience of renewal and cleansing. For many years he was a missionary in Africa, doing good wherever he could. Later he left the priesthood to marry his wife, who'd been a nun.

It was another of those exhausting emotional experiences for Dan. Had he been too empathetic to this son of a monster?, he wondered. But Bormann was only fifteen at the end of the war, so how could he be blamed? And he became a priest, to do good and make amends. Dan sat on the train on the way back to Wuppertal, thinking first this then that, wrung out.

His next interview was in a small town near Wuppertal, and it was quite different. The man Dan came to see was born in 1930 and he'd been a keen member of the Hitler Youth. He loved it all: the marching, the singing, the sport, the summer camps, the torch-lit processions. But his father wasn't so sure, he said. He worked on the *Reichsbahn* (railway) and the day came when he was told to join the Nazi Party if he wanted to keep his job. '*Vater!* You must join!' I told him, 'I couldn't understand why he was hesitating. And in the end he joined. When war broke out he was posted to Poland, where he saw terrible things – the ghetto at Parafjanów near Smolensk being liquidated, people told to undress before being shot into pits, children too. But he didn't have the courage to object, he said. 'He ran away and wept, he told me. He was sent home. He never recovered.'

Apparently the man's father wrote an account of it all. He called it 'Our Guilt' and it was dated 16 May 1945. He showed it to Dan, but the handwriting and German was too difficult for Dan to read. 'Shall I read it to you?

He started, hands shaking. 'On 9 February 1942 I was transferred to Poland. There were Jews living in the town. The Germans had a Jewish cook called Dolla, a sweet young girl with red hair, who was very, very clean. We became friends. Also there was Rita who had been a teacher, and the pharmacist called Herr Belzik. And a family called Aaron.' All before Himmler and Heydrich got going with their racial cleansing.

It was one woe after another. The man was with them on their last night. The man's son was crying now, searching for his handkerchief, but he went on reading. 'The Jews were herded together and forced out of the ghetto. They had to take off their shoes, coats, jackets, and they began to weep loudly. A boy of about fourteen tried to run away, but he was shot immediately. The men were forced to dig a large pit in the ground, and everyone – children and women, young and old – had to lie face-down to the ground.'

The man's son was sobbing now. Dan didn't know what to do. Again he tried not to think about his own family, who might so easily have been there, shot into a pit. Years later he tried to explain it to me: 'I was so stunned. So distressed. I didn't know what to do.'

The man went on reading, as though he wanted to do it in spite of the sobbing. 'I went as fast as I could to my barracks,' he read, 'heard shots again and again, and collapsed at the foot of my bed. Now I lost everything. I had followed the Lord faithfully for twenty-eight years, and now this terrible thing occurred. I wanted total oblivion . . .'

'He was sent to a field hospital,' said his son. 'A total collapse, but not allowed to tell anyone. Then he was sent home. Back home his condition got worse, he could hardly walk. He was accused by a Party official of having the wrong attitude. Accused of being a "dirty saboteur". People thought he was insane. He never recovered.'

Dan didn't know what to do but wait. In silence. The one thing not to do, he told me, was to speak. Intrude on the man's sorrow. He couldn't anyway. There were no words.

'He suffered till the day he died,' the man said once he'd gathered himself. 'But you must understand. The thing that shaped *me* was that I was unable to comprehend what my *Vater* was talking about when he came home. He told me never to hurt the Jews! I was disgusted. For me the Jews were the dregs of humanity. *Vater* said "Rudolf, Rudolf! Listen to me! Never attack a Jew!"'

The man was so agitated now, weeping and weeping, that Dan got worried. He managed to calm him down by reminding him he was just a young boy at the time who knew nothing but the Nazis. The past is the past, they finally agreed. It was time to leave. They shook hands warmly and Dan went his way.

Later that week he travelled by train across Germany again, to meet Klara. Living as he did in the dry Negev Desert, he still couldn't get over the fertile beauty of the countryside: those green meadows, those rivers, those dark forests. Klara lived on the outskirts of Munich in a leafy neighbourhood with gardens of flowers and vegetables. When she opened the door to him Dan could sense her hesitation, he told me. Had she done the right thing? Would she regret it? Could she trust him? She'd come to Dan through a friend who'd already been interviewed by him. She wasn't at all sure it was a good idea.

Klara was born in 1943 at that point in the war when things were turning once and for all against the Germans. Her father was the *Kommandant* of an *Einsatzgruppe*, those SS units which followed in the wake of the regular German Army, mopping up – or, to name it accurately, exterminating: Communists, Socialists, partisans, local officials who resisted, town mayors, army officers, intellectuals, police, first in Czechoslovakia, then Poland, then Russia. And Jews of course. Always the Jews. By the end of the war her father had disappeared into the anonymous crowd, like so many other members of the SS. And by 1948 the family – mother and three young children – were among an endless stream of refugees, walking on foot, carrying their bundles, pushing their wooden carts, from East to West Germany, fleeing the Communists. 'I was five. *Mutti* got us out over the border, one by one, in the night. I don't know how she did it! I know she paid some people...'

Klara was beautiful: tall, athletic, wavy light-brown hair and fine, strong features. She was clever too, a lawyer given to left-wing causes, forever defending people who couldn't easily defend themselves – a paid-up left-wing activist, including supporting the Palestinian cause against the Israelis. She was divorced with one child, a girl, now grown and off at university.

'In 1948 we ended up in a refugee camp near Hanover,' she told Dan once they were settled at her kitchen table, having decided to trust him, because Dan had that way with people. 'A year later *Vater* turned up, out of the blue. He said he'd been a regular soldier and then a POW in Italy, near Rimini. Later it turned out not to be true of course. But at the time we believed it. He managed to find a one-room apartment, for all five of us. I remember the local people were really nasty to us refugee children. There was a large garden with fruit trees, but we weren't allowed in there, we weren't even allowed to pick an apple off the ground. If we tried, a man with a whip would run after us. Later we got an additional room and I started school. That's one thing I can thank *Vater* for: he wanted us girls to go to the *Gymnasium*, just as much as the boy in the family. *Mutti* didn't care. She said we'd get married anyway. But he made sure it happened. Which was difficult because it cost money and we were very poor. *Vater* tried everything to get a job but he couldn't find anything. He ended up digging peat.'

Dan listened quietly, imagining what it must have been like in those early post-war years in Germany. So much hate and recrimination. So much despair. So much guilt.

'Finally we moved to Hamburg. I was twelve.'

Hamburg, thought Dan. Hamburg, his parents' home till 1933, when they fled to Palestine. It was mostly Socialist and Communist then, as his father told him. Not many Nazis.

'*Vater* had managed to get a better job, as a travelling salesman, always on the road. He only came home once a month. We didn't mind because he was so strict. He wanted to get a job as a civil servant again, but it didn't work. That's when I found out he'd been in the police before the war. But nothing else. When I was sixteen we moved to Düsseldorf, and he finally got his job back with the police, in the criminal investigation department, which is what he'd been before the war apparently. So that's when we started living together as a proper family, in 1959.'

'What was that like?' asked Dan.

'Very difficult. *Vater* was so strict. My sister was his favourite. She was a good girl, never caused him any trouble, sweet-natured, training to be a nurse. Whereas I was always fighting him, arguing with him, rebelling. My brother was more like me, and he got the worst of *Vater*'s bullying. But it was bad for me too. Once I came home a bit late from a date and he was so angry he slapped me, hard.'

Dan noticed the colour rising in Klara's face. It still hurt, that slap.

'Then, one evening in 1962, I'd been out on a date at the movies, a few weeks before my final *Abitur* exams. When I came home my boyfriend and I started to neck a little downstairs by the door. And then some man came down the stairway and asked was I so-and-so? I said yes, and he said, "I'd like you to come upstairs right away. Something has happened." They were all sitting in the living room, *Mutti*, my brother, my sister, *Vater*, the whole family. There were two other detectives there as well. They'd come to arrest *Vater*. They'd been waiting for me so he could say goodbye to me. They'd been there quite long time, but he asked them to wait for me. Not much was said then. So he went along with them.'

Later her mother told her a bit more: it was something to do with her father's activities during the war, she said. Apparently she knew there was an investigation going on and that he might be arrested, but she'd said nothing to the children. Then Klara remembered that her father got passports for all of them some weeks back which she'd thought strange at the time since they never travelled abroad. Her mother admitted he'd thought of taking them all to South America to avoid arrest, but they didn't have the money. She wouldn't say any more.

'All she said was: he had to do it. Had to shoot people. Just following orders. So she knew he'd been in the SS, and then headed an *Einsatzgruppe* in Ukraine during the war. But she always defended him. It was a terrible injustice, she said, that he was arrested. Others had done much worse.' Klara shook her head, close to tears. 'The arrest was like a bolt out of the blue. He'd always told us he was a soldier and then a POW with the Americans in Italy, and that he'd somehow escaped. He was tried in Düsseldorf and sentenced to four years. The charges were that he had been part of an SS firing squad and had also been its *Kommandant*.'

After the main Nuremberg Trials, where twelve of the top Nazis were sentenced to death, came the lesser trials, lasting from 1946 to 1949. There were twelve such trials in all, conducted by the Americans, known as the Subsequent Nuremberg Trials, and concerned different branches of the Nazi state such as industrialists, doctors, lawyers, civil servants and *Kommandanten* of the *Einsatzgruppen* extermination units, who were all members of Himmler's SS. The indictment for the *Einsatzgruppen* trial was threefold: crimes against humanity, war crimes, and membership of the SS and other criminal organisations. It was estimated that between them the *Einsatzgruppen* murdered some 2 million people. Later there were Denazification trials, run locally by Germans. It was at one of these trials that Klara's father was found guilty. The Russians ran their own trials, and continued to track down Nazi war criminals long after the Americans and the British and the Germans had ceased. For the Allies, Communism soon became the greater enemy, just as it had in Germany in 1933, allowing Hitler and the Nazis to come to power.

Klara stopped and searched for a cigarette. From her forced smile Dan could see how tense she was. '*Danke*, but I don't smoke,' said Dan when she offered him one.

'I can still recall the first time I visited *Vater* in prison,' she told Dan. 'Then he only complained how bad things were in jail, and the fact that he had to be with common criminals. I remember very distinctly his expression and that he, "a decent and proper German civil servant", was locked up along with criminals.'

In spite of all this Klara did well in her *Abitur* exams and went on to Cologne University, and later to Tübingen, studying Law. 'It's hard for me to remember that period,' she said. 'Actually, I wasn't around much any more. First I was at university. Then I went to France. Then I got married, in Tübingen, and had a child. After I had a family of my own I didn't really belong to them any more. I guess I put a certain distance between us. And when *Vater* came out of prison there were occasional visits, but we always got into terrible arguments whenever the topic of his trial was broached. And what I always found so awful in these conversations is that he felt sorry for himself. I always hoped he'd say something about his victims, but it never happened. I believe I could have made myself speak to him if that had been different. He even suggested he'd done it for us, for his family, to stay alive for us. He said that if he hadn't obeyed orders, they would have shot him. That was the worst of all!'

Klara began to cry. There was a long pause. Then clever Dan said: 'He seems very dear to you. Were you looking for some kind of justice?'

The question took her by surprise. 'Sometimes I think that – my *Vater*'s been dead for three years – that now I'd like to deal with this matter, because it can't burden my relationship with him any more. For example, there was one day at the trial when all the witnesses said he'd tried to get a transfer, but it was refused. And apparently by the time war broke out all the *Kriminalpolizei*, Criminal Police units, had automatically been taken into the SS.'

From his research Dan knew this was true. Into the Gestapo, then the SS. 'What about your mother?'

'She's been in psychiatric clinics four times for depression.' Klara lit another cigarette, drawing in the smoke, calming herself. 'She was a woman who, on her own, was always terrific. She kept things going through the entire period of the war, with three small children. My brother was only a baby when we fled as refugees. We were on the brink of starvation. And when *Vater* was arrested she went to work in a store.' Klara hesitated, unsure whether to reveal the worst. But then: 'She tried to kill herself when he was released from prison. I realise now that's when the depressions started. She always submitted to him. He was the boss. They'd known each other since childhood, you see. She'd spent her entire life with him. But he treated her in a condescending manner much too often. He made her feel she was inferior to him. That upset me very, very much. Perhaps that's why I'm divorced.' She smiled a small smile and looked away. 'Then he died, suddenly, of a stroke, in the street. And that's when her depressions started again.' Klara was close to tears. 'The death of my mother would be a terrible blow.'

Klara was tense and tired. They parted with a formal handshake. But a few weeks later Dan got a letter from her, thanking him and saying their talk had done her good. She was seeing a therapist. A year later they met again, in a restaurant not far from her office.

It was Dan's fourth and last visit to Germany. It was a beautiful, warm day, so they sat outside, in the shade of a chestnut tree. She realised now, she said, that her anger and disappointment in her father had led to many things in her own life, including her left-wing views and becoming a political activist. She looked happier and more relaxed. Dan was relieved.

Half the time Dan wasn't sure he should be doing what he was doing, unsettling people, stirring things up. And causing plenty of trouble for himself in Israel too.

His next visit was to Cologne. Again he went by train. Again he felt that mix of nervous tension and excitement as he walked down a leafy street and rang the bell of the top flat in an old-style apartment building. What would this Renate be like? Who knows?

She was waiting for him at the top of the stairwell, looking down. When he reached the landing, puffed, they shook hands formally and she smiled a hesitant smile. She was a fine person, Dan could see it immediately, not only in outward looks but inside too – thick brown hair, eyes very blue, medium height, dressed simply in jeans and T-shirt. She led him into a small hall with a kitchen on the left and into the sitting room, which looked out over the road shaded by the trees. It was light and airy, walls white, Persian rugs on the floor, plenty of books. Her partner Edi was already sitting there, a dark-haired, good-looking woman who'd been an actress, now a therapist. She stayed throughout the interview.

'I was an illegitimate child,' stated Renate in that compulsively honest way of hers as soon as the tape recorder was running.

But the reader is ahead of Dan this time. We already know Renate's story. Now Dan was finding it out for himself: about the unknown father who'd been an SS general in Latvia, Himmler's right-hand man in northern Russia, shooting the Jews of Riga into deep pits in the forest, responsible for thousands of deaths in Salaspils concentration camp. And about the mother, who'd had a long affair with him and loved him still. Renate talked as though it was only through painful honesty, ducking none of the detail, that she could even begin to come to terms with what he did – what she'd inherited. She started searching for answers early on, in her teens she said, but she found nothing. 'No one talked about it in Germany in those days. It was taboo.' Later, much later, there were some articles, and the Institut für Zeitgeschichte in Munich published a book.

'When did you first find a reference to your father?' asked Dan.

'It was a shock, reading Krausnick's *Anatomie des SS Saates* and his *Die Truppe des Weltanschaung skrieges*, but a relief too in a way – finally having some concrete evidence. Finally knowing who my father was, and what he did. Even though...'

And then she got up and left the room.

Dan and Edi sat there in silence, waiting. It had started to rain. Edi was watching Dan, trying to discover what effect Renate's monologue – because it had been a monologue – was having on him. Dan was immersed in his own thoughts, his horror at what Renate's father had done, his admiration at what the daughter, in all her honesty and courage, was trying to do. Then Renate came back into the room.

'Two years ago we went to Riga because I thought I could get documents about my father there,' Renate continued where she'd left off. 'But normal mortals can't get hold of such documents.'

'How is it possible that a person, once upon a time a decent enough person, can do such things?' asked Dan, who had a way of moving things on, taking his subjects by surprise with the next question.

'That's the question!' Renate responded immediately. 'How is it possible for people to do such things? How is it possible? And later, afterwards, how is it possible for an entire people not to come to terms with it? Then they have the argument: what right have you youngsters got to talk about it? You weren't involved! You don't know! All you know is what you've read in books! We were there!'

Edi stretched out a hand to calm her.

'It's not a question of accusing people,' Renate went on. 'It's simply a matter of thinking about it afterwards, of asking how is it possible, what sort of processes were involved? My interest is not in accusing people.'

By the time Dan left to go back to the railway station the rain had stopped. He walked instead of taking the tram because he needed time to digest the conversation. Renate was the first person he'd met in Germany who was asking the same questions as he was, and she was the daughter of one of the Reich's most terrible murderers! Years later, talking to me about it, he was still astonished.

We agreed then that once power gets into the wrong hands, it not only promotes all the 'bad' people, it can apparently make even 'normal' people who would lead normal, decent lives do utterly abnormal things.

Gerda lived in a town not far from Bonn. When Dan arrived her husband greeted him warmly, shaking his hand, but then left them to it. Gerda was one of those instantly likeable people, large-built, short greying permed hair, thick glasses, smiling. She'd heard about Dan from another interviewee, so news of the project was apparently spreading by word of mouth now. Once she'd served the coffee and a slice of her home-baked cake they settled down in two armchairs to talk. 'You have to imagine it,' she said. 'On our sitting room wall at home when I was growing up there was a large photograph of Hitler in a black frame.'

She indicated the size by spreading her arms wide. 'It dominated our lives, whatever we did. Whether we were eating, or reading, or talking, he was always there, watching us. My *Vater* had a little Führer moustache, just like Hitler. He did his hair just like Hitler. He wore his uniform just like Hitler. He was a total imitation. I can still hear the sound of his boots, those shiny black SS boots, always highly polished, banging up our stairs. I have never seen a face more filled with hate than my *Vater*'s. And he always said: it's the Jews! Just imagine how well-off we'd all be without the Jews!'

Gerda's father ran the local euthanasia clinic. The killing of the mentally and physically disabled had begun in 1939, on Hitler's personal order. The Master Race should be pure, not defiled by the defective, said the Führer, often repeated by Gerda's father to his children. Exact numbers are hard to establish, but some 150,000 disabled people were forcibly removed from their families and killed in the clinics over the next two years. Another 400,000 with hereditary diseases were sterilised. Another 10,000 homosexuals were killed, and thousands more castrated. The euthanasia programme was referred to as *Aktion T4* for those in the know. *T* for *Tiergarten*, that charming park in the centre of Berlin, 4 for the number of the villa from which the programme was administrated. Everything disguised and code-named. Everything leading back in secret to Department II of the Chancellery, and thence directly to the Führer. Euphemism was the name of the game. The Community Foundation for the Encouragement of Asylums handled the properties and hired the personnel, most of whom used false names and false jobs.

A company named the Community Patients Transport Service Ltd used innocent-looking postal vans and buses to remove the 'patients' to the killing centres. These had been adapted by SS teams from ordinary asylums to their new purpose, after which carefully selected nurses and doctors and administrators like Gerda's father were moved in. Hadamar, Bernburg, Grafeneck, Brandenburg, Hartheim, Sonnenstein – all busy with their 'mercy killing', all secret. The added advantage of the clinics was that they could experiment with the use of gas chambers, disguised as shower rooms, in preparation for the later killing of hundreds of thousands of Jews and other racially inferior people, not just a few thousand disabled people.

But news soon got out. Not least because of the foul smell from the chimneys when the wind blew in the wrong direction.

'All God-fearing people feel this extermination of the helpless is an almighty crime,' wrote the Bishop of Limburg to the Minister of Justice, risking his own life in so doing. 'Officials of the Gestapo are trying, as one hears, to suppress talk about what is going on with severe threats. The conviction is multiplied by the bitter knowledge that the talk is banned by threat, but the actions themselves are not prosecuted under law.' By 1941 the clinics were shut down, due to public outrage.

When Dan rang up his next interviewee, Dirk Kuhl, it was his wife Lena who answered the phone. 'You can talk to me in Hebrew,' she said, 'I'm from Israel.' They arranged to meet that Friday.

The Kuhls lived in a small town not far from Wuppertal, where Dan was again based. He took the local train and, sitting in a carriage surrounded by robust Germans, many old enough to have lived through the Nazi period and the war, he told me he couldn't stop himself asking silently: 'So, what did you do in the war?' Then he stopped. It was stupid and useless and unfair. He knew that less than a third of the population had ever voted for the Nazis. He'd checked the election results. So he turned his thoughts to Israel, and home. Normally he'd be putting on a clean white shirt, preparing for the Shabbat. They weren't religious, but they liked to have a traditional, festive atmosphere on Friday evenings. They sat round the table, lit the candles and sang the songs. In the old days Tammy used to bake challah, the Jewish bread, but after Yariv died the previous year she didn't do it any more. That's how it took her, the terrible grief. But they still did the rest.

Dirk Kuhl was at the railway station to meet him. He was a wiry man, energetic, stylish in a 1960s sort of way, with an expression of sceptical curiosity, sharp and humorous. He was about the same age as Dan – a teacher at the local *Hochschule*. His handshake was brisk and friendly. He'd written a letter to the local newspaper about his father, who'd been the Gestapo Chief in Braunschweig. That's how Dan had first heard about him.

At the house they sat round the table drinking coffee, the three of them: Dan, Dirk and Lena, all much the same age, each with their different stories of survival. It made Dan feel at home, sitting there with Lena, a Jew who, it turned out, was hidden as a child during the war by her gentile grandmother in Ukraine. After the war she'd set off with her mother for life on a kibbutz in Israel. Her mother was still there. But Lena wanted to come back to Europe. She and Dirk met at a student party in Düsseldorf. Her mother still didn't know that Dirk's father had been a big fat Nazi, he said. Well, perhaps not fat, but big. Dirk smiled his humorous smile.

'It wasn't a quick decision,' he said about going public. 'I simply feel we have to put an end to our silence.' An article in *Der Spiegel* had prompted him to write his letter.

'What's your earliest memory?' asked Dan

'I can only remember four meetings with my father. Once we were short of food at home, and he came in his uniform – that was an exception, he never wore uniform off-duty. I'd left my teddy bear in the bathroom and when he left, lo! there was a big sausage right next to the bear. At the that time that was something sensational, really. By 1944 people were starving in Germany. And then I remember a long trip in a car with him – checkpoints, roadblocks. It was dark

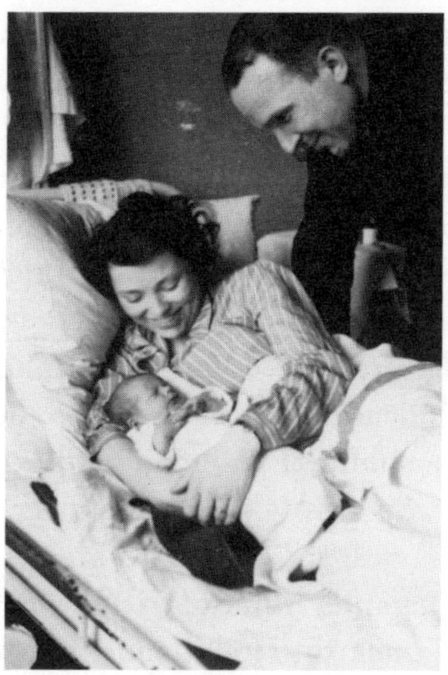

and there were soldiers. Then I recall a visit with my mother to a POW camp, run by the British, near Hanover. That was at the time of the Camp 21 trial, as a result of which he was arrested.'

Dan knew that Camp 21 was the camp run by the Nazis to 're-educate' people who opposed the regime, committing acts of so-called 'treason' – Communists, Socialists, priests, teachers, artists, army officers, Jehovah's Witnesses – any brave person who'd dared to fight the regime, risking their lives.

'All I can remember is that he was wearing a British khaki uniform. It had a typical British style.'

'Yes, I know what you mean,' said Dan. 'My father was in the British Army during the war, and I remember him in a similar uniform.' But with rolled-up shirtsleeves, he thought, because of the intense desert heat. Small world, as they say. As Dan told me this part, we smiled at one another. My father had been in the war too, all six years of it.

'They'd given him some sort of a job,' said Dirk, referring to the British. 'He knew English well, was a trained lawyer. He gave me a box of crayons as a present, and I did a drawing. That's the last time I saw him. He was executed shortly after.'

There was a pause then.

'Do you remember your mother at the time?'

'Not really. I remember being in the Black Forest, Christmastime 1948. It was our first vacation after the war. My mother told me then that my father had died in British captivity. I believed it at the time. As much as a child can tell, he hadn't been looking well when I saw him in the camp. He had lost a lot of hair, and he wasn't the man I remembered. I knew that many men were dying all around us at that time. Someone even shot himself in front of our house. So I accepted what she said.'

'How did she tell you the news? Did she cry?'

'No, I don't think so. We were sitting in a room and she said, "You've always said a prayer for your *Vater* to return. But he won't be coming back. He's dead. You'll have to live with that. And so will I."' It's true her voice sounded very troubled.'

Lena said she thought Dirk's mother had never got over it.

'We'd gone to live with my grandfather in Lübeck by then. My mother's father. When the Americans who'd commandeered the house left, he moved back in. There was plenty of room. I liked my grandfather a lot. He never approved of my father. He was a monarchist in orientation. Very liberal in political terms. Very upset that the Nazis had outlawed his Central Party. He was a factory owner, a manufacturer body and soul. He didn't approve of my parents' marriage, wasn't happy about it.'

Probably Dirk resembled his grandfather, not his father, thought Dan. 'What about your grandmother?'

'My grandmother was a very independent-minded woman. She didn't have much to do with the Church, nor the Nazis – with anything in fact which smacked of ideology. She was very self-confident, which is just what my grandfather needed: someone who would contradict him, stand up to him. Actually she had a very formative influence on me because my mother was away at the family factory all day, and would come home in the evening exhausted, with a headache.'

Lena added a comment now and again. 'Gradually, as we looked through all the letters and papers, it has become evident why she had her condition,' she said. 'She was a fighter by nature, but she'd been ruined, for all practical purposes, by this entire thing. Actually, she was the positive factor in the marriage.'

'I have a letter my father wrote in which he talks about his ideal when it comes to a wife. His notions are so narrow-minded, so antiquated, so petit-bourgeois, it's really awful,' said Dirk. 'My mother wasn't that kind of woman at all. I assume that marriage was some enormous mistake.'

'When did your father join the Nazi Party?' asked Dan

Lena thought 1933. Dirk thought it was a bit later. 'His goal was to become a judge, but it was impossible because he did so poorly in his final exams. So the only way he could get into the civil service was through the Party. He joined the police detective branch, which was later integrated into the Gestapo.'

They took a bit of a break then. Dan went into the garden. Lena into the kitchen. Dirk sat and read the newspapers. Then they picked up where they left off.

'Yes. My mother wasn't able to deal with the situation,' said Dirk. 'And then the business went bankrupt. My grandfather had died and my mother had to deal with it. It was a double strain, and she couldn't handle it.' He paused. 'My mother was a problem for me.'

'Actually they used to fight all the time,' said Lena. 'Naturally that was bound up with his father. She was very sensitive about it.'

Dan noticed how they talked almost as one, Dirk and Lena, each picking up from the other.

'My father's father, I also knew him of course, he was an old high school music teacher. I didn't like the man. He was a rigid old-fashioned man who talked enthusiastically about the First World War. Somehow I had the feeling something was wrong. After he died we didn't have any more contact with that side of the family.'

How complicated things were in post-war Germany, thought Dan, everyone at odds with each other, stuck with their terrible guilt. Or their resentments and denials, like Dirk's paternal grandfather.

'After the bankruptcy, my mother started all over again,' said Dirk, 'as a secretary at a psychological advisory service. Soon she was running the place. During that period our relationship was good. I had decided that if I couldn't love my mother, I could be fair and try to be a friend to her. I wasn't afraid she would have any influence over me any more. And at some point she no longer tried. She was opposed to our marriage, but it was because she didn't want to see any woman at my side, anyone serious. Not because Lena was a Jew. I know it had to do with the fact that I was an only child, and that my father had died. In the end, though, she accepted Lena. When she retired she moved in with us.'

People are remarkable, each in their own small lives, thought Dan.

'But at any family celebration she would start talking about Dirk's "wonderful" *Vater*,' said Lena. 'She would tell these beautiful stories about her engagement, her marriage. He would be presented as a very lovable, sweet and harmless person.'

'She fought for him tooth and nail,' said Dirk. 'I suppose she loved him. I don't know why. She even wrote to Chancellor Adenauer, pleading for his pardon.'

'She had this notion that he had atoned for his sins with his death. That those who had committed worse crimes had not been brought to justice,' said Lena.

'She thought it was unfair that they hadn't taken anything into account,' added Dirk, 'and had shot him as a scapegoat, because they hadn't been able to catch the others.'

So he was shot, noted Dan. Well, there was a lot of scapegoating after the war in Germany, he knew that. It was the same everywhere, after every war. Israel. Palestine.

When Dan returned to Israel after this fourth and last research trip to Germany in 1987 he felt it was high time to try and analyse his data, like the social scientist he was. He'd interviewed fifty children of Nazi perpetrators by then, mostly members of Himmler's SS. It turned out that the excuse given by many in Germany after the war – that it was mostly the SS who had committed those crimes against humanity, whether in the concentration camps, or in the *Einsatzgruppen* extermination units, or upholding the terror regime at home – had some truth to it.

So what were they like, these children of perpetrators? Were they born before the war? Or during? How old were they during the Third Reich? How and when did they learn about their fathers' wartime activities? Had they managed to be loving parents to their own children? What did they tell them? Were they religious? What backgrounds did they come from?

Night after night he sat at his desk, compiling graphs and tables. His analysis included the euthanasia programme and the transportation system. He discovered that many of the children of perpetrators were childless. He noted many came from the middle classes, fewer from the working or upper classes, and that the fathers were nearly all members of Himmler's SS. They were, by definition, members of the Nazi Party. He knew that the original membership of the Nazi Party, some 2 million, came largely from the lower section of that middle class – shopkeepers, white-collar workers, small officials – but that later it grew, encompassing a wider range of backgrounds, because people joined the Party to keep safe their jobs, their homes, their children. To be promoted.

Again and again he heard that the children of perpetrators grew up surrounded by silence. The parents said nothing, society said nothing. The schools said nothing. History stopped with Bismarck. It was a collective silence. Or, as Dan put it, a conspiracy of silence. 'The parents have erected a wall around their feelings about the atrocities they have witnessed or carried out, and the children have reacted by building their own protective wall,' he wrote. 'For several interviewees the interview process itself became an opportunity for exploring and integrating the past.' He noted that many of them feared some inherent 'bad seed' of evil or abnormality. Their conflicting feelings towards their fathers were a heavy weight, holding them in the dark past, interfering with their attempts to disentangle themselves and move forward.

He worried that he'd been too empathetic towards the children of Nazi war criminals. He reminded himself again and again: only evaluate a person within their own context. Don't impose anything of your own. He worried that the sample was too small for any proper assessment. He came to a decision: he would write a letter to each of his interviewees, inviting them to Wuppertal University for a conference on his research, along with some of his professional colleagues. Most wrote back refusing, giving a variety of excuses. But a few said yes, including Renate and Dirk, Gerda, Martin and Klara. In July 1988 he set off for Germany again, this time accompanied by his daughter from his first marriage at the kibbutz all those years ago in another time and another place. Yaarah was a student herself now and had followed her father's progress with interest. On the way, they stopped off in Heidelberg to visit the old family home again, the one built by Dan's paternal grandfather in 1909, before all the horrors of two world wars and the Nazis' attempt to exterminate the Jews. Dan wanted Yaarah to understand where she'd come from. Who she was.

The conference was highly emotional. How could it not be, with all that death and extermination, guilt and shame? But out of it came a decision: the children of perpetrators would form a self-help group. Because they'd discovered for the first time, listening to one another, that they shared the same horrors and nightmares, grew up surrounded by the same silences, felt the same troubling mix of hate and love for their parents. For the father because of what he did. For the mother because of her complicity in hiding it. Many times they reached an impasse. Finally it was Dirk's wife Lena who challenged them. 'Look!' she said. 'Accept your feelings! What is happening here, which, after all, is what makes living in this country possible for someone like me.' Dan felt a sense of shame, he told me. Once again it was a Jew who took the initiative, who gave everyone encouragement. 'Slowly we felt a sense of mutual affection.'

They always kept in touch after that. And Dan continued his research. And wrote his book. And he met Joe Albeck's One Generation After in Boston. Then came the moment he stepped over the edge, into more darkness.

With the help of his German colleague he organised a reconciliation meeting with the Wuppertal group of children of Nazi war criminals and the Boston group of children of survivors of the Holocaust. It took a great deal of persuasion and reassurance on both sides. 'It's just an initial effort,' he told them, 'an experiment in reconciliation, which is the only way forward, surely?' Because that's what Dan believed, heart and soul. Military and political means failed again and again. In big ways and small – big wars, and then those small lives ruined, leaving nothing but unresolved, silent pain. He knew it from his own story, and the story of Palestine.

Dirk Kuhl and Lena were with him. So was Gerda. And Renate. And Klara. So was Joe Albeck, after giving it careful thought. So was Charley Munn. So was Julie. They were the pioneers, the pathfinders. Dan smiled and raised his eyebrows at that one. He'd been a pathfinder once upon a time. Perhaps he was again now, but in another way. They met in Wuppertal.

You will want to know how it went, of course. But that will have to wait for the next chapter. Except for one thing: Renate, at that preparatory meeting, made an extraordinary decision – typical of her perhaps, given her bravery and her almost obsessive honesty. She decided to show the group the BBC documentary we'd made about her: *A Child for Hitler*.

It stunned everyone in that room. There was Renate's mother, a delightful woman, insisting she still loved 'Fried' whatever he was supposed to have done. There was Renate herself, searching for the truth about her father. The truth. Finally going to Riga with Edi, to the Salaspils concentration camp. And the deep pits dug in the forest. And talking to Isaac Kleinmann, one of only twelve Jews who'd escaped Jeckeln's massacres. And there was Friedrich Jeckeln himself, in the archive film, looking as though he were alive, emerging from his field caravan somewhere in Latvia to work at a table out in the sunshine, the very image of Renate. And then later, thin and haggard at his trial.

Yes, the Wuppertal group was stunned into silence, deeply moved.

Once the film was over Renate ran from the room and hid in the toilets, weeping. 'I wouldn't come out,' she told me later. 'I was so ashamed.' Then there was a knock at the toilet door and many voices, all encouraging her to come out, praising her for her bravery and her honesty. Finally she emerged. 'They were all waiting for me, a line of them, all hugging me, one after another. But do you know, I couldn't believe it: they were all Jews. Not one German!'

After that meeting, back in Boston, Joe sat down to write one of his poems. 'Winds of Reconciliation', he titled it. 'Celebrating the first encounter between children of Jewish Holocaust survivors and children of convicted Nazi war criminals, Wuppertal, Germany.'

Winds of Reconciliation

Six million winds died to bring us here now,
A half-century after your fathers murdered mine,
though we were innocent or unborn then.

From opposite edges of the abyss,
fearful of dangerous, heated passions
blowing in the historic gap between,
we cautiously approached each other,
though we were innocent or unborn then.

Horrors done to, and endured by parents;
we children were left too long with only
anguished and misbegotten solitude;
searching for even a trace of solace
in that appalling piece of history;
unable to grasp, undo, or redeem
a past we too felt responsible for,
though we were innocent or unborn then.

Twin heirs to Europe's infamous era,
we are its tainted offspring, set apart,
our silent isolation only recently relieved
by peers who could bear the pain of listening,
so we could, at last, feel fully heard,
though we were innocent or unborn then.

Children of murderers and survivors
dared encounter each other, while the world
held its breath; we bonded and befriended

wounded offspring, all still bereft, ashamed
and bewildered by that bloody epoch,
though we were innocent or unborn then.

Together we transformed isolated,
lonely, individual children, to
proud co-captains of a team which may yet
soothe the sores and scars of history with
our words and winds of reconciliation,
though we were innocent or unborn then.

CHAPTER NINE

NEVE SHALOM

Wind on Time, wind on. It is April 1993.

A white minibus far in the distance drives up a long country road, dust rising either side. The afternoon sun is beating down. The brown earth of the land is heavily irrigated to produce crops of olives, vines, vegetables, orange groves. This is Israel. The minibus is making for Neve Shalom, a Peace Village halfway between Jerusalem and Tel Aviv – the land which had seen so much fighting during the 1967 and 1973 wars.

Inside the minibus sit nine people, two from Wuppertal University, the rest children of Nazi war criminals. One is Gerda, whose father was a doctor administrating the Nazi policy of euthanasia. Her daughter Hella has come with her to support her and translate from English into German. Another is Klara, the daughter of the SS commander in charge of an *Einsatzgruppe* extermination unit in Russia. Another is Martin Bormann, son of Martin Bormann, Hitler's right-hand man. Another is Dirk Kuhl, whose father was the Gestapo Chief of Braunschweig, sentenced to death by the Allies after the war. He is accompanied by his wife Lena. Another is Renate Röder.

The minibus climbed higher and higher till the Germans could see the green Ayalon Valley far below. They hardly spoke. The land was mostly rock and stones now as the minibus turned another bend and Neve Shalom came into view – a cluster of simple white buildings in the shade of pine trees. Hella held her mother's hand. Dirk and Lena exchanged a few words. Renate looked out of the window, apart. Martin sat calmly, hands folded. Klara twisted her handkerchief in anxiety.

Neve Shalom, also known as Wahat-as-Salam, was founded in 1970 by Father Bruno Hussar, a Dominican priest, to show that two peoples, Israeli Jews and Arabs, could live together in harmony in an 'oasis of peace'. It began with one Palestinian Arab family and four Jewish families, living in tents. By 1994 some fifty families were living there, largely self-sufficient, helped by international volunteers, providing a centre for education and for meetings of reconciliation between former enemies. 'My people shall dwell in an oasis of peace,' quoted Father Hussar from Isaiah 32:18. And who better than he, born a non-religious Jew in Egypt who later converted to Christianity – living proof that what matters is how a man lives, not by which religion.

Waiting to greet them at Neve Shalom was a Jewish group – the children of survivors of the Holocaust, mostly from the Boston One Generation After, and three younger Israeli Jews, the grandchildren of Holocaust survivors. And Dan Bar-On. They stood about in the gravel car park, tense, watching the white van come round the last bend, dust rising. They have met before, for that preparatory session, but this meeting will last four days, and everyone was nervous. 'When Dan asked me to join this group I first said no. I had a good life, my children were young, I didn't need it, I didn't want it,' said Julie, speaking for most of them. 'I was so scared. How could I shake them by the hand?' She shook her head in horror. Perhaps it was against her better judgement, but here she was, a Boston Jew waiting to shake the hand of a child of a Nazi war criminal.

It was Dan who persuaded them, convening this meeting as a further step in his work of reconciliation, a risky undertaking in every sense and causing him plenty of trouble at home in Israel – hate mail included. But he reckoned it was necessary – a next step, following his four visits to Germany seeking out the children of Nazi war criminals. Was he mad or bad, his Israeli friends and colleagues asked themselves. Some refused to talk to him ever again. But not the community at Neve Shalom. They knew for themselves that the only way forward was for people to talk to one another, tell each other about their lives, gain an understanding of who the other side was. Reconcile. And, if possible, forgive.

As the minibus stopped and parked the Germans got out one by one, hesitant, blinking in the bright sunlight. The Jewish group stood by, equally hesitant. Neither side knew quite what to do. Their initial meeting in Wuppertal had left so many questions unanswered, so many stories half-told.

Dan moved forward to greet Martin Bormann, shaking him by the hand, German-style. The others followed. Julie welcomed Gerda and Hella. Joe walked Dirk and Lena to their room. Deena, from

New York, walked with Klara. Charley Munn went up to Renate, offering to carry her suitcase. 'No, thank you,' said Renate. 'I can manage.' They spoke English to one another – the lingua franca of peace, for once.

The rooms were ranged in a row of concrete blocks, Israeli-style, basic and functional yet pleasing in their way, painted white, with lovely views over the rocky land below. They were small rooms, airy and pleasant. Most were for two people, sharing a bathroom. Renate and Klara were sharing. So were Hella and her mother. Dirk and Lena too, of course. Julie was sharing with Sylvia, another of the Boston group. Charley Munn was sharing with Nitai, one of the younger Israelis. Martin Bormann, being older, was on his own. Likewise Dan.

Once the Germans had showered and changed, they made their way to the canteen as agreed, wandering along chatting about the village and the landscape and their rooms, anything, really, rather than the reason they were there. So this was Israel, they were thinking. This is the land to which the Jews fled from us Germans. And now here was the Jewish group, waiting for them in the canteen. The Germans hesitated to enter. Dan came forward, welcoming them in and making sure the two groups mixed, sharing one long table, not sitting apart.

The American group looked more confident, more sophisticated – one a psychiatrist, another a radiologist, another a teacher. They had a generosity of spirit about them, the generosity of children who've been deeply loved by their parents. The Germans looked cramped in comparison, unsure, guarded. But the two groups had one thing in common: none of their families had wanted to talk about the past. They didn't want to burden their children, they said, but really, they couldn't bear it for themselves either. So they forgot, or they denied, or, in the case of the Germans, they lied. The Jewish group knew more than the Germans, but little of the real darkness. The Germans knew hardly anything. It wasn't till the late 1960s that the Holocaust was mentioned in schools and the press, and even then it was mostly skirted over. As to their own fathers' part in it, that remained a locked secret.

In the canteen on that first strained day, the Jews made an effort to talk in a friendly way, putting aside their parents' dark pasts for the moment. The Germans tried hard to be as relaxed as the others, but they couldn't. Their past was dark in quite a different way and their present was laden with guilt. As to the future, who knew? Everything lay in shadow for the Germans, filled with doubts and fears.

That first afternoon was the introductory session. The meeting room was in a separate building a short walk from the canteen along a path lined with wild rosemary and thyme, through the shade of the pine trees. The building was simple, a single room with a corrugated roof and windows on two sides. Once inside, out of the glaring sun into the cooler interior, everything was basic and functional – a sink to the right of the door and a small table with a kettle and mugs, teabags, coffee, sugar, biscuits. Many folding chairs, stacked along the wall. It had been agreed that the eighteen – Germans, Americans and Israelis – would sit in a wide circle, facing one another.

The two groups walked into the room unsure of what to do, where to sit. Dan settled himself as a kind of anchor. Charley went to sit one side of him, Martin Bormann on the other. Julie sat next to Gerda, who had her daughter Hella on her other side, ready to translate. Renate and Klara sat side by side, perhaps to support one another in their anxiety and give each other courage. Nitai, just arrived from his kibbutz, sat on Renate's right. Sylvia sat next to Lena. Dirk sat next to Hani, another Israeli grandchild, but he looked cut off, isolated, head down. Everyone was nervous, Jews and Germans alike. Only Dan seemed steady and collected, as he remained throughout the four days, quietly guiding the meeting.

We, the BBC team, had already set up the microphones and a camera on tracks which could move round the outside of the circle. We were there to film a documentary for the History Unit, unexpectedly requested by the group, who'd seen the documentary we'd made about Renate and trusted us. We couldn't be in all the sessions all the time, but we tried to film as much as possible, hoping not to miss anything important. Ron Brown, the sound recordist, had the difficult task of constantly adjusting the microphones, depending on who was talking. He sat in a corner at his own small table for the purpose, tense at the challenge. John Goodyer, on camera, had to change focus all the time as well as adjust to the changing light from the windows because we'd decided on natural light only, lights being too intrusive. We were still using film in those days and each roll only lasted ten minutes. So Ray Forsythe, our assistant cameraman, had the double task of changing rolls fast, and also of pushing

John smoothly round the tracks. It was amazing how quickly the group forgot our presence. I had met most of them before, separately, whether in Germany or America or Israel, getting to know them. And I'd been to Neve Shalom too, to view the site and prepare the filming. 'Don't worry about always focusing on the person who's speaking. Listening faces are just as interesting,' was about the only advice I could give John. I might have added weeping – there was so much of it.

'Welcome,' said Dan.

There was silence in the room, heads down, eyes averted.

Dan said he wouldn't lead the conversation – that it was up to them. 'I didn't prepare any programme in this process,' he explained, his accent an Israeli one with no trace of the German of his childhood. 'It is very important that each person speaks for himself, not for someone else. We have this afternoon, we have tomorrow, we have Friday, we have Saturday, we have Sunday till noon.'

There was another long silence. The afternoon sun shone through the windows. You could hear the birds singing outside.

Then, out of the silence, like a bullet: 'When we sit here, it is hard to explain, even in Hebrew – there is something of death in this room.'

It was Tal, one of the three Israeli grandchildren, a young, serious kibbutznik, speaking the unfamiliar English deliberately, looking from person to person – living proof that the horrors of the past were passed on silently from generation to generation. 'I don't know if other people can feel it like me, but I can feel it in the air. Although we are here to talk about ourselves, our emotions our feelings, our thoughts – almost all of them concern dead people.' She was leaning forward, frowning with the effort of expressing the unspeakable.

Julie smiled at her in sympathy, nodding, but did not speak. No one spoke. Then Joe Albeck broke the silence, his tone quiet and level in that typical Joe way.

'What you say is profound, Tal,' he said. 'There is death, and there is also evil, and it is always there.'

'It has to do with the point in history that brings us here,' said Sylvia, nodding emphatically. Her parents had survived Auschwitz. She was a teacher from Boston – a pretty woman with dark curly hair, and perhaps just because of her prettiness what she said next was especially shocking: 'The point in history where our families were being murdered by your fathers... And it's right in the middle of us. That's why we're here.'

The Germans shifted in their seats and looked away, all but Martin Bormann, who remained still and immobile, as he did for most of the sessions. Renate and Klara, side by side, looked wary and guarded, like boxers in the ring waiting for the next blow. Dirk folded his arms, absenting himself. Gerda wept. Hella put her arm round her mother protectively.

'I feel it too,' said Charley, an instinctive peacemaker. 'But there is one point which might be different for some of us... I think in my own home there was more of an air of death than in this meeting...' And he began telling his story.

'I noticed early that my parents were different,' said Charley, facing the circle openly, wanting them to understand his point. 'But it wasn't long before I noticed that my mother in particular was different. She had difficulty handling stress. Certainly I as a six-year-old could handle stress better than she could. But she still managed to provide quite well for the physical functions of two boys. But, you know, she wouldn't be able to get together a complex meal, for instance, or follow complex directions. And my brother or I would always help her out with that kind of stuff. But one of the major manifestations of her stress was that she hears voices, usually Nazi voices, but sometimes condemnatory Jewish voices, but... voices. She has no visual hallucinations, but she hears voices, sort of just around the corner, usually threatening to take her money away, or, particularly, her children away from her... And it lends insecurity in the moment, because intellectually she knows it's bogus, but emotionally she can't convince herself of that unless she hears my voice or that of her therapist.'

Renate shifted in her seat. Klara looked away. Dirk sank his head in his hands. They knew from the Wuppertal session that Charley's mother had been well educated, spoke good English and was training to be a nurse before the disaster of the Holocaust engulfed her, destroying her life and any chance of 'normality' forever. Someone asked Charley if he remembered any specific examples.

'Hundreds! Hundreds!' he said. 'For instance, we might be in the car and she thinks she hears Nazis in the next car and asks me to figure it out because she didn't want to distract herself from driving.

And, you know, when I was quite young I used to do it for her, and look out of the window and try and understand why she heard those voices. But after a while I caught on to the fact that there really wasn't anything there.' He paused. No one spoke. 'It never extended any further… she never really, deeply lost touch with reality. There were just these momentary questions about voices heard. Very troubling for her.'

Everyone in that room except the Israeli grandchildren, who hadn't attended the Wuppertal meeting, knew what he meant. They knew that his mother, just eighteen when she was transported to Bergen-Belsen, had been found buried deep down in a pit filled with naked corpses. 'It was the British who liberated Belsen,' Charley reminded them, 'and a British Army officer was walking around the camp on the day of liberation, inspecting it, reeling from the horror of what he was witnessing, when he heard a voice calling from deep under that pile of corpses. And they managed to pull her out from that tangle of naked limbs and gaping mouths. And they…' he paused, momentarily unable to continue, '…they saved her'. He knew too well that the rest of her life never amounted to much more than a living death. Renate and Klara, side by side, wept.

The sunlight was beginning to fade. Dan called the session to an end, and everyone filed out in twos and threes, saying little, making for their rooms or the canteen.

The next morning there were more parents' stories, mostly from the Jews, the Germans still too anxious to do much more than listen. Julie talked about Łódź and Auschwitz, Joe about the Warsaw ghetto and Poniatowa, Charley about his father. The Germans listened and wept and kept their silence.

Charley picked up the story of what happened to his father after the family decided to come out of the hiding place which he, the inventive carpenter, had built for them in the ghetto. They simply couldn't bear being cramped in that small space any longer, he said, with no place to move or hardly breathe even. Rather die, they said. So out into the street they went, hands raised above their heads. Only his father, still young and strong, was saved from the first selection that day, not his mother or his sister. So he made it alive to Auschwitz, if you can call it alive, clambering out of the cattle truck and on to that infamous ramp. Here again, being young and strong, he was sent off to one of the barracks, ready for work. Best not to ask what kind of work. But by January 1945 the Russians were coming closer and closer, and the SS guards were frantically mopping up, barrack by barrack, before fleeing themselves.

'It was actually at the end of the day and it was time for his barracks to be exterminated, brought to the gas chamber.' Charley spoke in his clear way, paying careful attention to detail. 'And his group of Jews had been assigned to the *Zigeunerlager*, gypsy barracks, because the others were full. Anyway, they marched them all to the gas chamber. And when they arrived at the end of the day the whistle blew, and there ensued an argument between the guard who had marched them to the gas chamber and the guard who was running the gas chamber, because the gas chamber guard felt he was done for the day, but the barracks guard didn't want to march everyone back to the barracks. Ultimately the gas chamber guard won the argument. The barracks guard marched everyone back, expecting everyone to be gassed in the morning. But that next morning someone arrived from the factory to requisition workers, which was a common procedure, and his barracks was sent off to Görlitz, where he remained till they were liberated.'

Julie nodded, knowing what Charley meant. 'After Auschwitz,' she said, 'my father was looking through the women's quarters in the Displaced Persons camp, to look for women from Łódź, because he was hoping to find his little sister. And he didn't find her. But he met my mother.' She smiled around the room, making things better, lighter, which was typical of her as it turned out. 'And he liked her. And so he came back the next day. And they started to date, and that was that. Yes, that's how they met. Very often, meeting someone from your home place was enough. When you think about it, they had nothing. Absolutely nothing. And to meet somebody who came from the town that you came from was an important connection ...'

The Jewish group were picking up the story, one from the other, like reading familiar passages from the Bible. The Exodus. 'My parents walked through the mountains to Czechoslovakia and up the other way to the Allied Zone in Germany,' said Joe of Lonia and Mendel's story following the terrifying weeks in the Warsaw sewers which the group already knew from the Wuppertal meeting. 'Which is how they got to Germany where I was born. So we wound up staying in Germany till I was about three, which was how long it took to arrange to come to the United States.' He didn't have it with him, but there is a heart-rending photograph, probably taken by Lonia, of the family, including little Joe, looking out of the train window in Hamburg station, all smiling hopefully, off to their new life in America. Their golden future after their dark past.

Charley picked up the thread of optimism. 'Both my parents were in Displaced Persons camps for a couple of years,' he said. 'And in 1947 they both came separately to the United States and met in the United States. And they married and began new lives. And in 1949 they had a son, my brother, and in 1952 they had another son, me, and that's it for children.' He omitted the fact that his brother had tried to commit suicide in his late teens, so deeply and silently was the dark past handed on. And that he now lived, impaired, with their mother.

There were long silences in that room as they tried to take in all the stories – too much, really. Sometimes someone got up to make a cup of coffee or tea. Often they stopped, waiting for a speaker who was momentarily lost for words, or weeping. They broke for lunch in thc canteen. It was a relief.

'My parents were very intent on creating as normal a life as possible for us,' said Julie, back after the lunch break. 'Since they were living in Germany – I was born in Germany – they insisted on speaking to us in German. Not Polish. Or Yiddish. Because they were concerned that if we started talking in Polish, people would start looking at us. They wanted us to blend in and be as normal as possible.' She paused, thinking about it, and about her parents now, still living in Germany. 'I don't understand how they can be even a little bit normal. Mom did all the things a good mom does – she took care of us, she took us to dance classes, she fed us all, she clothed us, and talked to us, and played with us. But somehow there was always a sadness in her. Which makes total sense when you think what they'd gone through. But part of that being normal was not telling us what happened to them,' she went on. 'As a result, I didn't really find out what happened to them, I mean consciously, until I was in my late teens. And yet I can't think of a time when I didn't know.'

All the Jews in the group knew exactly what Julie was talking about – you could see it in the way they nodded and gave each other knowing smiles. As for the Germans, 'normal' wasn't in it for them, in any form. So they kept silent, just listening to the others.

Dan already knew the stories of course. He also knew they had to be told and retold, again and again. With his own story he marvelled, yet again, that his father had had the foresight and courage to get out of Nazi Germany – after only two months of the Nazi regime. How did he know? Most people, apart from the diehard Nazi Party members, thought the 'little corporal', as Chancellor Hindenburg called Hitler in private, would only last a year at most – fatally underestimating what could happen once power gets into the wrong hands. But not Dan's father. Against his wife's resistance and the disbelief of most of his family and friends – many of whom subsequently died in the Holocaust – he insisted. As soon as there was a ban on Jews working in the professions in April 1933, he knew they had to leave. Why did others, so many they knew, decide to stay? Was it disbelief? Was it fear? Was it simply unbearable for them to leave their homes and Germany, their *Heimat*? His father thought about going to Holland, Denmark, France, England, America – anywhere, in search of a haven. Finally, it was Palestine. How extraordinary life is, thought Dan, looking around the circle of people, each with their own stories of their fateful inheritance from the Holocaust, sitting in a meeting room at Neve Shalom, no longer Palestine but Israel now.

'Children of survivors that I know in general, and me specifically, there is a powerful tendency in our parents to protect us, beyond what's rational. To prevent harm from coming to us, every day going to school, to prevent harm coming to us coming home on the bus and in every aspect of life. And it's not reasonable. But it makes sense, in light of their irrational experiences.' This was Charley again.

All the Jews in the room nodded in recognition again. Yes, that's how it was.

Hani, who might easily have passed for a gentile in the Warsaw ghetto with her blond hair and blue eyes and red lipstick, just like Joe's aunt Yadzia, reminded them that it didn't stop with the children but passed on silently, even to grandchildren, born in Israel, like herself.

'You are not allowed to live your life the way you want,' she said, 'because I think somewhere in your heart and in your mind you feel that people have died, and those who survive never really live, still they behave like they died in the Holocaust – so you must do this and this and this.'

Thank God for the English language, thought Dan. Without it, how could they have a meeting like this? Only Gerda needed her daughter Hella to translate. For everyone else the inherited memory of the past could be expressed freely, in all its horror.

The next day the Germans began to speak, hesitant and fearful at first but gaining courage as they found, again to their surprise, that they were listened to with sympathy. By the time we, the BBC team, slipped back into the room and took up our positions, Gerda was trying to describe what it was like growing up in a fanatical Nazi family. She had a broad, intelligent face partly hidden behind her big spectacles, and you could sense that she was minded to speak clearly, honestly, not shying from any difficult facts. Hella was translating, comforting. Gerda had a horror of euphemisms – she'd grown up with them. The group already knew her father had been a doctor in charge of the local euthanasia clinic. 'Mercy killing', as they called it. And they knew, because they were well read, that the technology of killing developed at the euthanasia clinics was seen as a useful experiment for the later 'Final Solution' extermination of the Jews and the Gypsies – a way to purify the Aryan race of subhumans of every sort. Mainly Jews.

'You have to imagine,' Gerda said, with Hella translating. 'A huge wall in our house at home, completely covered with a Führer picture.' She spread her arms wide to indicate the size. 'And whether you were eating, or reading or talking, he was there, dominating everything. And my *Vater* did his hair like Hitler. He had the little moustache like Hitler. It was a total imitation.' Dan had heard this before, of course. But repetition was key to healing and, apart from reconciliation, these meetings were about healing.

Gerda looked around the room, telling them how it was. 'I don't know a face more filled with hate than my father's. I remember the boots, *ja*? Shiny, and they banged on the floor, and this face – well, it was always the Jews' fault. *Immer*, always! Once we get rid of them, what do you think? Everything will be all right.'

She looked from one Jew to the next – Charley, Joe, Tal, Sylvia, Hani, Nitai, Julie – sitting in that circle at Neve Shalom, listening closely to her, trying to explain: 'There wasn't much that was civilian in our life, it was all uniforms. So when I was ten, at my sister's wedding, I was allowed to wear the necktie for the first time with my *Bund Deutscher Mädel*, League of German Maidens, uniform. And I stood there, super proud, that I was allowed to wear that necktie.' She smiles at the memory, shaking her head. 'We were told: you *Junker* women of the Master Race, once the east is free of the subhuman, you *Junker* women will colonise the land to the east, infinite areas...' She stretched out her arms again to indicate the infinity. 'We were told that again and again.'

A murmur of understanding went around the circle, some more willing to accept these German stories than others. But, yes, they could understand that if you'd never known anything else, that if there was no free press to tell you different, no television of course, and constant Nazi propaganda, well... Nevertheless, they also knew that there were others who fought the terror regime and lost their lives often enough. Socialists, Communists, Catholics, Lutherans, shopkeepers, Prussian aristocrats, businessmen and army officers. What, they at Neve Shalom wondered, would I have done?

Later Martin Bormann started to describe something about his own childhood. Everyone in the room already knew that Hitler had been his godfather, that the Bormann family lived in the Führer enclave up at Berchtesgaden along with the Göring and Speer families, and that Martin had attended a Hitler Youth boarding school. But they didn't know much about his father. No one did. *Vater* Bormann was one of those crafty invisible ones. Some said he was Hitler's only true friend while the others were all either opportunists like Albert Speer and Leni Riefenstahl, or fanatic ideologues like Heinrich Himmler. 'He was a short, stocky man with rounded shoulders and a bull neck,' as Walter Schellenberg, who'd been high up in the Gestapo, put it in his memoirs written after the war, once all the danger was over. 'His head was always pushed forward a little and cocked slightly to one side, and he had the face and the shifty eyes of a boxer advancing on his opponent. He seemed to me like a pig in a potato field.' Not that Bormann's son Martin agreed. He had little critical to say about his *Vater*, certainly not about his appearance.

'I can remember Hitler visiting us once, at Christmas, and I got a box of tin soldiers,' Martin said, looking around the circle, smiling at the memory. 'And we went to congratulate the Führer every birthday. On one occasion I got a whack from my father. Because I said, "*Heil Hitler, mein Führer*", which wasn't right. So – whack! Why? Because the correct form was "*Heil, mein Führer*". And I said, "*Heil Hitler, mein Führer*". So I got whacked!' He smiled and didn't look in the least bit bothered about it.

Someone asked him if he therefore thought his father had been a bad father, which is just what Dan had asked him. Martin shook his head. No, he didn't.

'The important memory of him: a strict but a good and fair father who unfortunately was rarely at home,' was his surprising reply. Apparently his *Vater* was always off somewhere with the Führer, increasingly at Hitler's triple-secure HQ near the Eastern Front, the Wolf's Lair, as the war turned worse and worse for the Germans. 'Then it might be for a day or two, and he'd have a few hours for us,' Martin added. 'I read in a text that my mother's influence had been a bad one, of a fanatical wife to my father. I would reject that absolutely. She may well have been a devoted follower of Hitler, but she was definitely never a fanatical Nazi.'

'When Hitler died,' said Gerda, 'I think I sat at our dining table and cried, for three or four hours. I knew, in my childish mind, I knew: it's over. You are nothing now.' She looked around at the circle while Hella translated, her hands gesticulating a wiping-away of the past. 'Something has gone wrong. Something has broken. You're no longer who you were. Uniforms and all that, no more. All gone. I didn't know what. But I knew it had ended.'

'Jenbach was the place where the remains of the Party directorate gathered, at an inn,' said Martin. 'And it was there at one o'clock at night that I heard the news that Hitler had died, "fallen surrounded by his faithful followers" as it was put. So I had to reckon my father had died there too.' He stopped to think, shaking his head. 'It was bad. There weren't more than two dozen of us there, but in the next hour eight people shot themselves. And one of the others, an old school *Kamerad* of mine, he was apparently thinking of doing the same. Me too. But then, as sometimes happens, we met up there and talked, and stopped each other from doing it. We both wept. And stopped each other.' He smiled, remembering the young boy he'd been then.

The light was fading as they left the meeting room, the birds chirping, off to roost. They walked down the path together in twos and threes, Jews and Germans together now.

The next morning Renate and Klara, sharing a room, took turns in front of the bathroom mirror, doing their hair, putting on a little make-up and, in Klara's case, her earrings. Renate wore shorts and sandals, Klara white linen trousers and a cool sleeveless top. They joined the others coming out of their rooms into the bright sunshine, made brighter by the whiteness of the buildings. 'Morning! Morning!' they greeted Charley and Nitai, walking along the concrete path together, past a row of other small white buildings, up some steps and on to the canteen. Was that another settlement in the hazy distance, they wondered, pointing, each looking out over the rocky land, past the cypress trees?

That morning Deena Harris, a psychoanalyst from New York, began to tell her mother's story. Deena always wore dark glasses, inside and out. She was stylish and clever and humorous. She said her mother had been a hidden child, saved by some neighbours, some good Germans. After the war she'd made her way to the United States like so many others, married Deena's father, brought up her family, got on with her life. She hardly talked about what it had been like, first hidden, then on the run in Nazi Germany. Deena, the psychoanalyst, thought it was repression – a denial of the past.

'In the story of my mother, I got such a view of repression, and how that works,' she told the group. 'A friend of mine had been to an exhibition in Berlin, of art from the Jewish childrens' schools, all over Germany, during the Nazi period. And he got a catalogue, which I have here.' She held it up to show everyone, pointing to a particular page. 'It was my mother's Jewish school, in Düsseldorf! And in the catalogue there is a list of all the pupils in her school, all the teachers, what happened to them, *ermordet*, *ermordet*, *ermordet*, murdered, murdered, murdered, and by my mother's name it says nothing, because no one knew what happened to her.'

A murmur of astonishment went through the room. The coincidences of history! The things which survive against the odds!

'She sat in my dining room for two days, she did not leave the table, it's all in German, page by page she's reading it. This teacher, Julo Levin, was the art teacher in the Jewish school, and he saved all the paintings by the children and hid them. And he died in Auschwitz. And then there's a photograph of a class in the school, and I thought: that's my mother! And I showed her. But she said – you know, this is my mother – "Oh no! it can't be!" Everything's "it can't be", everything's ridiculous with her.'

Klara was amazed: 'Your mother? And did she recognise herself?'

Deena smiled. 'She said, oh I don't know... But even my father said he could just see her.'

Julie was nodding. 'My mother says she remembers all the stories, but she can't really believe they're true, that it really happened. She says it's because nobody can imagine it. It's just not possible to imagine it, even if you read a hundred books, she says, you just can't believe it. My father often says he sometimes thinks he's telling a fairy tale!'

At the lunch break Deena sat outside the meeting room in the shade of the pine trees and showed everyone the catalogue. It was a large, shiny one, filled with vibrant pictures in vivid crayon – two boys in *Lederhosen* short trousers and braces on a happy hiking trip in the Alps, some Gypsies, landscapes with bright-blue skies and big yellow suns.

'They're not really thinking what's happening with the Nazis,' said Deena.

And then she showed them the photograph of the class with her mother, perhaps aged nine, in the back row, leaping up out of her seat, hand in the air, waving furiously at the teacher: I know the answer Herr Levin! Ask me! Ask me! I know the answer!

Deena, pointing to it, laughed: 'She's sort of, very eager…'

Renate was standing behind Deena, leaning over: 'Does she recognise the class?'

Deena: 'Yes, it's definitely her class.'

Deena turned to the index. 'And there's a list of what the pictures were.' She ran her finger down the list, searching for her mother's name.

'Look! Here!' Renate spotted it first. Klara put on her glasses to get a closer look. Everyone crowding round Deena was amazed. Yes! There was her name! It was a painting of a gypsy, in bright colours, smiling a big smile.

'Yes,' said Deena. 'And then she says, "Ah nah! I never made a gypsy!"'

They laugh together, Deena sitting on a bench with Klara and Renate, two daughters of Nazi war criminals, on either side.

'And I hear, coming from the room: "Oh my God! Pesha Bernbaum, I went to gymnastics with her! Oh my God, here's Stephan – I had a crush on this boy!" And then she said: "You know, until this moment I always thought I was making it up."'

In the canteen everyone sat mixed up together now with no need for intervention from Dan. It being self-service, each had a tray:

cold meats, salads, bread rolls, butter. Fruit. Coffee. Water in jugs on the long table. Small vases of flowers. Everyone talking. Lena was telling Martin Bormann about her mother's story, Jewish, born in the Ukraine. Nitai was talking across the table with Sylvia about life on a kibbutz. Joe was listening in his intent way to Gerda. Dan was with Tal and Hani, talking about Israel. Renate was laughing with Charley, which is not something the group often saw: Renate laughing. Though at home with Edi there was plenty of laughter. Those dimples, as Edi said.

But under the chatter there was tension. That afternoon had been put aside for a visit to Yad Vashem, the Holocaust Remembrance Center in Jerusalem.

They went together, by bus. We went in our hired crew van, taking as little equipment as possible. John would have to film everything hand-held, Ray guiding him so he didn't trip or get in the way of other visitors, Ron following behind with his mic on a pole, poised to step in each time we stopped to film something. We agreed not to film too much and never to be too close – just try and capture the feeling and significance of the event.

The Germans in the group were steeling themselves. They were extremely anxious, feeling the weight of their fathers' crimes heavy on their shoulders. Their only consolation: although Yad Vashem was Israel's official memorial to the Jews murdered by the Nazis, it also honoured those who had saved the Jews at that time – hiding them, helping them escape, protecting them from the very worst in the concentration camps. It was a document centre too, with an extensive archive and thousands of recorded testimonies from survivors, including Lonia's. And it was a research centre, focusing its work on genocides everywhere, not only in Nazi Germany, producing many publications on the subject and offering educational courses. It was opened to the public in 1957 and had undergone many extensions since then. But its main purpose remained to commemorate the 6 million Jews murdered by the Nazis during the Holocaust. Dan had got the permissions needed for us, the BBC, to film there.

By the time we caught up with the group inside Yad Vashem they had split up – some going this way, some that. The first we found were Dirk and Lena standing side by side, silently, in the Hall of Names, which commemorates the 6 million Jews with lists of names and photographs and testimonies. Dan and Lena moved from picture to picture – old-fashioned studio portraits for the most part, black and white or sepia, some in oval frames, some rectangles, some full-length, some seated with studio props, of old men with beards, city women in hats, young men and women looking out, smiling at the camera, their whole lives ahead of them. The photographs rose higher and higher into the dome above: teachers, businesspeople, civil servants, craftsmen, housewives, fathers, mothers, children. All gone.

Klara was standing further along the chamber, alone, weeping. Filming her from a distance, we saw Hella go up to her and put her arm round her. In the Hall of the Eternal Flame, with the names of the concentration camps carved into the stone floor in Hebrew and English – Dachau, Sachsenshausen, Auschwitz, Ravensbrück – we found Renate, also alone, head bowed. Joe was further along, again alone, lost in contemplation of the Eternal Flame. Then we saw Martin Bormann come up and join him and hold him close, and Joe letting him do it, which was somehow unbelievable, and hard to watch. We left and moved on to the museum section, where we found Deena and Julie and Gerda. 'That's how my parents were transported to Auschwitz,' Julie was telling Gerda, pointing to some cattle trucks and barbed wire, with emaciated Jews looking out between the slats. Deena spotted the famous picture of the ragged little boy with his hands raised in the air, giving himself up in the Warsaw ghetto. 'That's my cousin!' she told Gerda. 'And he's alive! He lives in New York. But we don't know what happened to his mother . . .' Gerda said nothing, just nodded. What was there to say?

As we left, we walked through the Garden of the Righteous Among the Nations with its lovely trees and pathways and memorials to honour those who had risked their lives to save Jews during the Holocaust, including Janusz Korczak, who left the Warsaw ghetto with all the children he'd so far been able to save from transportation, but no longer. It was a relief to find something beautiful and inspiring amid all the horror. We walked along as a group, no longer filming, a mix of Germans, Americans, Israelis and BBC crew, profoundly affected, deeply moved.

By the time they went into the canteen for supper that evening the talk had turned to family life after the war, once all the horror was over. Or not over, more like.

'When we arrived in the United States we had a railroad flat,' said Joe the next morning. He smiled, but there was some anger too, well covered up. 'It was literally over the railroad. The noise of the subway, day and night, you know? First couple of years, neither parent spoke English.' He told them how his dad had to find a job so they could live, and that he was fired from six different handbag factories before he got the hang of making a perfect clasp, and that he did it for the rest of his working life, seven cents a clasp. Again Joe smiled, hiding his pain and humiliation. 'I think it was too bad. He was a great man.'

He paused, trying to put it into words. 'There was something missing that everyone else takes for granted,' he said. 'When other people have extended family they don't have to choke or put out of mind associations and memories of people – to put it correctly – who have been murdered. Sometimes you . . .' he searched for the right way of putting it again: 'not just stories, but real places and names. People you know. So that's something that colours . . . everything. So it introduces a level of holding back which is motivated by protection, which is a problem. The side-effect is a kind of distance, because unfortunately the children know something is missing . . . there is a kind of silence.'

The Germans knew all about silence, of course, but in their case it was accompanied by denial. 'And secrecy,' Dan now pointed out in a rare intervention.

'I think the difference between secrets and silence is very important,' said Dan. 'Secrets can be the secrets of one family. Silence – the characteristic, that you don't talk about it, your neighbour doesn't talk about it, the other neighbour doesn't talk about it.' As he spoke he pointed at people around the circle. 'So it becomes a conspiracy of silence.'

'Of course it was like that in my case,' said Renate, pointing to herself. 'All the time I felt that there was something wrong. And my mother always told me in the nicest words about my father. That he was a wonderful man.' She gestures a smoothing-over with her hand, shaking her head. 'But I always felt something was wrong.'

Most people in the room had seen the BBC documentary we'd made about Renate at their preparatory meeting. So they already knew the story of her father. But still she needed to go over it again. 'One day I discovered he had killed a lot of people – Jewish people, Communists, partisans, Gypsies. During his trial he didn't try to hide any information. The way he stood there – I think he couldn't imagine to go on with his life, because everything was broken, not only Germany, and all the leaders, but also his ideals had gone, and he knew Germany was totally broken.'

'So there was secrecy in your childhood?' That was Joe.

'My mother said he was missing,' said Renate. 'But other fathers were coming back from Russian captivity. So she said he was probably no longer alive. She didn't understand that it was the stupidest, the worst thing she could have told me. I always dreamed up these stories of when he'd come back . . .' Renate paused, gathering herself. 'Always she would tell me how wonderful he was, how much she still loved him. That he was a courageous man, a good man. But at school I saw that the *Hinterbliebene*, the children whose fathers were killed in the war, or still in captivity, got extra food. And I never got it. And the other kids would laugh at me and say, "Ha ha, she doesn't even know her *Vater*'s name!" So I knew something was wrong.'

'I was sixteen when he was arrested.' This was Klara. 'And I think if he had not been arrested, I would never have known. I'm sure my family would have kept the secret forever.'

Everyone in the room was quiet, waiting for her.

'Once *Vater* was back home from serving his prison sentence nothing more was said about it, except that it had been a terrible injustice,' she went on. 'My family just said he'd been forced to lead an *Einsatzgruppe* SS extermination unit against his will because he was part of the Criminal Police before the war and they were all automatically transferred.' She shook her head and bit her lip. 'I left home as soon as I could and went to university. During this entire period, I learned nothing more about my father because I was considered something of a traitor in the family. They always said, "All you want to do is tell your dear left-wing friends about it." So I was cut off, excluded.' She looked wretched, close to tears. 'Sometimes I think that – my father's been dead for three years now – that now I'd like to deal with this matter, because now it can't burden my personal relationship with him. But I must also tell you, something I always found so terrible was that my father said he'd done it all for us, for his family. He said if he hadn't obeyed these orders they would have shot him. He never mentioned the victims. That's what I thought was the worst thing of all!'

She sat weeping, covering her face with her hands. A murmur of sympathy went around the room. 'I know he did it,' she said finally, looking up. 'But until today I cannot, really I cannot imagine my father standing there and giving the order to shoot.' She stopped there, shaking her head. 'I know that he did it, but I cannot imagine him in that role.'

The German group had found their voice by now. It was shaky and fearful and fraught, but it was there. One after another they spoke of what had happened, and of how they tried to lead their own lives by facing the truth, not lying about the past, and not making excuses for what their fathers, and by complicity their mothers, had done. But everyone could see how the guilt of their fathers went on blighting their lives.

'In my father's case, the trial was already over and he'd been sentenced to death,' said Dirk. 'And this is the farewell letter to my mother.' He picked the letter up and cleared his throat. 'I'll read it out.' Then he realised he wasn't wearing his glasses. He took them out of his pocket smiling his wry smile, cleared his throat again, then began:

> My beloved, sweet Kathe, we have just said goodbye to one another, my beloved, for the last time. When you receive this letter I will no longer be alive. I know how terrible this news is for you, because you never gave up hope. But you promised me you'd be brave, even if the worst happened. So now I take my leave from this world in the knowledge that you will be my same brave wife after my death as you always were

> before. We are all human, and my fate is too hard. But think of our son, the most precious thing I leave behind for you. He will need you all the more now that he has no father. May you have pleasure in him always, and when you look at him, you will be looking into my own eyes. I was so happy when you showed me his photograph, but I had to pull myself together not to break down. [Dirk stopped for a moment, steadying himself.] In my last words to you, I swear to you that I never ordered or committed a crime. I only hope and pray that the day will come when I will be rehabilitated. Try to wipe the tragic end of my life from your mind. Remember me as we were in happier times, when we made plans, and took pleasure in our life together. In a moment I shall be having my last meal. Then I'll spend the last hours on this earth with you in my thoughts, stroking your hands and pressing you to my heart, together with our son. Then come greetings…

He choked, reaching down to put the letter on the floor and took off his glasses, wiping his eyes. 'So, it got to me after all!' Another wry laugh. He looked up at the group of people sitting in the circle and smiled. He could feel their sympathy, and their respect for his courage.

'*Ja, ja,*' he said again. 'But how many lies are there in there? *Ja!*' He shrugged in disillusion. Shook his head. 'Of course he's lying. Or he can't see what he did was a crime, because he saw himself as just a tool, *ja*? And that's particularly terrible for me. I've also read the text of his defence statement at his trial, where he describes the Gestapo as a normal administrative body with normal duties.' He shook his head again. 'That was even more shocking for me because it was such a stupid argument. He seems to have had such a naive attitude to this system. I was really shocked, *ja*? I would almost have preferred a cleverer father.' He stopped for a minute, seeking out Lena in the circle. 'As Lena and I read that, we were really shocked. Compared to other fathers in our group,' he looked around: 'Renate's father knew what he was doing! Mine… it's shaming.' He smiled his wry smile again, shaking his head.

Dan called the session to a close. It was surely enough horror for one day. But the next morning the theme was quickly taken up again.

'I think this is an important story,' said Gerda about life at home after the war, Hella translating. 'All those concentration camps, all the photographs and reports – and at home after the war my parents said, "This is the Jews. They're lying. This is the left-over Jews, lying."' She looked around the circle, from Jew to Jew. Hella put her arm round her mother. 'And then my father went on using the Hitler salute, till 1957, till the day he died.' She looked disgusted, shaking her head. 'The Hitler salute,' she repeated. 'A bit disguised, of course. But, for example, when relatives came to visit, bidding them goodbye outside the house, he did it. I can prove it! I have home movie of it. I can prove it! *Mutti*, *Vater*, standing side by side. A bit disguised, but absolutely, he did it, arm raised high. And *Mutti* laughing. So late – twelve years after the end of the war!' She stopped. 'Today, today I would stand in front of him, straight as an arrow, and say, "*Vater*, with me, no more! Get back in your tomb and stay there till the weeds grow over it for all I care. But with me, it's over. Forever."' Then she wept.

'When the Denazification trials started in the 1950s all my father's colleagues in the SS were put on trial,' said Klara. 'My father was dismissed from the civil service after his trial and when he came out of prison he couldn't find a job anywhere. He ended up digging peat. We were very poor. My parents only knew how to complain. My mother kept repeating it was unfair, that in many cases people who had done much worse were not brought to justice.' Klara sighed. 'They learned nothing!'

'Are you sure?' someone asked, because it was hard to believe, as it was hard to believe Gerda's story about her father's Hitler salute.

'Yes, I am sure,' said Klara, 'from the way they talked about it. When they were watching a TV programme they'd say: "Oh, that old topic, they're bringing it up again." My *Vater* was a convinced anti-Communist and anti-Semite.' She hesitated briefly, unsure whether to go on, but then she did: 'It came up once in connection with your country,' she said, looking at Dan and then past him to the Israeli grandchildren. 'I myself was very critical of Jewish policies in the Middle East. I took part in demonstrations against Israeli policy toward the Arabs. And once my father suddenly agreed with me, enthusiastically. "Well, you're finally wising up!" And I thought, my God! It was clear to me it was the old anti-Semitism in a new guise, provided with new fuel.'

Dan already knew this story. But it was shocking to the others.

'He'd got his old job back in the police by then. Later I discovered he'd become a member of the Gehlen Organization.' Klara could see not everyone in the group knew what it was. 'It was a kind of Intelligence secret service, organised by the Americans, directed against Communism.'

A murmur went around the room.

'He always told us he was working for an insurance firm. He was somewhere else during the week, came home only at weekends. But during that entire time he was actually working for the Gehlen Organization, maybe even killing... with the support of the Americans. Because people found the anti-Communist attitude of these old SS and their practical knowledge and skills about the Soviet Union quite useful. What terrible cynicism!' She was close to tears, but went on. 'So he lied to us about more than one period in his life... I don't know if he could have lived so well, keeping up appearances till he died, if he had been living with inner conflict...'

'Well, you know I am a schoolteacher,' said Renate. 'Some students are very interested in this period. I've talked about it several times. The persecution of the Jews, they are very interested in that. But the parents soon start complaining. They ask me to let this period of history rest, to let it be. Some even say there were also some good things about Hitler. They mention the autobahns and solving the unemployment problem. And crime. A typical complaint is that I don't talk about what the Allies did. "How about Dresden?" Then there's also the argument: what right have you youngsters got to talk about it? You weren't even involved! You don't know! All you know is what you've read in books. We were there!'

She looked around the circle of Jews and Germans and Israelis, and everyone knew what she was talking about. That conspiracy of silence again. 'There's been a big shift since the commemoration of the fortieth anniversary of the end of the war. Something different on TV each day. But it was really an attempt to whitewash the issues. Since then it's become an issue at school. Students say, "Stop, stop!" And they're right in reacting that way. It was the same old thing over and over again, no new insights whatsoever. You have to awaken interest, ask questions, wake people up. Then there's another much smaller group: the intellectuals. Their approach is making everything seem black and white. I try to explain a bit about my mother's situation. But they just say: "She must have known." But the crucial question is: how is it possible for people to do such things? How is it possible?' She was almost pleading. 'And later on, how is it possible for an entire people simply not to come to terms with it?'

Dan nodded. Yes, that's what he was asking himself that day on his way to the railway station in Cologne, after his interview with Renate. But not everyone in the room was sympathetic to the view. They felt deeply for Renate individually, but for the whole German nation, still trying to come to terms with what they did... Not really.

'I keep thinking,' Renate said, 'I keep thinking, what do I harbour deep within me? What am I capable of? That somehow there must be something evil in me.'

Charley, Julie, Joe, Hani, Nitai, Sylvia, Deena, Tal – all the Jews in the room shook their heads, smiled, sighed, or found some other way of conveying how wrong they thought she was, without rejecting the fact that she felt that way. The Germans knew just what she meant, of course.

'My father died suddenly,' said Klara, 'of a stroke, out in the street, in 1980.'

Again Dan already knew the story, but the others didn't.

'My mother's been having a bad time of it. She's been in psychiatric clinics four times because of depression,' she went on, not looking for sympathy, just to try and explain. 'I think it took her a long time to finally realise her husband was dead. They'd known each other since early childhood and had spent their entire lives together.'

In a strange way Julie and Joe knew what she meant. Their parents had been totally reliant on one another too, years and years of reliance, though for quite different reasons of course. Julie's parents were both still alive. Joe had lost his father.

'She tried to kill herself when my father was released from prison,' Klara went on, which was shocking and hard to understand for everyone except Dan who'd heard it already. 'That's when it started. She was a woman who, on her own, was always really terrific. She kept things going through the entire period of the war with three small children and everything. My brother was only a few weeks old when we fled as refugees from East to West. We were on the brink of starvation in East Germany. And when my father was arrested she went to work in a store. But after that, whenever he came home, she'd always submit to his will again, immediately. He was the boss.

Perhaps it was something she forced upon herself. I think my father treated my mother in a condescending manner much too often. He made her feel she was inferior to him. That upset me very, very much. On the other hand, I would have preferred a stronger mother…'

They broke for lunch. When we came back into the meeting room later that Saturday afternoon Charley was talking about the psychological disorder his mother had been left with after the war, following her horror in Bergen-Belsen.

'My mother's story gets much worse, not better,' he said in his even, rational way. 'When I was about thirteen my parents split up. Because, in large part in my view, my mother had this disorder. However, this disorder wasn't even a described entity at that time, so she was misdiagnosed, by several psychiatrists, as being simply a schizophrenic of some sort. And treated with medication, sometimes powerfully, and naturally the treatments did not work well. So my parents split up over one physical event when my mother slapped my father, and that had never happened before, but it was enough that it scared my father because he'd been warned by these various psychiatrists, if she ever became violent… So he got one slap, and he left. You have to understand, he had endured years of confusion and sadness, but he left. At the moment he left, I made an independent choice to go with him. I was fifteen. My brother made the same choice…'

Everyone in the room could see that Charley was in terrible pain and guilt just thinking about that decision he'd made, aged fifteen, to leave with his father, meaning his mother was abandoned by her family, her only family, and left to try and make sense of her life, alone, from one day to the next.

'We lived in New York for another two years or so and then moved to Los Angeles, which essentially severed contact with my mother. I can't speak for my brother, but I did that because I was a teenager, and I needed for my own selfish teenage reasons to just sort of fit in, and be a happy kid.'

Charley stopped there, close to tears. Everyone waited in silence till he gathered himself.

'Sadly my mother's life got terrible after that, but it was all unbeknownst to us. Ultimately she lost her job as a nurse, and then the house – too much stress – then lost all her money. Then became a street person in New York, not very known about at the time, and after some period and her psychological situation getting worse and worse, she...' he stopped again for a moment, struggling. 'She somehow managed to hold on to enough money to get herself back to her roots – in Germany. Her family had been successful members of German society, for generations. So she flew back to Germany. Hoping to somehow re-establish herself there. And ultimately of course became a street person in Germany. Somehow she was captured – not the right word,' he smiled, shook his head and changed the word to snagged, 'she got snagged by the social welfare system in Germany and, to their great credit, they managed to send her back to America. And this time she was snagged by the American social services. And someone recognised that this was an educated person who was a licensed nurse... and by then psychology had evolved a bit, and she was fitted back into a better system, and ultimately became a working nurse again. Saved up money. Got an apartment again. Became a member of society again.'

The room was in complete silence. Some were in tears. It really was the worst story of all – this poor, sweet woman, buried under corpses at Bergen-Belsen, treated as a schizophrenic in America after the war because no one knew what was wrong with her, then abandoned by her family... Really it was unbearable.

'It was around that time that she contacted me. I was already at Berkeley by then. I got a phone call and... it was a surprise. But I sort of rolled with it a bit, and we had a very nice visit. Now we talk on the phone perhaps once or twice a week and visit once or twice a year. And it's great.'

Charley finished, spent, felled by guilt, although it wasn't his fault – none of it. Of course it wasn't 'great', but it's the best he could do. He tried, with all his might and intelligence and American optimism, to mend the past. But the past wouldn't mend.

No one spoke, lost in thought and fellow feeling. And guilt – the terrible guilt of the Germans, the lesser guilt of the Americans who knew how brutal the treatment of Charley's mother must have been within their psychiatric system back in the 1960s.

'When friends of us asked, why do you go to Israel – there's Palestinians coming from Gaza stabbing Jews in Jerusalem, it might be dangerous. Really, I had no fear,' Klara said after a while. 'I thought if something would happen to me, it would be a kind of justice.' She paused, looking around the circle, trying to express what she meant:

'I thought, there have been so many Jews who have been killed in Germany, by the Germans, so a little, little payment...' she indicated the littleness with her fingers, 'you know, that if something happens here to me...' She shrugged.

'Klara, I'm terribly sorrowed by that feeling you had that it's almost OK if you were to die because so many Jews died at the hands of Germans,' said Charley, always generous, and somehow relieved now by the telling of his own part in his mother's story.

'It is a measure of how bad you feel about what your father has done that it takes his child's sacrifice to start balancing out the sides,' said Julie. 'I feel very sad for you...' She smiled at Klara in sympathy.

'What you say sounds familiar to me,' said Dirk. 'A short time after Lena's brother was going to die, then I had the feeling, why don't you take me? You can take me for him!' He gesticulated with his hand in despair. 'Because he has children, and so many Jews were killed, so keep him! It doesn't matter when I am going to die, because, why not!' He was agitated now, quite unlike his usual slightly distanced self. 'God, take me, why not! I don't believe in God any more, but I begged him, please take me for him, and everything will be OK. It was just this fantasy of... giving one for the other.'

'I was having these feelings for a long time,' said Renate. 'And more and more they got fainter, but when the animosities against foreigners in Germany came again, I again had those feelings...' She stopped and wept. 'Even if I knew it didn't help, doing that and thinking that,' she shrugged 'But they are here...'

'I'm not sure there are not parts of me that are happy you are feeling that way.' This was Hani, the Israeli grandchild of Holocaust survivors. 'I know it's ugly, and I hate this feeling, but it's a part of me that wants some revenge. It's a part of me that wants you to suffer. It's become harder for me the more I know you, but...'

'I know what you're talking about, because it was my first thought: let them suffer!' This was Julie speaking across the circle to Hani. 'But once you have a face...' She smiled and pointed to Renate, 'once you know a person, it's very hard to hold on to that feeling...'

'I was thinking about who of the Germans had similar experiences like me, and my imagination was that one who had not had these fantasies was Martin,' said Klara, looking along the circle to where Martin was sitting. 'Often I envy Martin his faith, you know, his belief in God. I really envy you this,' she smiled at him in a shy way. 'Because it gives you such a security. So... is that right, that you have never had these ideas?'

Dirk, further along, looked at her with some scepticism. Martin had been leaning back in his chair, arms folded. Now he leaned forward, face cupped in hands.

'No, that is not right,' said Martin. 'It was so, that I too had those thoughts... But then I entered into the religious congregation, I learned the theology of sacrifice, and the resurrection of Christ, and the resurrection is much more than the sacrifice. And when I entered Israel, now, on this journey, in the footsteps of the Exodus, when we came over the border in our Israeli bus at Eilat, our driver has an... *Ankleber*...' he couldn't find the right word in English, but raised his hand as though sticking something on the windscreen.

'Sticker,' offered Renate.

'Sticker,' repeated Martin, 'with a red heart, yes? It said: "I Love Israel". And when I saw that marvellous, wonderful land, that was what Israel made of that land, I said: I love Israel too.'

Dirk looked away. Gerda and Renate held their peace. But Dan took out his blue and white handkerchief and blew his nose, and wiped his eyes. It was an extraordinary moment, noted with some surprise by those of us who saw it. Dan, who rarely intervened, always remaining the objective mediator, was shaken with emotion. Was it the mention of Israel? Was it that he knew something of Martin's inner life that no one else did? It was hard to tell. Had they known of Dan's struggle to be a pioneering Israeli in his youth, they might have understood.

Martin went on: 'Life is stronger than all the shadows. And I believe life is stronger for each of us, also. Much stronger than all the shadows. That is my hope.' He looked up and around at the circle of people. 'And therefore I am very very thankful I can be here, with you, together with you all. And with Dan.' He bent his head. Like a prayer.

The light was fading again. Dan called the session to an end.

Sunday morning was the group's last session. Everyone was on edge, caught between two opposing feelings: happiness that the four days had unfolded so well, sadness that it was coming to an end. Some relief.

When we slipped into the room later and took up our positions – John Goodyer to his seat on the tracks, camera fixed, Ray Forsythe behind him at the ready, Ron Brown at his own table, more confident that he could manage all the different mics now – we were hardly noticed, as had been the case every day after that first introductory meeting.

Someone was asking Klara how long her father had been with his *Einsatzgruppe* extermination unit, in the *Säuberungsaktion*, 'mopping up' operation – of Jews, but also Communists.

'A month,' said Klara. 'At the trial he defended himself vigorously, saying he'd been assigned against his will and given the same rank as when he was a police officer, which is probably true. I really do believe that these men had no clear idea of what was going to happen to them. For example, the three men who were found guilty along with my father were people who had lived a proper and orderly life... a lawyer, a policeman... So these people were...'

She searched for the right word. 'Educated?' someone suggested. 'Normal people?'

'Yes, normal people,' Klara shrugged. How could anyone understand it?

That is what happens once power gets into the wrong hands, thought Dan again. His father had understood that and knew where it was likely to lead, especially for the Jews. But how many others did? And how many Jews went on living in Germany, hoping against hope the danger would pass? Until it was too late.

'Sometimes when I write about my relatives, my relatives who died during the Holocaust,' said Joe, 'I refer to them as lost love. And I wonder if that is both a difference and a similarity with the Germans, because when they think about the Holocaust and what happened, at least in one way, as the perpetrators decide to kill the other people, love is lost there – not only with the victims, but also for their own family. Which is real, but which we are only just beginning to be able to describe and understand.'

Renate and Klara, sitting side by side, both wept. Klara had for a long time been unable to tell her daughter about what her father did in the war because, she said, she wanted her daughter to be able to love her grandfather. Renate had lived a childhood filled with recrimination, sharing a small flat with her mother and grandmother, both caught up in their own troubles, with little time for love.

'Of course I'd have liked to have a father like others had a father and learned some of the lessons of life from him,' said Dirk. 'But that wasn't to be. On the other hand, I know it sounds really perverse – I am thankful I didn't have to deal with this father. It sounds terrible, but that's how it is. And another thing: it probably made my marriage to Lena possible. My father paid for what he did – you can't pay with more. And basically, through that, he freed me.' He looked around the circle, almost challenging them to disagree. But no one did.

'In Germany it's like that,' said Renate, 'they did not yet really face the past. We have lots of books and we have a lot of reports on TV, but they are only bringing facts.' She shook her head. 'And people are fed up with facts. They say, "Oh, we know everything!" No need to listen. They don't want any longer to listen to all that stuff! So we have to find another way... Maybe this way, which we are just doing, is a way, a new way, not exchanging facts, but facing each other as individuals, with different experiences, and really talking about our feelings. Because the past is not yet done!'

'It's only the next generation, the children, that can do something,' added Martin, speaking as one who knew. 'The actual perpetrators and victims can't do it. But if the children can reconcile, can come towards one another, then we can have peace. And only then can we have peace.'

There was a murmur of agreement, though perhaps not everyone felt that the son of Martin Bormann was the right person to say it.

Now they all, one after another on that last Sunday, began to describe what had happened to them over the past four days – was it only four days? It seemed so much longer.

'Just what occurs to me,' said Klara, the lawyer who defended the defenceless – often left-wing activists. 'I can't bear to see violence, people being beaten up. My sense of pity, of compassion, is very strong. I can't stand seeing people suffer. Verbally either, any kind of violence. I think I have quite a pronounced sense of social injustice. Maybe my chosen profession has something to do with it: a small personal contribution, a form of reparation,' she smiled around the room, happier and more open now at the end of these four days. 'I see my profession very much in terms of a struggle against authority and the exercise of power, state power. I do think my divorce has something to do with being free of my husband's authority... But now I don't freeze up when someone asks me about my father. What is important for me now is my own future. And the future of my daughter, who is also very politically involved. I have taken over the guilt my father didn't feel, or didn't show me he felt. In rational terms, it's absurd, I mean, I had nothing to do with it.'

'Many, if not all the members of the children of the perpetrators in our group,' said Charley, 'they have to think through more pain, and when they ultimately get to the end of the nightmare, you know, I get to a good person, or a good pair of people, and they get to at least one terribly evil person, and sometimes two. And so...' He stopped for a moment before expressing it: '...and so there's no solace at the end for them. And they end up living with pain. Forever.'

Then Julie spoke. 'When we first came to meet you, I was terrified.' She looked across the circle, across the divide, at the Germans. 'I kept thinking: how can I greet them? How can I shake their hands? How will I not hate them?' There were silent nods all round – from the Jews because they'd all felt the same, and from the Germans because, in their guilt, they felt they deserved it. 'But then I saw how badly you suffered, how destroyed you were by it, and I found I couldn't hate you...'

'I think it's that feeling which also allowed me to feel open to you all,' said Deena, 'knowing that you suffer... Knowing that you are here, and that you came because you suffered, and felt guilt, was the only way I could accept you and like you. If you were, in my mind,' she put her hands to her head, 'like those other Germans, who don't care, then I think I could never like you, so...'

'After the first days, all the fear had gone.' This was Klara. 'There was such a feeling of warmth and trust. I think I have never talked so much about my past. It took a lot of pain from me. A great part of the pain was not being able to talk about it. And so, I felt accepted.'

Later we filmed the group as they parted, each making for their own bus, hugging, smiling, promising that this meeting was the start, not the end of something. It was moving to watch. Incredible, too, that just four and a half days could make such a difference.

'When I planned this workshop,' Dan told us later, 'my three questions were: will they be able to face each other? Will they be able to help each other go ahead? And talk about issues none of them have confronted fully until now? And if so, will some common agenda evolve which is beyond their own personal struggle?'

The common agenda, a new method of resolving conflict, nationally as well as personally, was what Dan was all about.

The answer was surely 'yes' in terms of personal reconciliation and growth. As to the 'common agenda', it lay in the future.

CHAPTER TEN

AFTERMATH

In 2008 I got a most upsetting email from Dan. I'd retired from the BBC by then and had started writing non-fiction books on much the same subjects as I'd made the documentaries, namely twentieth-century European history.

Dan's email told me that he'd been diagnosed with a brain tumour and given three months to live. It didn't take me long to decide what to do. I sent an email back asking whether he and Tammy would like me to come to Tel Aviv to film him talking about his life and his work – his life's work. He replied that same day: yes, he'd like a chance to make a record of the thing which had mattered most to him in his working life: the importance and power of reconciliation. His whole life, from his start in Haifa following his parents' decision to flee Nazi Germany to his end in Tel Aviv, which had once been in Palestine and was still in turmoil – all of it told him that military and political might left terrible death and destruction in its wake which only the reconciliation between former enemies could mend. To Reflect and Trust, or TRT as the Neve Shalom group named it. Listen to the 'Other', that was his message. Always had been. I rang John Goodyer, the cameraman at Neve Shalom in 1993, and asked whether he would come to Tel Aviv with me. He said yes.

The Neve Shalom meeting had ended on a note of euphoria. We, filming it, could see it and feel it. People who had hesitated to even shake each other's hand now hugged one another, smiling and crying, bidding goodbye in English and German and Hebrew. They already had a date for their next meeting. And the next, and the next, over several years, sometimes in Germany, sometimes in America, sometimes elsewhere. Soon they were including others from other conflict zones: from South Africa, from Northern Ireland, later from Palestine and Israel. Sometimes as a group, sometimes separately, they teamed up to address conferences, schools, churches, they spoke on the radio and appeared together on television, sitting side by side on a stage, telling their stories, explaining how it was that people destined to hate one another had learned to love one another instead, just by listening to the other, coming to understand. To Reflect and Trust.

Charley Munn decided during that Neve Shalom meeting to change his name to Samson. He wanted to honour his parents' suffering, the one from Bergen-Belsen the other from Auschwitz, and he wanted to acknowledge his Jewish heritage – drop American Charley, even though it had been his mother's fervent wish to give him a new life in the New World, leaving the dark past far behind. He also decided at that same meeting to start up his own group in Austria. He called it The Austrian Encounter, run along similar lines to the TRT meetings, and it was so successful, so rewarding and important to the participants that it continued for twenty-one years. It also spawned another group called The Encounter which expanded beyond the borders of Austria, to Paris, Berlin, Trieste and Łódź in Poland – all places still traumatised by their years under Nazi rule, whether as victims, Jewish or political, or as perpetrators either through their active collaboration with the Nazi occupation or merely as silent bystanders. And he teamed up with Dirk, the two appearing on stage together in Germany to tell their stories, side by side. Sometimes it was filmed too. Along the way he got married to Rachel and had two children, which was not something Samson had ever thought personally possible for him before the TRT meetings, which released him in some way.

For Dirk, sharing the stage with Samson required an extra act of courage – to speak the unspeakable in Germany to a German audience about his father, the Gestapo Chief of Braunschweig. Knowing his audience, he would tell them about his mother, who'd always maintained her husband had done no more than many others who were never caught or sentenced. These others were living their anonymous lives in suburban villas, or in the city, or in a village tucked away in the countryside, fathers and grandfathers, husbands, brothers, sons, the ones who got away. 'Of course I'd have liked to have a father like others had a father,' as he'd said at Neve Shalom, 'and learned some of the lessons of life from him, but that wasn't to be.' Perhaps, in the end, he began to forgive him.

As for Renate, the daughter of Friedrich Jeckeln, the SS general in charge of the whole of Northern Russia, she went on working as a teacher in her progressive secondary school which included disabled children. And she went on attending the TRT meetings, including the ones extending to other conflict zones, and she went on speaking out. 'In Germany it's like that: we did not yet really face the past,' as she said. 'People are fed up with facts. They don't want any longer to listen to all that stuff. So we have to find another way.' That was always her message, and it went on being her message till the day she died on 5 June 2010, with Edi at her side, holding her in her arms. Extraordinarily, Else, Renate's mother, had died only two months earlier, on 6 April 2010. Still loving her Fried.

Martin Bormann, the son of Hitler's deputy, wrote a book about his life and his beliefs, and went round schools and prisons and churches spreading the word. 'I'm fairly certain today that my father knew about everything, or almost everything,' he told Dan during their first interview. 'I'm also fairly certain he approved of it all, more or less. I can only explain it by the fact that he grew up and into this ideology as a young man.' How hard it is for a son to blame his father. 'It's only the next generation, the children, that can do something,' he would repeat again and again, like a mantra. 'The actual perpetrators and victims can't do it. But if the children can reconcile, can come towards one another, then we can have peace.' Martin, being a former priest, had no children of his own. Or perhaps it had nothing to do with being a priest. Many children of Nazi perpetrators had no children of their own.

After the Neve Shalom meeting Sylvia was another who decided to tell her story to others. By way of introduction she told her audience her parents were living in Warsaw and engaged to be married when the Germans invaded Poland in September 1939. 'They were what could be classed as the upper-middle class, business and professional people. They spoke Polish, not Yiddish, though they understood Yiddish. My mother was a pianist, having gone to the Warsaw Conservatory.' When the Germans invaded they fled eastwards, to Russian-occupied eastern Poland, where they were sent to a Russian labour camp. People died of malnutrition, she said, but at least they weren't slaughtered. When they war ended they managed to get back to Warsaw but there wasn't anything left, not people, not buildings, just rubble. So they decided to leave, making for America. She too had a childhood, safe and loved, but living in silence about the past. It was her main reason for joining the TRT group. 'Personally it was a breakthrough, confronting assumptions and fears.' Like the others, she began giving talks, telling others about it. Sometimes with Renate. Sometimes with Klara. Sometimes with Joe. Often she joined forces with Julie.

Julie was the only child of Holocaust survivors in the TRT group who grew up in Germany. The other parents had mostly made for America, except for the grandparents of the three Israeli participants, who went to what was then still Palestine, and Dan's parents, who'd left Hamburg to make a new life in Haifa. But Julie's parents, both originally from Łódź in western Poland, both in the ghetto there, both later transported to Auschwitz, decided to stay in Germany. Who knows why? Perhaps because they'd met in Germany after the war, in a Displaced Persons camp, and fell in love there. Or perhaps they couldn't bear to leave their home, their *Heimat*. Whatever the reason, Julie's parents decided to stay. They put the past behind them, not talking about it, especially not to the children. 'What's that on your arm?' Julie remembers asking her father when she was a child, pointing to the number tattooed there. 'My father never hid his arm from me, so why did I not ask before?'

After Julie married, she and her husband moved to America, to Boston, and raised their children there. Like the others, she continued the TRT group over many years. She attended conferences. She wrote articles. She wrote a book, *Den Abgrund Überbrücken* (To Overcome the Abyss) with others about their reconciliation stories. She'd already trained as a therapist. But in 1995 she went to Germany on her greatest venture. Adventure, even. 'A Jewish therapist guides her German colleagues in confronting their heritage: a recipe for disaster or an opportunity for healing?' went the title of an article she wrote about it later. 'I first conceived of running a seminar for German therapists when I learned from German friends that when they wanted to work on their feelings about their parents' role in the Nazi era, their therapists would change the subject,' she wrote. 'On reflection that makes perfect sense. After all, who are the therapists? Don't they share with their clients that same heritage? Who was supposed to have helped the clinicians do their work?' It was organised through the Fritz Perls Institute in northern Germany, and there were many times when Julie wondered if it had been a good idea. Many of the group knew their fathers had been in the SS, all suspected their fathers knew much more than they would admit, and might have participated in atrocities about which they claimed only to have 'heard'.

And so to Israel and the three grandchildren of Holocaust survivors whose families had chosen to remake their lives in what was then Palestine, though not for much longer. It turns out that trauma can be passed from generation to generation, as they said, albeit growing fainter as time goes on. All three of them were Dan's students in the Department of Behavioural Sciences at Ben-Gurion University, so perhaps they were more open and willing to embrace the Germans, by way of reconciliation and healing. And yet . . . 'There is something in our families that will not allow you to lead your life as you want,' as Hani had put it at Neve Shalom. 'Because somewhere in your mind and in your heart, you are surrounded by people who died, people who don't live, or people who live like dead people. So you must do this and this, and not this . . .' And at the end of the meeting at Neve Shalom it was Hani who added, looking from one German to the next: 'I am not sure there are not parts of me that are happy you are feeling that way. I know it's ugly, and I hate this feeling, but it's a part of me that wants some revenge. It's a part of me that wants you to suffer. It's become harder for me the more I know you, but . . .' But, but.

All three of these Holocaust survivor grandchildren went on with the TRT meetings over several years, gave talks about it to schoolchildren and students, and gave guided visits to Holocaust museums.

Soon the TRT group decided to widen its scope and include members of other conflict and reconciliation groups: South African, Northern Irish, and Palestine/Israeli. The structure was based on the same principle as before: talk to each other, listen to each other, try to understand the Other. Members of the original group were each assigned to a smaller group from another conflict, showing the way. They met in different countries just as before, victims and perpetrators in the same room together.

Often they were hearing the stories of the Other for the first time. Once a Palestinian woman from the West Bank asked: 'How do you know the Holocaust happened?' It caused turmoil. On another occasion someone wanted to know what was the connection between the past Holocaust and the present Israeli–Palestinian conflict. Some of the Jewish group discovered they felt more at ease with the Germans than with the Palestinians, and that it was easier to be a victim than a victimiser. It was shocking. But most shocking of all was the meeting in Derry in 2002, with the Irish Catholics and Protestants.

That meeting had to have a different structure, mixing the separate groups into one large group, because the Northern Irish group felt more comfortable telling their stories to members of other conflicts rather than to their own. Now the Palestinians sometimes lined up with the Catholics of Northern Ireland, as did the Black South Africans. Victims all, they felt.

As for Dan, in the mid-1990s he did what he always had done: he stepped over the edge again, crossed that red line once more, this time bringing with it even more criticism, even more alienation, even more hate mail than when he'd decided to go to Germany to interview the children of Nazi war criminals. Because this time it was about Israel and Palestine.

'Euphoric' is the word Dan used about the time following the Oslo Accords, signed between Israel and the PLO: the first in Washington in 1993, the second in Taba, Egypt, in 1995. What's in a photo? But there stands Clinton, President of the United States of America, beaming, one arm round Yasser Arafat, the other round Yitzhak Rabin, both terrorists at one time or another, now shaking hands, talking to one another, on the brink of a peace process which would lead to the PLO recognising the State of Israel, and Israel recognising the PLO as the representative of the Palestinians to negotiate a future two-state solution to the intractable problems of the region ever since Ben-Gurion had proclaimed the State of Israel in 1948.

Why wouldn't Dan feel euphoric? Dan, the son of parents who'd fled Hamburg in 1933, arriving in Haifa, Palestine, to start a new life safe from the dark past. Dan, the man who'd always believed that talking to one another, learning to understand the Other, was the only way forward. How was he to know that Yitzhak Rabin would be dead within two years, assassinated by an extremist Israeli incensed by the idea of a two-state solution? How was he to know that the conflict would go on and on, to this day? No, he felt euphoric, and being who he was, he soon set about adding his own small effort to the bigger one of international politics. Because, for the time being, the situation looked full of hope. The Palestinian Authority was created, giving significant Palestinian governance over the Gaza Strip and the West Bank, and there was international agreement that the PLO and Israel would be equal partners aiming at an eventual two-state solution.

So Dan set about applying his usual method of Trust and Reconciliation, of storytelling, to the most important political movement of his life. Again he began with his own students at Ben-Gurion University, both Israelis and Palestinians. The Palestinians weren't from the Gaza Strip or the West Bank, they were Palestinians who were citizens of the State of Israel, but it was a start. Talking about it later, Dan would smile his smile and raise his eyebrows. You had to start somewhere didn't you? Talk to each other. How did the Palestinians see the Israeli experience, their need for a home, a safe haven, after the horrors of the Holocaust? How did the Israelis see the Palestinian experience since 1948, Al Nakba, the Catastrophe, as the Palestinians called it?

And then Dan met Sami Adwan. As he told it to me later, in 2008 when I went to Tel Aviv to interview him, he was at another of those conferences to further the peace process. Was it in Germany, was it Norway, was it Switzerland – in any case it was sometime in 1997, and the mediator, addressing the assembled delegates, suggested they introduce themselves by standing up, starting with the oldest. Were there any grandparents present?, he asked. There were two: one Israeli, one Palestinian. Dan and Sami. They laughed and smiled at each other across the hall, and afterwards they went off together for lunch, talking and talking. 'Convivial' is how Dan described Sami. 'Remarkable' is how Sami described Dan. 'Friends' is how they described their relationship from then on. In a sense they reflected what was happening in Israel at that time: a certain shift among the younger generation who were more open to a wider perspective, in spite of the First and Second Intifadas when Palestinians rose up against the continued Israeli occupation. This younger Israeli generation were more open to the idea of a two-state solution than their parents and grandparents, especially those who were Zionists and those in the more traditional Orthodox Jewish communities.

Through all this Dan and Sami's friendship continued and grew. 'Sami and I also got our families involved,' wrote Dan in his book *Tell Your Life Story*. 'In November 1999 my youngest son Haran was about to join the Israeli Air Force rescue unit as part of his military service. Haran had already befriended Sami's oldest son Tariq by then. Before Haran's recruitment Sami invited us all to a Bethlehem restaurant. During the dinner he got up and spoke, addressing Haran: 'I know how concerned your parents are for your health and safety, as you are joining the army. But now, since we are friends, I will be concerned just as they are, because we are now one family.' Dan was choked with emotion at Sami's generosity, as he told me. 'Haran was joining the army which was still controlling most of the Palestinian territories – the army that Sami himself fought not many years earlier.'

Not only fought. Sami was captured and imprisoned. 'I was kept inside a prison cell with two soldiers positioned outside the door,' he told me later. 'The door had a single hole, no more than five centimetres in diameter. The soldiers called out to me and there was a paper that I had to sign. The paper was written in Hebrew and I said: no, I'm not signing a document I cannot read. There was another soldier there who asked the officer, "How can we ask him to sign something he cannot read?" I began to realise that even soldiers wearing the same uniform could have different opinions and ways of thinking. This is what being in prison gave me the opportunity to learn: that I should not look at others and assume they are all the same. This was an extremely important experience.' Once he was let out of prison Sami decided to change tactics.

Then came the Oslo Accords. And meeting Dan. And working together. Supported by the Frankfurt Peace Research Institute, they began by arranging exchanges between Sami's students at Bethlehem University and Dan's at Ben-Gurion University. Later they decided to set up PRIME, the Peace Research Institute for the Middle East, with a £40,000 sponsorship from the World Bank where Dan's brother Michael used to work. The key to change in the future was the youth, Dan and Sami agreed, the schoolchildren. It was they who needed to be enabled to tell their stories to one another, to learn about the Other. And the key to them was the teachers. There was a Lutheran high school, Talitha Kumi, near Beit Jala, close to the border with Israel on the Palestinian side which offered to help. With the sponsorship money they were able to set up a base there, in two rooms, and pay Fatma, a young Palestinian woman, to be the part-time administrator. Then they opened a bank account with the Bank of Bethlehem, because peace costs money.

They began by inviting six Israeli and six Palestinian teacher/researchers to a three-day meeting in Antalya in Turkey, and then another in East Jerusalem. The teachers were asked to write their own histories/stories. It was shocking how different these stories were, in every detail, starting with the Balfour Declaration. So the first decision of the group was never to say the other version was 'wrong'. Later came the decision to write a textbook for schoolchildren with the two versions of the history of Palestine/Israel on the same page, in two separate columns. So in one column there was Ben-Gurion's victorious declaration of the State of Israel. In the other column, side by side, was the story of the same moment, but now called Al Nakba, the Catastrophe. There was a space in the middle for the students to write their own comments.

By the time John Goodyer and I went to film Dan in Tel Aviv in 2008, the Talitha Kumi high school students knew the PRIME textbook well. It was charming to see them walking out of class and down the path, Palestinians and Israeli Jews, arm in arm, at the end of the school day, talking and laughing together just like any other schoolchildren. By then we'd already filmed Dan at home, interviewing him about his life and his work, and later with Tammy, sitting in a café, relaxed, talking and smiling, Tammy smoking, Dan drinking his coffee, for all the world as though Dan might live forever. Now we were standing outside the school, setting up the camera to film Sami arriving to see Dan. It was the first time they'd met since Dan's diagnosis with a brain tumour.

We filmed Dan walking towards Sami, who had just parked his car in the shade of pine trees. They met and kissed on both cheeks like the old friends they were. Sami reached out his hand and rubbed Dan's bald head.

'Your hair is gone ...' He stood back and looked into Dan's face. 'So how do you feel?'

Dan smiled and raised his eyebrows.

We followed them into the school, up a flight of steps and along the corridor leading to one of the schoolrooms put aside for PRIME, filming them back-view, two old friends talking and laughing together, quite forgetting John walking behind them, camera on shoulder, tracking them.

We sat them side by side at one of the desks in the schoolroom, a simple two-shot which told you everything you wanted to know about them: their friendship, their closeness, their respect for one another, their shared purpose and, without exaggeration, their love. Dan with his bald head and Sami with his glasses and moustache, listening to one another, nodding and smiling, picking up the story from one another like brothers.

Dan explained the idea of the two perspectives on the one moment in history, two narratives which were diametrically opposed, and how the students had to learn to accept the Other. And, most importantly, the role of the teachers within it. 'It's quite a revolutionary idea for history teachers,' he said. 'Because normally they deal with the past. But this is now. In the middle of the conflict. Because we didn't want to wait till the conflict ends before acting. We wanted to act now.'

'We try to widen the scope of the teachers as well as the students,' said Sami, in good English, with his Palestinian accent. Not many schools had taken up their offer, he conceded. Not yet. But it was a start, and the schools were on both sides of the border. 'Different locations, girl as well as boy students, different levels,' said Sami, making the point that girls were not excluded.

They showed me their PRIME textbook, which we filmed close-up. It has a charming cover, a simple painting of two men, facing away from one another, each watering a tree with a watering can. The one is a Jew, the other a Palestinian in his robes and headdress. The trees are leafy and joined at the top. Dan opened the book and showed the pages with two texts and the lined space in between for the students to put down their own thoughts. It was their great achievement, a concrete one, managed during, not after, the difficult times of conflict.

'It was a time, you see . . . they were so optimistic,' said Sami, looking up, smiling. 'Oslo days. And we wanted to be part of it.'

'We wanted to create a mechanism, you see, a method for resolving future conflicts,' said Dan, finishing Sami's sentence.

So what were the difficulties?, I asked.

'Teachers on one side could not always accept the terminology of the other side,' said Dan. 'Is it Eretz Yisrael, in 1948, or is it Palestine?'

'Did they (Palestinians) flee or were they uprooted?' added Sami.

Dan: 'Was it the War of Independence or was it the Nakba? This year is the sixtieth anniversary of the founding of Israel for us. For the Palestinians it's the Nakba, the Catastrophe.'

Sami: 'The Palestinians were living in their homes, on their land...'

They sat in silence for a while. It was time for a change of shot. I asked John to take the camera to the side, for a close-up of the two faces, Dan in profile, Sami facing him. I stayed where I was so they went on talking to me.

'Now we must look at those feelings.' That was Sami.

Dan nodded, yes, it was the only way to deal with the past. To acknowledge it. 'Till a few years ago the word Nakba was not known in Israel,' he said. 'Things are changing. But very slowly. It becomes at least known about now... We felt we wanted to do something now, while the conflict was still on. But it is quite risky. The Holocaust ended a long time ago. But this is ongoing.'

'I was in Israeli jails,' said Sami. 'Israelis were destroying our homes. Limiting our freedom of movement. Then to find an Israeli who wanted change. To work together. It was very risky for me, endangering my family, my children. A lot of uncertainty, and that uncertainty, it makes you feel impotent. Without hope.'

'First of all, I knew all the time Sami risks more than I do,' added Dan. 'But it's similar in my society. I knew certain doors would not be open to me. Certain people... But I knew that what I do with Sami was more important to me.'

I wonder about the heritage of the Holocaust in Israel. And Palestine. Dan smiles at me, nodding. We both know how those children of Holocaust survivors had the courage to listen to the children of Nazi war criminals. The Other.

'We are still under the psychology of the Holocaust,' said Dan. 'Victims... Even families who were not directly affected by the Holocaust. The fear. No one is going to help us. No one is going to rescue us. The Palestinians have nothing to do with this. Nevertheless...'

'I agree with Dan,' said Sami. 'In order for the Palestinians to sympathise with the Holocaust, it's very complex. They recognise, but find it difficult to sympathise. They fear it can play down their own right to sympathy…' He turned to face Dan. 'We also feel we are alone. The Arab nations, the West, the Americans, they all neglect us. We feel our identity is suffering. Very few people are listening to us. We too are dispersed, like the Jews!'

He turned his palms upwards, in a gesture of… of what? Resignation? Despair?

Dan smiled at him. Nodded.

'This,' said Sami, indicating the room and PRIME, 'this is our hope.' He paused for a moment, thinking about it. 'It's more than a hope… it's a dream. A dream for change.'

A dream.

We seemed to have come to the end of our interview. And it was time for lunch. We were going to one of Sami's favourite restaurants in Ramallah. We did a last shot of the two of them walking through the pine woods, hand in hand, talking, talking.

Dan died three months later.

> One shouldn't either ignore or forget the past. But, on the other hand, one shouldn't relive the entire past every time there's a suicide bombing in Tel Aviv. We need to work our way through the Holocaust. We must understand that not everything that was important back then is important now. Now it is important in a different way. Now it is the Israelis and the Palestinians. Then it was the Jews and the Nazis. But our business is to learn to forgive one another, liberate ourselves from the past, and move on.
>
> Dan Bar-On
> Tel Aviv, April 2008

ACKNOWLEDGEMENTS

To Renate, Joe and Dan, my grateful thanks. Without you, this book, along with its warning about what can happen once power gets into the wrong hands, could never have been written. It took courage for all three of you to speak out, tell the truth and trust me. Two of you are dead now, but who says we can't thank the dead? In their place, on earth, I must thank Edi Seebauer, Renate's partner, for her constant help, not least by allowing me full access to Jeckeln's (Renate's father's) extraordinary letters to her mother, Else. Likewise, I must thank Yaarah Bar-On, Dan's daughter, for her help, most especially with the lovely photographs of Dan as a child in Haifa, and later on his kibbutz, among the fruit trees. Joe can speak for himself, of course. And so he did, fully and generously, including three of his beautiful and moving poems, now published on Amazon under the title *Living with Lost Love*.

This has been a lucky book. Lucky to have three such powerful and important stories to tell. And lucky to have excellent publishing support, both from Clare Alexander, leading literary agent of Aitken Alexander Associates Ltd, and likewise the team at Weidenfeld & Nicolson. Clare has a powerful personality, which she somehow combines with a light touch, for which many thanks are in order. Ed Lake, my editor at Weidenfeld & Nicolson, is given to making highly imaginative suggestions, which seem to make little sense at the time, but later… Ciara Mongey has guided this book seamlessly through production. Natalie Dawkins has a fine eye for a good image. Nina Sandelson is a perfect editor. And Linden Lawson is a copy-editor who doesn't change the style of the author but makes some judicious suggestions and meticulously checks the facts. As to our proofreader, Sam Stocker, his eagle eye spotted errors large and small. Where is a book without good publicity? Happily Elizabeth Allen has been the perfect choice. Lucky, as I say.

So, on to the back stacks of the London Library in St James's Square. Much of my research for this book and my past ones has been done there, because their German collection is wonderfully extensive, presumably thanks to Nazi Germany as more and more intellectuals – Jews, Socialists and Communists – fled the country during the 1930s before it was too late, bringing their books with them. But this time my favourite from the back stacks came from another section: Israel. Laurence Oliphant's *Haifa, or Life in Modern Palestine*, published by William Blackwood and Sons. In 1886. No one had taken it out since the 1950s. I held it in my hands with intense pleasure, anciently leather-bound, musty with years of happy neglect. Useful too, given that Dan was born in Haifa way back in 1938. As for the front desk at the London Library: always helpful, always friendly. If you can't find a book, they'll find it for you. If you're out of the country, they'll send it to you. What more does an author want?

Thank you, all.

Catrine Clay
London, January 2026

LIST OF ILLUSTRATIONS

Sources and permissions (by reference to photo number)

The families of our characters have very kindly allowed us to reproduce the personal photographs in this book. The Neve Shalom photographs were supplied by the BBC camera team, John Goodyer and Ray Forsythe. The below images have been reproduced with the permission of the following agencies:

1: Alamy/Süddeutsche Zeitung Photo
2: Alamy/World History Archive
6: Bundesarchiv N 1126 bild 33.052/Entaraffin Ana
7: Alamy/INTERFOTO
10: bpk-Fotoarchiv/Fotograf unbekannt

NOTES

PART ONE: DARK PASTS

CHAPTER ONE: Renate: A Child for Hitler

5 'Every mother of good blood…': Hrabar, Tokarz and Wilczur, p. 193.

6 'We believe in the God of all things…': Lilienthal, p. 100.

6 'Yes, I think I had a Naming Ceremony…': Author interview.

7 Secret addresses: Lilienthal, p. 80.

8 C Company: Author interview, 1992.

9 '*Grüss Gott.*': Housden, pp. 50–1.

9 'The way in which Youth…': Housden, p. 74.

10 'As part of our mission…': Rauschning, p. 140.

10 Von Feury: Author interview, 1992.

11 'All that baloney…': Author interview, 1992.

13 'A marriage with few children…': Ackermann, p. 242.

13 'The unmarried woman': Lilienthal, p. 22.

13 Hereditary health laws: Burleigh and Wippermann, p. 49.

14 The *Lebensborn* home names: Ackermann, p. 129.

15 *Lebensborn* statutes: Lilienthal, p. 43.

17 'When determining racial characteristics…': Clay and Leapman, p. 46.

18 Number of children born in *Lebensborn* homes: Ackermann, p. 130, Lilienthal, p. 229.

20 'As you know…': Clay and Leapman, p. 76.

21 'The popularity of these trips…': Housden, p. 41.

22 '*Liebes Elsele!*': Letter from Friedrich Jeckeln to Else Röder, 20 July 1937.

25 'We are all men here…': Ackermann, p. 242.

26 Funeral of a Communist: Mason, p. 315.

27 Sabotage: Mason, p. 722.

27 'There have been complaints for several months…': Housden, p. 37. The output was double in England.

27 'Pilgrims flocked…': Housden, document 50.

29 'Every war is a loss of the best blood…': Ackermann, p. 240; Appendix document 4.

32 'The following will be executed ...': Krausnick, *Anatomie des SS Staates*, p. 62; Nuremberg document PS078; and IMT, International Military Tribunal, 76 and 79.

34 Shooting the Jews in pits: Fleming, pp. 78–9, 80–1 and 96, citing Jeckeln's trial.

CHAPTER TWO: Henrich Himmler: The Great Aryan

43 Diary entry: Ackermann, p. 24.
43 Himmler's childhood: Frischauer, chapter 1.
44 Heini's godfather: Frischauer, p. 16.
44 'School was difficult for Heini': Ackermann, p. 21.
46 'A book that expresses ...': Padfield, p. 69.
49 'Like a schoolmaster ...': Schellenberg, pp. 72 and 165.
49 Working for Gregor Strasser: Frischauer, pp. 23–4.
49 'Looks like a half-starved shrew ...': Strasser, *Mein Kampf*, p. 15.
50 'That's just like him ...': Lüdecke, p. 268.
51 Meeting Marga: Frischauer, p. 25.
51 'Size 50 knickers ...': Höhne, p. 165.
52 Albert Krebs: Ackermann, p. 29.
52 'Typical Jewish arrogance ...': Frischauer, p. 27.
52 Walther Darré: Burleigh and Wippermann, p. 57.
53 'For us ...': Padfield, p. 162.
54 Early SS: Krausnick, *Anatomie des SS Staates*, p. 140.
55 Heydrich: Frischauer, p. 38.
56 Kersten on Heydrich: *Memoirs*, p. 90.
56 'Schoolmasterly ...': Aronson, p. 62.
56 'Far superior ...': Schellenberg, p. 30.
56 Engagement and Marriage Decree: Ackermann, p. 262.
58 *Sieg Heil!*: Engelmann, p. 51.
60 'We are dependent ...': Strasser, *Mein Kampf*, p. 64.
61 'Woke his chauffeur': Frischauer, p. 43.
62 'Wolffie': von Lang, *Top Nazi*, p. 1.
62 Wewelsburg: von Lang, *Top Nazi*, p. 44; Frischauer, p. 68.
63 'My first aim ...': Clay and Leapman, p. 67.
63 'The ideal German ...': Housden, p. 168.
64 'In my opinion ...': Padfield, p. 167.

64 '*Geheim!*': Padfield, p. 240–8, including the Roberts quote from his book *The House that Jack Built*, published by Methuen in 1939.
66 'It is not only . . .': Padfield, p. 238.
66 The 1936 gamble: Engelmann, vol. 1, p. 229.
67 'In Berlin . . .': Shirer, p. 124.
68 Himmler to Gürtner: Padfield, p. 183.
69 Henderson: Clay and Leapman, p. 169.

CHAPTER THREE: Lonia, Mendel and Joe

71 The Goldfeld/Albeck story is based on author interviews with Joe Albeck, Lonia and Mendel's son, and Lonia.
71 'This is the Polish rebel force!': Padfield, p. 265.
73 Ghettos in Poland: Hrabar, Tokarz and Wilczur, p. 154.
74 'The Jew is a *Schmarotzer* . . .': Ackermann, p. 159.
74 'As soon as I have the power . . .': Housden, p. 12.
75 For an analysis of anti-Semitism in Nazi Germany as a political tool, see Krausnick, *Anatomie des SS Staates*, p. 21.
75 Himmler's *Harte Reinigung*: Ackermann, p. 155.
76 Heydrich quote: Krausnick, *Anatomie des SS Staates*, p. 52.
78 Ghetto statistics: Krausnick, *Anatomie des SS Staates*, p. 59.
79 Witness statements: Hrabar, Tokarz and Wilczur, p. 158.
79 'I saw a little girl . . .': Ackermann, p. 165.
80 Dr Korczak: See Yad Vashem histories.
82 Himmler memo, 20 Jan 1943: Krausnick, *Die Truppen des Weltanschauungskrieges*, p. 66; Nuremberg document NO2405, copy in Institute fur Zeitgeschichte.
82 Wannsee: Padfield, p. 357–8.
86 Poles saving Jews: Hrabar, Tokarz and Wilczur, p. 173.
86 Warsaw uprising: Hrabar, Tokarz and Wilczur, p. 161.
86 Stroop quotes: Hrabar, Tokarz and Wilczur, p. 161.
87 Stroop to Krüger and Himmler quote: Ackermann, p. 164.
87 Selection and transport to Poniatowa: Author interview with Lonia Albeck. Further interviews with Joe Albeck.
90 'There have been complaints . . .': Housden, p. 37.
90 'Try to obtain . . .': Lifton, p. 359.
92 Norway, *Lebensborn* Homes: Lilienthal, p. 262.
92 Himmler's *Erntefest*: Browning, p. 240.
94 Massacre at Poniatowa: Krausnick, *Anatomie des SS Staates*, p. 121.

CHAPTER FOUR: Heinrich Himmler: Rise and Fall

99 'Obviously it is possible ...': Padfield, p. 287.
100 'The sadly unavoidable loss': Ackermann Document No. 4.
101 Himmler's 'Über die Behandlung der Fremdvölkischen im Osten', written on a train, 28 May 1940.
101 'I showed the Führer my paper ...': Padfield, p. 301.
101 Rascher to Himmler: Frischauer, pp. 177–87.
103 'Camps for Jews ...': Fleming, p. 71.
105 'You will receive more detailed instructions ...': Broszat, p. 153.
105 Jeckeln testimony: Fleming, p. 96–100.
106 The 'new Europe': Ackermann, p. 185–90.
106 'Only girls of good blood ...': Padfield, p. 366.
107 Himmler reaction to death of Heydrich, Schellenberg, p. 323
107 '*Meine Herren* ...': Padfield, p. 382.
108 'For the *SS-Führer* ...': Broszat, p. 182.
109 'Himmler viewed ...': Broszat, pp. 171–83, for the full account.
110 Wolff evidence: von Lang, *Top Nazi*, p. 338.
111 Germanisation of children: Hrabar, Tokarz and Wilczur, chapter 3 for full account; Hillel, pp. 152–3, Dr Roman Hrabar headed the Polish Mission seeking the stolen children after the war.
111 'All the good blood ...': Ackermann, pp. 205–8.
114 'Separate police registration office': Clay and Leapman, pp. 97–100.
115 Hitler Youth: Ackermann, introduction; Klonne, pp. 28–34.
115 'This youth will learn nothing ...': Kater, p. 18, Klonne 17–34.
116 'Some 200,000 children': Hrabar, Tokarz and Wilczur, p. 147.
116 German public opinion: Boberach, p. 4903 and p. 14, p. 5561–3.
116 'We have only one task ...': Padfield, p. 340.
117 Jeckeln and Riga: Krausnick, *Anatomie des SS Staates*, p. 478, also pp. 235 and 62; Fleming, p. 75. Also Padfield, p. 624, footnote 34 on the liquidation of Riga ghetto.
117 Pohl: Frischauer, p. 11; Aronson, pp. 62–3, note 360.
119 Himmler on the run: Frischauer, pp. 247–9; Himmler's disguises: Ackermann, p. 232.
120 Himmler's capture: Frischauer, p. 9.

PART TWO: THREE FUTURES

CHAPTER FIVE: Renate Tells Her Story

125 Renate's story: Based on author interviews with her and her mother, Else.

125 For a more detailed read about post-war Germany, see Jähner, p. 132.

127 Nuremberg: Ackermann, p. 167; Lilienthal, p. 7; and Thompson.

128 Tattooed human skin: Frischauer, p. 146.

128 'The defendants in this case...': Frischauer, p. 183.

129 The *Lebensborn* trial: Hrabar, Tokarz and Wilczur, pp. 142 and 200; Ackermann, p. 128, footnote 172, re: Nuremberg document PS2825.

142 Jeckeln, *Kristallnacht*: Author and Dan Bar-On interview in *Legacy of Silence*, p. 153.

146 'Then she found...': Fleming, pp. 44 and 75–99.

CHAPTER SIX: Joe Tells His Story

157 Joe's story: Author interview with Joe and his mother; Joe's memoir, *Living with Lost Love: Poems for Survivors and their Children*, published on Amazon.

157 'So that this nation...': McCullough, p. 586.

163 'These Republican gluttons...': McCullough, p. 658.

163 'I believe...': McCullough, p. 676.

182 Joe's poems are featured in his memoir, *Living with Lost Love: Poems for Survivors and their Children*.

CHAPTER SEVEN: Dan: Child of Israel

190 Description of Haifa, late nineteenth century: Oliphant, pp. 1–40.

192 'I don't regard...': Morris, p. 9.

192 Population of Palestine, 1918: Ingrams, p. 44.

193 The 1920s Jewish population: Bregman, p. 4.

194 Early Zionists: Ingrams, pp. 3–5.

194 'We will conquer...': Segev, p. 116.

194 'A land without a nation...': Segev, pp. 127 and 140.

194 'It was suggested...': Ingrams, p. 10 and War Cabinet minutes; Ingrams, pp. 11–18.

195 'My general impression...': Ingrams, p. 45, and chapters 2 and 3 for general background. See also MacMillan for a fine and detailed account of the Paris Conference.
195 Clayton and Allenby: Ingrams, pp. 63 and 105.
196 Ben-Gurion in America: Segev, p. 124.
198 Bruno memoir: With thanks to Dan Bar-On.
201 Jewish population: Segev, p. 244.
201 Arab revolts: Bregman, p. 9.
201 Dan's story: Author interviews.
204 Jewish settlements, 1939: Bregman, p. 4.
205 'If England does not want...': Segev, p. 390.
205 'We need to prepare...': Segev, pp. 404–7.
206 Khalidi: Morris, pp. 18–20.
206 Fatwa order: Bregman, p. 4.
206 'Establish a Jewish state...': Bregman, p. 11.
207 'The land of Israel...': Segev, introduction and p. 406.
207 The 1948 war: Palumbo, prologue; Morris, p. 1.
208 'Lands have been taken quite unlawfully...': Palumbo, see footnote United Nations Archives 13/3.3.1 box 10. Report of the 'Special Investigating Team'. Negev Report.
208 Haifa: Morris, pp. 40–2.
211 The USS *Liberty*: Bregman, prologue.
213 Children of survivors stories: Author interviews; Bar-On, *Legacy of Silence*.

CHAPTER EIGHT: Dan Enters the Dark

221 Author interviews with Dan.
221 Children of Nazi war criminals: Author interviews; Bar-On, *Legacy of Silence*.
226 'Hitler was my godfather...': Author interview; Dan Bar-On interviews for *Legacy of Silence*.
241 Euthanasia statistics: Browning, *NYB*, October 2018.
242 'The added advantage of the clinics was that they could experiment': Burleigh and Wippermann, pp. 102 and 148.
242 'All God-fearing people...': Housden, p. 57.
247 'A conspiracy of silence...': Bar-On, *Dark Side of the Mind*, p. 321.
250 Joe's poems and memoir: With my thanks to Joe, who kindly gave me permission to use both.

CHAPTER NINE: Neve Shalom

258 'Hundreds! Hundreds!': Many of these quotes come from the interviews we did for the BBC documentary, in the breaks between the sessions.

263 'Mercy killing...': Lifton, p. 306.

264 'A pig in a potato field...': Schellenberg, p. 359.

CHAPTER TEN: Aftermath

291 'A certain shift among the younger generation...': Segev, introduction.

BIBLIOGRAPHY

Ackermann, Josef, *Heinrich Himmler als Ideologe*, Musterschmidt, Göttingen, 1970.

Ambrose, Stephen, Eisenhower, Vols 1 and 2, Simon & Schuster, London, 1984.

Aronson, Shlomo, *Reinhard Heydrich und die Frühgeschichte von Gestapo und SD*, Deutsche Verlags-Anstalt, Stuttgart, 1971.

Bar-On, Dan, *Legacy of Silence*, Harvard University Press, Cambridge, MA, 1989.

Bar-On, Dan, *Tell Your Life Story*, CEU Press, 2006.

Boberach, H., *Berichte des SD und der Gestapo über Kirchen und Kirchenvolk in Deutschland 1934–1944*, Matthias-Grunwald, Mainz, 1971.

Boberach, H., *Meldungen aus dem Reich 1938–1945*, Pawlak Herrsching, 1984.

Bormann, Martin, *Leben gegen Schatten*, Bonifatius Kontur, 1996.

Bregman, Ahron, *Israel's Wars: A History Since 1947*, Routledge, London and New York, 2002.

Broszat, Martin, ed., *Kommandant in Auschwitz: Autobiographische Aufzeichnungen von Rudolf Höß*, Deutsche Verlags-Anstalt, Stuttgart, 1958.

Browning, Christopher, *Ordinary Men: Reserve Police Battalion 101 and the Final Solution in Poland*, HarperCollins, New York, 1992 and 2017.

Browning, Christopher, *The Origins of the Final Solution. The Evolution of Nazi Jewish Policy*, September 1939–March 1942, University of Nebraska Press and Jerusalem Yad Vashem, 2004; William Heinemann, 2004.

Burleigh, Michael and Wippermann, Wolfgang, *The Racial State: Germany 1933–1945*, Cambridge University Press, 1991.

Clay, Catrine and Leapman, Michael, *Master Race*, Hodder & Stoughton, 1995.

Engelmann, Bernt, *Im Gleichschritt Marsch*, Kiepenhauer & Witsch, Cologne, 1982.

Ezergailis, Andrew, *The Holocaust in Latvia, 1941–1944*, Historical Institute of Latvia (in association with the United States Holocaust Memorial Museum,) 1996.

Fleming, Gerald, *Hitler and the Final Solution*, Hamish Hamilton, London, 1985.

Fraenkel, Heinrich and Manvell, Roger, *Heinrich Himmler*, William Heinemann, London, 1965.

Fried, Albert, *McCarthyism, The Great American Red Scare: A Documentary History*, Oxford University Press, Oxford, 1997.

Frischauer, Willi, *Himmler: The Evil Genius of the Third Reich*, Odhams Press Ltd, 1953.

Fulbrook, Mary, *Reckonings: Legacies of Nazi Persecution and the Quest for Justice*, Oxford University Press, 2018.

Goebbels, Joseph, ed. Elke Fröhlich, *Tagebuecher*, De Gruyter Saur, Zurich, 1992.

Henry, Clarissa and Hillel, Marc, *Children of the SS*, Hutchinson, London, 1976.

Hirst, David, *The Gun and the Olive Branch*, Faber & Faber, London, 1977.

Höhne, Heinz, *Der Orden unter dem Totenkopf*, Verlag der Spiegel, Hamburg, 1966.

Housden, Martyn, *Resistance and Conformity in the Third Reich*, Routledge, London, 1997.

Hrabar, Roman, Zophia Tokarz and Jacek Wilczur, *The Fate of Polish Children During the Last War*, Interpress, Warsaw, 1981.

Ingrams, Doreen, *Palestine Papers, 1917–1922: Seeds of Conflict*, Eland Books 1973.

Jähner, Harald, *Aftermath*, WH Allen, London, 2021.

Kater, Michael H., *Hitler Youth*, Harvard University Press, Cambridge MA, 2004.

Kersten F., The Kersten Memoirs 1940–45, Hutchinson, London, 1956.

Klonne, A., *Hitlerjugend: Die Jugend und ihre Organisation im Dritten Reich*, Papyrossa Verlag, Hanover, 1960.

Koch, H. W., *In the Name of the Volk: Political Justice in Hitler's Germany*, I.B. Taurus Publishers, London and New York, 1989.

Koop, Volker, *Rudolf Höß: Der Kommandant von Auschwitz*, Boehlau Verlag, 2014.

Krausnick H., Buchheim H., Broszat M. and Jacobsen, H., *Anatomie des SS Staates*, Deutscher Taschenbuch Verlag, Munich, 1979.

Krausnick, H. and Hans Heinrich Wilhelm, *Die Truppen des Weltanschauungskrieges*, Deutsche Verlags-Anstalt, Stuttgart, 1981.

Kuby, Erich, *The German Betrayal*, Hoffmann & Campe, Hamburg, 1982.

Lang, Jochen von, *The Secretary: Martin Bormann: The Man Who Manipulated Hitler*, Random House, New York, 1979. First pub in German 1977.

Lang, Jochen von, *Top Nazi, SS General Karl Woolf: The Man between Hitler and Himmler*, Enigma Books, 2005.

Lifton, R. J., *The Nazi Doctors*, Macmillan, London, 1986.

Lilienthal, Georg, *Der Lebensborn e.V.* Geschichte Fischer, Stuttgart and New York, 1993.

Lüdecke, K., *I Knew Hitler*, Jarrolds, London, 1938.

MacMillan, Margaret, *Peacemakers: Six Months that Changed the World*, John Murray, London, 2001.

Mason, T. W., *Arbeiterklasse und Volksgemeinschaft*, Westdeutsche Verlag, Opladen, 1975.

McCullough, David, *Truman*, Simon & Schuster, London, 1992.

Morris, Benny, *1948 and After: Israel and the Palestinians*, Clarendon Press, Oxford, 1990.

Noakes, J. and Pridham, G., *Documents on Nazism*, Jonathan Cape, London, 1974.

Oliphant, Laurence, *Haifa, or Life in Modern Palestine*, William Blackwood and Sons, Edinburgh and London, 1886.

Padfield, Peter, *Himmler, Reichsführer-SS*, Macmillan, London, 1990.

Palumbo, Michael, *The Palestinian Catastrophe*, Faber & Faber, London, 1987.

Rauschning, H., *Hitler Speaks*, Thornton Butterworth, London, 1939.

Schellenberg, Walter, *Memoiren*, Verlag fur Politik und Wirtschaft, 1956; Andre Deutsch, London, 1956.

Segev, Tom, *A State at Any Cost, The Life of David Ben-Gurion*, Apollo, London, 2019.

Shirer, W., *Berlin Diary*, Hamish Hamilton, London, 1941.

Strasser, Otto, *Hitler and I*, Jonathan Cape, London, 1940.

Strasser, Otto, *Mein Kampf: Eine Politische Autobiografie*, H. Heine, Frankfurt am Main, 1969.

Thompson, Larry V., Lebensborn and the Eugenics Policy of the Reichsführer-SS, *Central European History*, Vol. 4, No. 1, 1971, 54–77.

Turner, H. A., *German Big Business and the Rise of Hitler*, Oxford University Press, 1985.

Waite, R. G. L., *The Psychopathic God: Adolf Hitler*, Signet, New York, 1993.

INDEX

Page numbers in *italics* refer to illustrations.

RAISING READERS

Books Build Bright Futures

Dear Reader,

We'd love your attention for one more page to tell you about the crisis in children's reading, and what we can all do.

Studies have shown that reading for fun is the **single biggest predictor of a child's future life chances** – more than family circumstance, parents' educational background or income. It improves academic results, mental health, wealth, communication skills, ambition and happiness.[1]

The number of children reading for fun is in rapid decline. Young people have a lot of competition for their time. In 2024, 1 in 10 children and young people in the UK aged 5 to 18 did not own a single book at home.[2]

Hachette works extensively with schools, libraries and literacy charities, but here are some ways we can all raise more readers:

- Reading to children for just 10 minutes a day makes a difference
- Don't give up if children aren't regular readers – there will be books for them!
- Visit bookshops and libraries to get recommendations
- Encourage them to listen to audiobooks
- Support school libraries
- Give books as gifts

There's a lot more information about how to encourage children to read on our website: **www.RaisingReaders.co.uk**

Thank you for reading.

hachette UK

---

[1] OECD, '21st-Century Readers: Developing Literacy Skills in a Digital World', 2021, https://www.oecd.org/en/publications/21st-century-readers_a83d84cb-en.html

[2] National Literacy Trust, 'Book Ownership in 2024', November 2024, https://literacytrust.org.uk/research-services/research-reports/book-ownership-in-2024